*THE BUILDING BLOCKS
OF THE EARLIEST GOSPEL*

"Bellinzoni invites study groups on a splendid journey, preparing them for informed discussion of the multiple sources and story forms used by the Gospel of Mark's author. Understanding their use helps us distinguish what are Jesus' authentic teachings, historical facts, and teachings of the nascent church. Readers are invited to struggle with Mark's deeper meaning in order to hear his proclamation of the good news, summed up in Jesus' commandment to love God and one's neighbor."

—**Nancy Lane**, Reverend Mother, Life-Professed Solitary

"In his latest book, Bellinzoni accomplished for me what five years of study at a main-line theological seminary did not—to pull together into a coherent whole all I knew, supposed and doubted on the subject. His method is rigorous while crystal clear, at the end culminating in a graceful, even moving summary of what he takes to be the evangelist's method and motive."

—**Turhan Tirana**, Reverend Father

"With intellectual rigor and heartfelt passion for the text, Arthur Bellinzoni gives his audience what he has always offered to his students: a chance to let the text speak first in its own context. What follows is a journey toward faith for seekers and a fresh perspective for pastors, engaging mind and spirit. Deep faith is nurtured by good information. Through this unique insight into Mark's view of Jesus we are enriched and challenged."

—**Virginia Miner**, Transitional General Presbyter, Presbytery of Lackawanna, Scranton, Pennsylvania

"Bold, Informative, Deep—Bellinzoni combines decades of scholarships to produce a systematic analysis of the first Christian gospel. He conclusively proves that Mark was a compilation of earlier written texts and that this 'gospel' was not meant to be an unbiased historical account. Like many powerful sermons, the writer of Mark calls upon historical facts, but also myths and ethical sayings to promote Jesus as the messiah. Bellinzoni's work is a must for serious students of the bible!"

—**Rick McLain**, PhD, Professor at State University of New York, Ononodaga Community College

THE BUILDING BLOCKS OF THE EARLIEST GOSPEL

A ROAD MAP TO EARLY CHRISTIAN BIOGRAPHY

By
Arthur J. Bellinzoni

WIPF & STOCK · Eugene, Oregon

THE BUILDING BLOCKS OF THE EARLIEST GOSPEL
A Road Map to Early Christian Biography

Copyright © 2018 Arthur J. Bellinzoni. All rights reserved. Except for brief quotations in critical publications or reviews, no part of this book may be reproduced in any manner without prior written permission from the publisher. Write: Permissions, Wipf and Stock Publishers, 199 W. 8th Ave., Suite 3, Eugene, OR 97401.

Wipf & Stock
An Imprint of Wipf and Stock Publishers
199 W. 8th Ave., Suite 3
Eugene, OR 97401

www.wipfandstock.com

PAPERBACK ISBN: 978-1-5326-4356-9
HARDCOVER ISBN: 978-1-5326-4357-6
EBOOK ISBN: 978-1-5326-4358-3

Manufactured in the U.S.A.

All translations of the Gospel of Mark are my own. All other biblical references are from The Harper Collins Study Bible: New Revised Standard Version. New York: Harper Collins Publishers, 1989.

CONTENTS

Preface | xi
Abbreviations | xiii

INTRODUCTION | 1
    The Text of the Gospel | 1
    The Literary Form of the Gospel | 2
    Literary Forms of the Building Blocks of the Gospel | 3
    Our Earliest Gospel | 4
    Authorship, Date, and Place of Composition | 5
    Chapters and Verses | 6
    Purpose | 7

CHAPTER 1 | 8
    The Superscription or Title | 8
    The Preaching of John and the Baptism of Jesus | 9
    The Temptation of Jesus in the Wilderness | 11
    The Beginning of Jesus' Teaching in Galilee | 12
    The Call of Jesus' First Disciples | 13
    Jesus Teaches with Authority and Heals the Man with the Unclean Spirit | 15
    The Healing of Peter's Mother-in-Law | 17
    The Healing and Exorcism of Many | 17
    Jesus Departs on a Preaching Tour of Galilee | 18
    The Cleansing of the Man with the Scaly Skin | 19
    Conclusions after Chapter 1 | 21

CHAPTER 2 | 23

    The Healing of the Paralyzed Man and Jesus has Authority to Forgive Sins | 23
    Jesus Calls Levi to be His Disciple | 26
    Jesus Eats with Sinners and Tax Collectors | 27
    The Question about Fasting and the New and the Old | 28
    Jesus' Pronouncement about the Sabbath | 30
    Conclusions after Chapter 2 | 31

CHAPTER 3 | 33

    The Man with the Paralyzed Hand | 33
    The Multitude at the Seaside | 35
    Jesus Appoints the Twelve | 36
    Jesus and Beelzebul | 38
    Jesus' True Family | 40
    Conclusions after Chapter 3 | 42

CHAPTER 4 | 44

    The Parable of the Sower | 44
    The Purpose of Parables | 47
    The Interpretation of the Parable of the Sower | 48
    A Collection of Miscellaneous Sayings | 50
    The Parable of the Growing Seed | 52
    The Parable of the Mustard Seed | 52
    Concluding Statement about Jesus' Parables | 53
    The Stilling of the Storm | 54
    Conclusions after Chapter 4 | 56

CHAPTER 5 | 58

    The Healing of the Gerasene Demoniac | 58
    The Woman Healed of the Flow of Blood and the Girl Restored to Life | 62
    Conclusions after Chapter 5 | 66

CHAPTER 6 | 69

    The Rejection of Jesus at Nazareth | 69
    Jesus Sends the Twelve out on a Missionary Journey | 71
    The Death of John the Baptist | 73
    The Feeding of the Five Thousand Men | 76
    Jesus Walks on the Water | 80

CONTENTS vii

    The Healing of the Sick in Gennesaret | 83
    Conclusions after Chapter 6 | 84

CHAPTER 7 | 87
    The Tradition of the Elders | 87
    More on the Tradition of the Elders | 89
    The Jewish Law of Ritually Clean and Unclean | 91
    Still Another Saying on the Subject of Ritually Clean and
        Unclean | 92
    A List of Vices that Come from within a Human Being | 93
    The Syro-Phoenician Woman's Request for her Daughter | 95
    Jesus Cures a Deaf Man | 97
    Conclusions after Chapter 7 | 99

CHAPTER 8 | 101
    The Feeding of the Four Thousand | 101
    The Demand for a Sign | 104
    The Yeast of the Pharisees and of Herod | 105
    Jesus Cures a Blind Man at Bethsaida | 107
    Peter's Declaration about Jesus | 109
    Jesus Foretells his Death and Resurrection | 112
    A Cluster of Eschatological Sayings of Jesus | 114
    Conclusions after Chapter 8 | 118

CHAPTER 9 | 121
    The Transfiguration of Jesus | 121
    The Coming of Elijah | 123
    The Exorcism of the Epileptic Boy | 125
    For a Second Time Jesus Foretells His Death and
        Resurrection | 127
    Which Disciple is the Greatest? | 128
    Another Exorcist, Followed by a Series of Unrelated
        Maxims | 129
    Conclusions after Chapter 9 | 134

CHAPTER 10 | 136
    Jesus' Teaching about Divorce | 136
    Jesus Blesses the Children | 139
    The Rich Man, True Riches, and the Kingdom of God | 140
    For a Third Time Jesus Foretells His Death and
        Resurrection | 144

James and John Ask for Precedence | 146
Jesus Heals the Blind Man Bartimaeus in Jericho | 150
Conclusions after Chapter 10 | 151

Chapter 11 | 153
Jesus' Triumphal Entry into Jerusalem | 154
The Cursing of the Fig Tree | 157
The Cleansing of the Temple | 158
The Lesson of the Withered Fig Tree and Additional Sayings on Faith and Prayer | 160
The Question of Jesus' Authority | 162
Conclusions after Chapter 11 | 164

Chapter 12 | 166
The Parable of the Evil Winegrowers | 166
On Paying Taxes to Caesar | 169
The Question of the Resurrection | 172
The Greatest Commandment | 174
The Question about David's Son | 176
Criticism of the Scribes | 178
The Poor Widow's Contribution | 179
Conclusions after Chapter 12 | 180

Chapter 13 | 182
The Apocalyptic Discourse | 182
Jesus Predicts the Destruction of the Temple | 183
Four Disciples Question Jesus Privately | 183
Jesus' Warning about Imposters | 184
Sayings of Jesus on Signs of the Beginning of the End | 184
Sayings of Jesus on Persecution | 186
The Abominable Desecration | 187
Warnings against False Messiahs and False Prophets | 189
A Prophecy of the Coming of the Son of Man | 189
The Lesson of the Parable of the Fig Tree in Summer | 191
Two Sayings about the Certainty of Imminent Consummation | 192
Saying on the Unknown Hour and Day | 192
An Exhortation to be Alert and the Parable of the Absent Householder | 193

The Application is to Everyone | 194
Conclusions after Chapter 13 | 194

CHAPTER 14 | 197
The Passion Narrative | 197
The Plot of the Priests and the Scribes to Kill Jesus | 198
The Anointing of Jesus at Bethany | 199
Judas Agrees to Betray Jesus | 201
The Preparations for the Passover Meal | 202
The Prophecy of the Betrayal | 203
The Institution of the Lord's Supper | 204
Peter's Denial Foretold | 207
Jesus and the Disciples in Gethsemane | 209
The Betrayal and Arrest of Jesus | 212
The Flight of the Naked Young Man | 214
Jesus' Trial before the High Priest and the Council | 214
Peter's Denial of Jesus | 220
Conclusions after Chapter 14 | 222

CHAPTER 15 | 225
Jesus' Trial before Pontius Pilate | 225
The Mockery before the Soldiers | 227
The Crucifixion of Jesus | 228
The Death of Jesus | 232
The Roman Centurion and the Women | 234
The Burial of Jesus | 235
Conclusions after Chapter 15 | 237

CHAPTER 16 | 240
The Discovery of the Empty Tomb | 240
Conclusions after Chapter 16 | 244

CONCLUSIONS | 245
The Literary Forms of the Gospel | 245
Pronouncement Stories | 245
Miracle Stories | 247
Parables | 248
Sayings | 249
Legends | 251
Constructions of the Evangelist | 254

The Text of the Gospel | 256
The Literary Form of Gospel or Biography | 256
The Author of the Gospel | 257
The Place of Composition | 257
The Date of Composition | 258
The Christology of the Gospel | 259
The Purpose of the Evangelist in Writing the Gospel | 264
The Historical Jesus | 265
The Aftermath | 267
Issues for Further Consideration or Discussion | 269

Bibliography | 271
Scripture Index | 273

PREFACE

As an undergraduate at Princeton University, I first developed a special interest in the Gospel of Mark. I wrote my two-semester senior thesis for my religion major under the guidance of Professor W. D. Davies on *The Gospel of Mark in Recent Scholarship* (1957). I was convinced at the time that Mark was the earliest gospel and that, as such, it was closer in time to Jesus and, therefore, more reliable in the quest for the historical Jesus. That is still partially true: the Gospel of Mark is certainly our earliest written gospel, but the issue of its historical value is far more complicated, as we will see in this volume.

My interest in the Gospel of Mark persists, even after sixty years. After the publication of my comprehensive study *The New Testament: An Introduction to Biblical Scholarship* (Eugene, Oregon: WIPF & STOCK, 2016), I vowed that my writing days were behind me. That delusion lasted for about two weeks, until I felt compelled to write a book that would introduce the average layperson to the probable process that resulted in the Gospel of Mark. I wanted to afford the reader some understanding of the building blocks of the gospel, the presumably oral and largely written material to which the evangelist had access and which he wove into a literary narrative—a story.

A friend of mine recently remarked it would be wonderful if someone could write a book about the Bible that could bridge some of the differences between more conservative and more liberal Christians. I had this challenge very much in mind in writing this book, but I am not really confident it is possible to build such a bridge because conservative and liberal Christians probably start out with different assumptions about what the Bible is and what it is not. I do not believe the Bible is inerrant, perfect in every detail, even in the original Hebrew and Greek, and certainly not in any English translation. If anything, I might say the Bible is perhaps something more like "The Word of God in the words of men."

My interest in the Gospel of Mark persists to this day. The fact that Mark is the earliest gospel may mean it has the least-developed theology and that it, therefore, reflects a more primitive and less-developed christology than the gospels of Matthew, Luke, and John. Clearer access to that less-developed Christianity may, in itself, be of merit.

I like to believe people will use this volume as a basis for discussion—church groups, seminarians, college students, reading groups, etc. I hope to introduce my readers to questions for which we do not know all of the answers in order to generate thinking and conversation.

Although I am ultimately responsible for everything in this book, I have been assisted by two good friends whose contributions I want to acknowledge. Dr. Marvin A. Breslow, Emeritus Professor of History at the University of Maryland and my roommate for four years at the Harvard University Graduate School of Arts and Sciences, read the manuscript and made innumerable corrections and invaluable suggestions. Only I can appreciate the value of his contribution. Dimitrios Dimopoulos contributed his technical skills in ways that were invaluable. I can barely type, no less unravel the intricacies of a computer for formatting, correcting, printing, and copying such a long manuscript. Both men's contributions are evident on almost every page of this book.

ABBREVIATIONS

Scripture Abbreviations

Old Testament

Gen	Genesis
Exod	Exodus
Lev	Leviticus
Num	Numbers
Deut	Deuteronomy
Josh	Joshua
Judg	Judges
1 Sam	1 Samuel
1–2 Kgs	1–2 Kings
2 Chr	2 Chronicles
Job	Job
Ps (*pl* Pss)	Psalms
Prov	Proverbs
Isa	Isaiah
Jer	Jeremiah
Lam	Lamentations
Ezek	Ezekiel
Dan	Daniel

Hos	Hosea
Joel	Joel
Amos	Amos
Mic	Micah
Hag	Haggai
Zech	Zechariah
Mal	Malachi

New Testament

Matt	Matthew
Mark	Mark
Luke	Luke
John	John
Acts	Acts
Rom	Romans
1-2 Cor	1-2 Corinthians
Gal	Galatians
Eph	Ephesians
Col	Colossians
1 Thess	1 Thessalonians
Heb	Hebrews
Jas	James
Rev	Revelation

Apocrypha

Wis	Wisdom of Solomon
1 Macc	1 Maccabees

Pseudepigrapha

Sib Or	Sibylline Oracles
4 Ezra	4 Ezra
2 Esd	2 Esdras
2 Bar	2 Baruch
1 En	1 Enoch
Ps Sol	Psalms of Solomon

Dead Sea Scrolls

1QpHab	An Essene commentary on Habakkuk found in Cave 1 at Qumran

INTRODUCTION

Before embarking on a study of the building blocks of the Gospel of Mark, the earliest gospel, it is important for the reader to understand something about the background of this remarkable literary creation.

THE TEXT OF THE GOSPEL

When the average reader picks up the Bible, it is not self-evident that he or she is reading a translation into English of 66 different books written between about two and three thousand years ago—in Biblical Hebrew with some Aramaic in the case of the thirty-nine books of the Old Testament, and in *Koine* or Common Greek in the case of the twenty-seven books of the New Testament.

In fact, before we can even begin to translate the Gospel of Mark into English, it is important to ask whether we are translating the text that left the author's pen when he first wrote the gospel almost two thousand years ago. The answer to that question is not self-evident because the books of the New Testament come down to us in the form of about 4,500 ancient Greek manuscripts, no two of which are identical. There are, additionally, thousands of early manuscripts of the New Testament that are translations from Greek into other ancient languages—Syriac, Latin, Coptic, Georgian, Ethiopic, Nubian, Sogdian (a Middle Iranian language), Gothic, Old Church Slavonic, etc.

Reconstructing the "autograph," the name given to the author's original text, is challenging, if not impossible; however, textual critics have been working at that task for almost two hundred years. Many scholars, including myself, are convinced that well-intentioned scribes made both inadvertent and intentional changes to the text they were copying, especially in the first century of its transmission and especially in the case of the gospels of Matthew, Mark, and Luke. It may not have been until the fourth century that the canon of the New Testament was essentially established, only after Christianity had been embraced by the Roman Emperor Constantine (306–337). It was probably only then that the text of the New Testament was regarded as no longer fluid, but essentially "fixed." We may be dealing in the case of the gospels of Matthew, Mark, and Luke, not with texts close to the author's autograph, but rather with texts of the gospels that were current in about 200 CE.

That said, in this volume I am working with the Greek text of Nestle-Aland (*Novum Testamentum Graece*), now in its 28th edition. Older English translations of the New Testament did not have access to the best manuscripts of the New Testament or to the important tools of textual criticism. Hence, older translations, including the revered King James Version (KJV), are less close to the author's original, the autograph, than more recent translations.

I decided that rather than select an existing English translation from the multitude that already exist, I will provide my own translation, following as closely as possible the Nestle-Aland Greek text. This edition of the Greek New Testament provides us with something that is at least close to the evangelist's original Greek of the New Testament, or to a text not later than about 200 CE in the case of the Gospel of Mark. At times I disagree with Nestle-Aland's Greek text of the gospel, but I will indicate those disagreements in my commentary and provide the reader with the reasons for my deviation from the Nestle-Aland text. I will also try in my translation to follow the Greek text as closely as possible, even in instances where the evangelist's Greek is awkward or problematic. It is likely that Greek was not the author's mother language, as his Greek is sometimes flawed, and some of his thoughts appear to reflect a Semitic or Aramaic background. Working with any book in anything other than the original language invites misunderstanding or at least lack of full understanding, especially when words have a wide range of meanings, and the translator must select a single word that misses the nuances of the original text. My commentary will, hopefully, address or explain at least some of these translation challenges.

THE LITERARY FORM OF THE GOSPEL

There are four distinct literary forms represented in the twenty-seven books of the New Testament: (1) four Gospels; (2) one History; (3) twenty-one Letters; and (4) one Apocalypse. We are obviously working with the first of these literary forms in the case of the Gospel of Mark.

The English word "gospel" comes from the Old English *godspel*, a compound word made up of *god* (meaning "good") and *spel* or *spiel* (meaning "news"). The Greek word *euaggelion* also means "good news" and first appears in the New Testament in letters by Paul, where it refers to the oral proclamation of the "good news" that Paul was preaching, perhaps as early as 38 CE.

The word *euaggelion* also appears in the opening words of the Gospel of Mark: "Beginning of the *good news* (*euaggelion*) of Jesus Messiah." This verse is actually the superscription or the title of the book. What follows in the book is all part of the "*good news*" of God's saving act in the life, suffering, death, and resurrection of Jesus. The author is not referring in 1:1 to his own work as a gospel, a specific literary form, because there was apparently no such literary form before the composition of Mark. The designation of "gospel" as a literary form occurred almost a century later.

Scholars recognize that our four canonical gospels (Matthew, Mark, Luke, and John) are similar in literary form to Greco-Roman biographies of the period, such as Plutarch's *Lives* and Suetonius's *Lives of the Caesars*, which come from the late first and early second centuries respectively. Greco-Roman biographies were not what we would regard as biographies in the modern understanding of that literary form. Ancient biographies were not intended to provide an accurate historical account of a person's life and work. They were rather concerned to provide positive accounts of a person's character in order to encourage readers to follow that person's example. Greco-Roman biographies stressed how great a person was. Exaggeration—indeed fabrication—was commonplace and even expected in these early biographies.

LITERARY FORMS OF THE BUILDING BLOCKS OF THE GOSPEL

Beginning almost a hundred years ago, scholars began to recognize that most of the written material in the gospels of Matthew, Mark, and Luke (the so-called Synoptic Gospels because of their similarity) appeared to be of five distinct literary categories or forms: pronouncement stories, miracle stories, parables, sayings, and legends (or stories about Jesus).

1. Pronouncement stories generally involve a discussion or dialogue between Jesus and an opponent in which Jesus resolves the issue with a final statement or pronouncement.

2. Miracle stories are accounts of wondrous events attributed to Jesus by the creative imagination of the church, often based on the fulfillment of alleged "proof texts" in the Old Testament. It is critical that modern readers understand the difference between "miracles" and "miracle stories."

3. Parables were a common form in both Jewish and Greco-Roman circles. A parable is a short story told to illustrate a simple truth—in this gospel often a simple truth about the coming of the kingdom of God, the period of God's rule.

4. Sayings refer to individual sayings or to clusters of sayings, usually attributed to Jesus.

5. Legends (or stories about Jesus) report alleged "events" in the life of Jesus often surrounded by miraculous or supernatural details.

It is important, especially with regard to miracle stories and legends, to take note of the invaluable contribution of David Friedrich Strauss,[1] who defined religious myth as "nothing else than the clothing in historic form of religious ideas, shaped by the unconscious power of legend, and embodied in a historic personality." In other words, miracle stories and legends should be understood for the religious ideas they contain, enshrined in what merely appears to be history, but is generally not a reliable report of an "event."

Scholars generally agree on these five literary forms, although some scholars try to refine the forms into even narrower categories or sub-groups. For our purpose, these five literary forms are sufficient for the reader to understand the material in most of the Gospel of Mark.

OUR EARLIEST GOSPEL

The overwhelming consensus of modern scholarship is the Gospel of Mark is the earliest of the gospels, and the authors of the gospels of Matthew and Luke used Mark as one of their written sources. The detailed arguments for the priority of Mark fall outside the scope of this book. Suffice it to say that the Gospel of Matthew reproduces about 90 percent of the subject matter of Mark, and the Gospel of Luke about 55 percent, with close verbal agreement and with individual stories in generally the same sequence or order.

---

1. Strauss, *Das Leben Jesus* (quoted by Albert Schweitzer, 79).

AUTHORSHIP, DATE, AND PLACE OF COMPOSITION

All four of the canonical gospels were written anonymously. There is no claim to authorship anywhere in the gospels of the New Testament. The attribution of the gospels to apostolic and subapostolic figures dates from the second century. In the case of the earliest gospel, the gospel was attributed to John Mark, a disciple or follower of Jesus' disciple, Peter. The actual author was likely no one known to us from the New Testament or early Christian literature. He was probably a person of standing in his own community, who was sufficiently literate to be able to read and write Greek. From this point forward in the book, I will not refer to the author by name, but simply as the evangelist or as the anonymous author of the earliest gospel.

The date of writing of this gospel is also not self-evident, although there may be hidden clues within the gospel itself. If the situation described in 13:5–23 reflects events that were known to the gospel's readers (or listeners), then the date of composition is probably after the Roman Emperor Nero's persecution of Christians in Rome in 64 CE. The lack of mention of or allusion to the Jewish war against Rome suggests a date before 70 CE, so sometime around 66–69 CE is a reasonable but by no means certain estimate.

As to where this gospel was written, the matter is even more uncertain. The author frequently explains Jewish customs to his readers and translates Aramaic words into Greek, so Roman Palestine was obviously not the place of composition. The gospel also uses a few Latin words, suggesting perhaps Rome or a Roman province, perhaps in Italy or Syria or elsewhere. Rome is an obvious candidate for the place of authorship, and many scholars have made that case. Some have suggested Alexandria, Egypt. Syria is also a good candidate, especially if there is any significance to the mention in 12:42 of the coins "lepta" and "quadrans," which suggest not Rome but rather one of the eastern provinces. Moreover, there is a great deal of Old Testament imagery in the gospel, so Syria may be a better candidate than Rome. We know there was an important church in Antioch of Syria relatively early in the history of Christianity. The church in Antioch had both Jewish Christians and Gentile Christians. It was a church where both Aramaic and Greek were likely spoken. Such an audience would account for both the preservation and the translation of some Aramaic words and phrases and for the clear importance of the Jewish Bible, especially for the Jewish-Christian members of the church.

Hence, my best guess—and it is little more than a guess based unfortunately on scant evidence and subject to legitimate differences of opinion—is the earliest gospel was written by an important but anonymous member of the church of Antioch of Syria in about 66–69 CE for a mixed Jewish-Christian and Gentile-Christian community. The evidence is not compelling, so we are forced to draw these conclusions somewhat tentatively within the limits of historical reason.

CHAPTERS AND VERSES

Ancient manuscripts of the New Testament were written first in Greek, a language written like English from left to right, but there were no spaces between words in the early manuscripts of our gospel, and there was no punctuation to indicate the beginning or end of a sentence or an idea. Words were written without spaces between them until the end of a line and then continued on the following line. Imagine trying to make sense of a text that read:

BEGINNINGOFTHEGOODNEWSOFJESUSMESSI-
AHJUSTASITHASBEENWRITTENINISAIAHTHEPRO-
PHETBEHOLDISENDMYMESSENGER

This convention of writing sometimes makes it unclear and open to question where one sentence ends and the next sentence begins. We shall see examples of this uncertainty in the text of the earliest gospel.

Neither, of course, were the books of the New Testament divided originally into chapters and verses. English Archbishop of Canterbury and Roman Catholic Cardinal Stephen Langton (1150–1228) and French Dominican priest and Cardinal Hugo de Sancto Caro (1200–1263) developed different divisions of the Bible into chapters in the 13th century. Langton's system prevailed and serves as the basis for our modern divisions into chapters.

Subsequently, Italian Dominican philologist and biblical scholar Santes Pagnino (1470–1541) was the first to divide the chapters into verses, but it was Parisian printer Robert Estienne (1505–1559) who created a verse numbering in his 1551 edition of the Greek New Testament and in his translation of the New Testament into French in 1553. That system prevailed. Estienne also produced in 1555 a Latin Vulgate that was the first Bible to include the verse numbers integrated into the Latin text rather than, as previously printed, in the margins. The first English translation to use verse numbers was a 1557 translation by English scholar and Bible translator William Whittingham (ca. 1524–1579). The first English Bible to use both chapters and verses was the Geneva Bible of 1560, creating the standard now in use in almost all Bibles since that time.

INTRODUCTION

PURPOSE

The purpose of this volume is relatively modest. My hope is to provide the reader with enough information about each story in the gospel and about the gospel as a whole to afford an informed reading of the earliest gospel. The evangelist was not writing a book for subsequent submission to a committee for possible inclusion in the canon of the Christian Bible. He was rather collecting already existing oral and written tradition into a coherent narrative to promote for his own Christian community an understanding of the "good news" of Jesus Messiah.

The church in Antioch (?) was likely already familiar with many of the individual stories or pericopes (the more formal designation for these units of tradition), probably from the evolving liturgy of the church. Christians gathered together in people's homes, as there were no churches as we understand that word as a specific building for Christian worship. It was likely in such gatherings in homes that stories would be told, perhaps as the basis for a sermon or message delivered by an elder or a leader of the church. Such stories might illustrate some truth about Jesus or address a question or issue of importance within the church. In other words, these individual stories or building blocks were developed within the church to serve the needs of the church. Regrettably from our perspective, historical accuracy was not a concern of the early church or of the earliest evangelist. We must, therefore, learn to read the gospel for what it is (a proclamation of the "good news"), and not for what we might like it to be (a reliable biography of Jesus of Nazareth). It is the author of the Gospel of John who said it best, when he wrote in 20:31 of his gospel: "But these things are written so that you may come to believe that Jesus is the Messiah, the Son of God, and that through believing you may have life in his name." The gospels are proclamations of the good news, not history books.

My hope is that individuals might be challenged by this modest contribution and might engage in dialogue with themselves and with others to discuss and debate the contribution, the meaning, and the purpose of this, the earliest gospel.

Chapter 1

THE SUPERSCRIPTION OR TITLE

1:1 Beginning of the good news of Jesus Christ (or Jesus Messiah).

THIS PHRASE, CLEARLY PENNED by the author, is actually the superscription or the title of this earliest written proclamation of the good news about Jesus Messiah. The word Christ (Greek *Christos*) is actually the Greek translation of the Hebrew word Messiah (meaning "the Anointed One"), and is a confessional designation about who Jesus was in the eyes of the anonymous author and of the early Jewish-Christian community for which he wrote (presumably in Antioch of Syria). Christ is not part of Jesus' name.

This proclamation of the good news about Jesus Messiah was written by an anonymous author, probably shortly before 70 CE. The traditional titles of our four canonical gospels were actually added in the second century, probably to ascribe apostolic authority to these anonymous writings: the Gospel of Matthew purportedly by one of Jesus' twelve disciples, the Gospel of Mark purportedly by a follower of Jesus' disciple, Peter, the Gospel of Luke purportedly by a traveling companion of Paul, and the Gospel of John purportedly by one of Jesus' twelve disciples.

The phrase "good news" first appears in Christian writings in letters of Paul to describe the early oral proclamation of the salvific death and resurrection of Jesus that early followers of Jesus preached first to Jews and then to Gentiles. It is the same word that was later translated into English as "gospel," but it is premature to understand this as a literary form in the instance of this early writing, the first such proclamation of the good news, which set the model for about two dozen later gospels.

The anonymous author is probably modeling his writing after the Greco-Roman lives of heroic figures, such as what appears in the near-contemporaneous Plutarch's *Lives* and Suetonius's *The Twelve Caesars*. These books were not historical biographies as we understand history and biography today but were rather glorified stories whose purpose was to present a positive portrait of great men of the ancient world without regard to historical accuracy. Plutarch makes it clear he is not concerned with history, but rather with the influence of character, whether good or bad, on the lives and destinies of men. In fact, he likened his craft to that of a painter and is more of a moral philosopher than a biographer in the modern sense of the word.

THE PREACHING OF JOHN AND THE BAPTISM OF JESUS

1:2 Just as it has been written in Isaiah the prophet: "Look, I am sending my messenger before your face, who will prepare your way;

3 a voice of someone crying out in the wilderness: 'Prepare the road of the Lord; make straight his paths,'"

4 John, the one baptizing, appeared in the wilderness, preaching a baptism of repentance leading to the forgiveness of sins.

5 And there went out to him all the region of Judea and all the people of Jerusalem, and they were baptized by him in the Jordan River, confessing their sins.

6 And John was clothed in camel's hair and a leather band around his waist, and he was eating locusts and wild honey.

7 And he preached, saying, "There is coming after me someone who is more powerful than I, the strap of whose sandal I am not worthy to stoop down and untie.

8 I baptized you with water, but he will baptize you in the Holy Spirit."

9 And it happened in those days that Jesus came from Nazareth of Galilee and was baptized in the Jordan by John.

10 And immediately, going up out of the water, he saw the heavens breaking apart and the Spirit descending like a dove into him.

11 And a voice came from the heavens, "You are my Son, the beloved; in you I take delight."

These ten verses constitute a discreet unit of tradition, which serves to introduce Jesus. There are no birth and infancy narratives of the sort that we find in the early chapters of Matthew and Luke. The anonymous author, writing earlier, is apparently unfamiliar with birth and infancy narratives. For the evangelist, the arrival of John the Baptist and his baptism of Jesus are the beginning of the story. I would identify this story as a legend, because it reports the intersection between the supernatural and the natural orders—not only John's baptism of Jesus, but also the descent of the Spirit into Jesus and God's call and designation of Jesus as his beloved Son.

The story begins with the ministry of John the Baptist, who is introduced as the precursor of Jesus in eschatological fulfillment of a prophecy of Isaiah. The quote in our text (1:2) is actually not from Isaiah but from a conflation of material from three different sources in the Greek translation (the so-called Septuagint) of the Hebrew Bible: Exod 23:20; Mal 3:1; and Isa 40:3. This conflation of texts suggests that the author is not quoting directly from the Old Testament but rather from a written Christian source that already contained a collection of proof-texts of Old Testament passages that, it was believed, looked ahead to the life and ministry of Jesus. Scholars call such a document *testimonia* or "testimonies." Decades before the writing of the earliest gospel, Paul's preaching already contained a traditional message that Jesus' death for our sins and his resurrection occurred "in accordance with the Scriptures" (1 Cor 15:3-4). This early claim apparently led Christians to search meticulously through the Jewish Scriptures for passages they could use to proclaim the good news about Jesus the Messiah. The practice of picking bits and pieces of Scriptures, totally out of their original contexts, and piecing them together was apparently not uncommon in contemporary Judaism. In the early 1950s, such a *testimonia* document was discovered among the Dead Sea Scrolls, usually dated to the middle of the first century BCE, the creation of a Jewish sect known as the Essenes. A similar conflation of Old Testament texts was likely the creation of Christian scribes, whose work served either directly or indirectly as one of our anonymous author's written sources.

The author is likely inserting here at the beginning of his work a story that recalls an actual event early in Jesus' ministry, his baptism by John in "a baptism of repentance leading to the forgiveness of sins." Jesus' baptism by John must be an historical fact, because it later posed some embarrassment for the early church. Why, after all, would Jesus submit to John's "baptism of repentance leading to the forgiveness of sins?" The report may reflect an historical memory that Jesus' call and commission occurred at his baptism by John, or shortly thereafter. Yet in his account, the evangelist makes it clear this was the occasion when Jesus was designated as God's Son, by recalling almost exactly the words of Ps 2:7 in the Greek Septuagint translation: "You are my son; today I have begotten you."

This early Christology of Jesus' *adoption* by God is found both in the writings of Paul, where, in the opening paragraph of Romans, Jesus "*was declared to be* Son of God with power according to the spirit of holiness *by resurrection from the dead*" (Rom 1:4) and in Acts 2:36: "God *has made him both Lord and Messiah*, this Jesus whom you crucified" (italics mine). Our anonymous author simply moved Jesus' messiahship or divine sonship back from the time of his resurrection to the time of his call and commission on the occasion of his baptism. By doing so, the anonymous author is claiming that Jesus' entire ministry was, therefore, *messianic*. According to the anonymous evangelist, Jesus was God's chosen one from the time of his baptism and, therefore, throughout his entire ministry.

The view that Jesus was "adopted" as God's "chosen one," whether by virtue of his resurrection or at the time of his baptism by John, is called Adoptionism and was an early belief of many Christians. Even though it is found in the New Testament both here and in Paul and in Acts, this Adoptionist Christology was condemned by the church as heretical with the acceptance of the Nicene Creed at the Council of Nicaea in 325 CE.

What is not clear is whether Jesus actually understood that his "call" came at his baptism by John, or whether this idea is merely a creation of the early church or of the anonymous evangelist. Neither is it clear how much of this story may have been influenced by the early church's ritual baptism of converts into the Jesus movement. What is clear is that Jesus submitted to John's baptism and may actually have been an early follower or disciple of John the Baptist.

THE TEMPTATION OF JESUS IN THE WILDERNESS

1:12 And immediately the Spirit drove him out into the wilderness.

13 And he was in the wilderness for forty days, tempted by the Satan, and he was with the wild animals; and the angels waited on him.

The story of the Spirit casting Jesus into the wilderness follows immediately upon the account of his baptism by John and before the story of the formal beginning of Jesus' ministry following John's arrest. The story of Jesus' forty days in the wilderness is reminiscent of Moses' forty days on Mount Sinai and Israel's forty years in the Sinai wilderness, the number forty meaning simply "a long time."

In the Old Testament book of Job, the Satan was a member of the heavenly council, where he acted as a kind of prosecuting attorney. However, under the influence of Zoroastrian dualism during the Persian occupation of Judah, the Satan evolved into an entirely evil opponent of God, as in this story of the temptation of Jesus. With the call of Jesus, the eschatological war between good and evil has officially begun. As such, this story should also be classified as a legend, a story about the intersection of the natural world and the supernatural worlds of both evil, represented by the Satan, and of good, represented by God's newly designated Son and the angels. The implication of the story is that good will ultimately prevail, but, as we will see, only after a very difficult struggle.

THE BEGINNING OF JESUS' TEACHING IN GALILEE

> 1:14 But after John was handed over, Jesus came into Galilee, preaching the good news of God,
>
> 15 and saying, "The time has been fulfilled, and the Kingdom of God is at hand. Repent, and believe in the good news."

Verses 7–8 above imply that John the Baptist regarded himself as the forerunner of someone more powerful, who was coming after him. But who was that someone for whom John was the precursor? Presumably Jesus, at least in the mind of the evangelist. Verses 14–15 state clearly that Jesus' ministry began immediately after John was arrested. But why? In fulfillment of John's proclamation? Yet, Acts 19:1–7 suggests that there were still followers of John the Baptist at the time of Paul, decades after Jesus' death. In fact, followers of John the Baptist seem to have survived into the second century and even beyond. If John had already acknowledged Jesus as his successor, then why didn't John's disciples simply become followers of Jesus? Something seems to be wrong here. The gospels of Matthew and John state clearly that John recognized at Jesus' baptism that Jesus was the one who was coming after him. The earliest gospel does not make that recognition quite as clearly as the later gospels of Matthew, Luke, and John.

I would like to propose a somewhat different sequence of events, one perhaps reflected, even if only innocently, in the earliest gospel. Perhaps John considered himself the precursor not of Jesus but of a figure known in some contemporary Jewish circles as the Son of Man, an eschatological figure who would usher in the age of God's rule or the kingdom of God. In that case, John's baptism of repentance leading to the forgiveness of sins was in preparation for the coming of the eschatological Son of Man, who was himself the precursor of the coming of God's kingdom.

With the arrest of John, Jesus, apparently a disciple of John and in deference to John, took up John's mantel and continued to proclaim the imminent arrival of the eschatological Son of Man and of God's kingdom. There seems to be a similarity in the preaching of John and Jesus given what little we can know when comparing 1:7–8 with 1:15. Let us at least keep an open mind about this question as we continue to delve into Jesus' teaching later in this gospel.

Why was John arrested, and why did his preaching come to an end? The anonymous author is aware that John was arrested by agents of Herod Antipas (see 6:17), who at the time was tetrarch of Galilee and Perea (4 BCE–39 CE). According to the account in 6:17–18, John considered Herod Antipas's marriage to his brother Philip's wife Herodias to be unlawful, clearly reason enough to anger Herod Antipas and Herodias.

Although this unit (or pericope) in its current form is likely a literary creation of the evangelist, it may contain an authentic saying or teaching of Jesus, possibly in imitation of John.

THE CALL OF JESUS' FIRST DISCIPLES

1:16 And while passing along beside the Sea of Galilee, he saw Simon and Andrew, the brother of Simon, casting [a net] in the sea; for they were fishermen.

17 And Jesus said to them, "Follow me, and I will make you to become fishermen of men."

18 And immediately leaving the nets, they followed him.

> 19 And going forward a little, he saw James, the son of Zebedee, and John, his brother, who were also in the boat putting their nets in order.
>
> 20 And immediately he called them, and leaving their father Zebedee in the boat with the hired servants, they went after him.

Now that "the time [of the Satan's rule] has been fulfilled" (i.e. is at its end), it is time for Jesus to call his first four disciples: Simon (Peter) and his brother Andrew, and James and John, sons of Zebedee, all fishermen in the Sea of Galilee, an area about 25 miles northeast of Jesus' hometown of Nazareth. In its current form, this story is a legend.

There are in our gospel actually three callings of disciples: this passage in 1:16–20, then again in 3:13–19 and in 6:7–13, and perhaps also in 2:14 (see below). Each of the three callings is followed by a literary unit containing several stories. This arrangement should probably be seen as a literary device of the evangelist and not as the historical record of three distinct callings, each followed by specific events in the life and ministry of Jesus.

The listing of Peter first among the disciples may be intentional because of his position of preeminence among Jesus' followers, the fact that he was the first person to experience the risen Christ after Jesus' death, and his role of leadership in the early Jerusalem church. The listing of James and John as sons of Zebedee may be to distinguish them from Jesus' brother James and John the Baptist.

The mention of the hired hands (v. 20) may be a literary detail to assure the listener that James and John did not abandon their father, thereby leaving him helpless; moreover, the suddenness with which the four men immediately drop what they are doing to follow Jesus is also a literary detail, as it is clearly not believable. The word "immediately" (Greek *euthus*) is a favorite of our author: in fact, it has appeared four times in just the first twenty verses.

The suddenness with which the four men leave everything to follow Jesus may also serve as a lesson to the author's audience as to the kind of uncompromising commitment Jesus expects from them as well.

CHAPTER 1

JESUS TEACHES WITH AUTHORITY AND HEALS THE MAN WITH THE UNCLEAN SPIRIT

1:21 And they entered into Capernaum, and immediately on the Sabbath entering into the synagogue, he taught.

22 And they were astonished at his teaching, for he was teaching them as someone having authority, and not as the scribes.

23 And immediately there was in their synagogue a man in an unclean spirit. And he cried out,

24 saying, "What do we have to do with you, Jesus Nazarene? Have you come to destroy us? I know who you are—the holy one of God!"

25 And Jesus rebuked him, saying, "Be quiet, and come out from him!"

26 And when the unclean spirit had convulsed him and cried out with a loud voice, he came out of him.

27 And they were all amazed, so that they debated among themselves, saying, "What is this? What new teaching is this? With authority he gives orders even to the unclean spirits, and they obey him.

28 And his fame spread immediately throughout the whole region of Galilee.

Capernaum was at this time a small fishing village at the northwest tip of the Sea of Galilee and appears to have served as the site of the beginning of Jesus' ministry. Jesus entered the synagogue in Capernaum and immediately began to teach. As is common in this gospel, the word "immediately" (v. 23) is misplaced in the sentence, an indication of the author's somewhat flawed Greek.

The synagogue served as a place for prayer, worship, teaching, the study of Scriptures, and other religious activity. The author reports that unlike the scribes, who at this time were primarily copyists whose teaching was based on tradition and precedent, Jesus taught "with authority." The phrase "with authority" implies a *freedom of choice* or *a right to act* beyond what one might expect in the synagogue. In other words, Jesus was breaking protocol in the way in which he was teaching. The phrase is repeated later in verse 27, where the people collectively acknowledge Jesus' authority following an exorcism, thereby providing a connection with what might originally have been two units, verses 21–22 and verses 23–28. By deviating from the prescribed way of debating about the Jewish law or Torah, Jesus was an iconoclast. He broke with tradition. We will see later in the gospel the nature of Jesus' radical teaching about the Torah, the nature of his authority. For the author, Jesus' *authority* is grounded in the descent of the Spirit at Jesus' baptism, when he was adopted as Son of God. The amazement of the people in verses 22 and 27 is a common device of the author.

Verse 23 begins again with the author's common connective "and" and his favored word "immediately." The reference to the man *in* (Greek *ev*) *an unclean spirit* is probably an Aramaism, inasmuch as the word *bē* in Aramaic (the language of Jesus, his disciples, and the earliest converts to Christianity) can mean both *in* and *with*. This and similar clues elsewhere in the text suggest the evangelist may have been a Jewish Christian, whose first language was Aramaic rather than the Greek in which he was writing his account of the good news. Likewise *unclean spirit* is Jewish terminology for a demon that has entered the man. In asking the question "What do we have to do with you?", the author is quoting a biblical idiom found in Judg 11:12; 1 Kgs 17:18; 2 Kgs 3:13; and 2 Chr 35:21, implying that the demons want to know why Jesus is acting in such a hostile manner toward them: "Have you come to destroy us?"

The demons recognize Jesus, because like Jesus they too are supernatural beings. Jesus then ordered the demon(s) to be quiet and come out from the man. The demon then tore the man to and fro, cried out, and finally left the man.

In the Greco-Roman world in general, and in Jewish literature and in this gospel in particular, stories about such exorcisms or healings often conclude with a phrase expressing the amazement of the crowd. The author again repeats here the authority with which Jesus not only taught, but with which he performed exorcisms. The eschatological war against the powers of evil has begun.

Once again, there follows the evangelist's favored word (v. 28): and *"immediately"* Jesus' fame spread throughout the whole region of Galilee.

This story, this unit of tradition (what scholars call a pericope [pronounced pe-ri'-co-pee]) is a miracle story, which is, of course, quite different from a miracle. The emphasis is on the word "story." This pericope is a story of an exorcism that the author has incorporated into his account of the good news.

CHAPTER 1 17

THE HEALIING OF PETER'S MOTHER-IN-LAW

> 1:29 And immediately coming out of the synagogue, they went into the house of Simon and Andrew with James and John.
>
> 30 But Simon's mother-in-law lay sick with a fever, and immediately they told him about her.
>
> 31 And approaching, he lifted her up holding her hand, and the fever left her, and she served them.

The story of the return to Capernaum, the home of Peter's mother-in-law and presumably the home(s) of Peter and Andrew, is interesting, because just a short time earlier Jesus asked the disciples to leave everything behind and follow him. Now they are back in Capernaum. Such clues reinforce the likelihood that we are dealing not with history but with pericopes or stories arranged in their current order by the evangelist.

In this brief miracle story, we once again see the author's use of the word "immediately" twice (at least the first of which is misplaced, as is often the case) and the use of the connective "and" five times, increasingly evident editorial characteristics of the anonymous evangelist.

The story itself is quite simple, although it follows the usual account of such a story: (1) the coming of the miracle worker, (2) the description of the sickness, (3) the request for a healing, (4) the healing itself, and often (5) the amazement of the crowd. In this story, there is no word from Jesus, just the touch of his hand.

THE HEALING AND EXORCISM OF MANY

> 1:32 But when it was evening, when the sun set, they brought to him all who were sick and those who were demon-possessed.
>
> 33 And the whole city was assembled together at the door.
>
> 34 And he healed many who were sick with various diseases, and he cast out many demons. And he did not allow the demons to speak, because they knew him.

These verses are probably a construction of the evangelist and not material drawn by him from a written source. The description of the "whole city assembled at the door" (v. 33) and of healings and exorcisms (v. 34) are general and lack the detail of most of the miracles stories we find throughout the gospel.

It is implied that the setting is still at the door of Peter's mother-in-law's house, although this too is probably nothing more than the way in which the author organized the two stories in sequence. If it is the author's intention to say these healings occurred in the evening, i.e., after the Sabbath, then the healing of Peter's mother-in-law occurred on the Sabbath, presumably in violation of Jewish law or Torah.

The detail that everyone in Capernaum who was sick or possessed by a demon was brought to Jesus and cured on the spot may be the evangelist's way of emphasizing the universality of the good news about Jesus the Messiah.

Jesus' decision not to allow the demons to speak is in contrast with the earlier exorcism in the synagogue, where the demon called Jesus by name. This story may be the first instance of the motif of the messianic secret, a theological theme the author seems to employ throughout the gospel in order to deal with the seeming contradiction between the belief that Jesus was Messiah and Son of God from the time of his baptism on the one hand, and the fact that it was only after his death and resurrection that his followers believed that he had been elevated by God to the position of Messiah and Lord on the other hand. In other words, by silencing those who recognize him as Messiah during his lifetime, the Jesus of the gospel tries to keep his messiahship secret until after he is raised from the dead in order to conform to the reality of when it is that Jesus' followers actually came to believe in his lordship and messiahship.

JESUS DEPARTS ON A PREACHING TOUR OF GALILEE

> 1:35 And early in the morning when it was still quite dark, having risen, he went out and went away into a deserted place; and there he prayed.

> 36 And Simon and those who were with him searched for him.

> 37 And they found him and they said to him, "Everyone is searching for you."
>
> And he said to them. "Let us go elsewhere into the neighboring towns, so that also there I may preach; for this purpose I have come forth."
>
> 39 And he came preaching into their synagogues into all Galilee and casting out the demons.

Like most of the pericopes or units of tradition in this gospel, this story begins with the word "and" (Greek *kai*). There then follows a report of time ("early in the morning when it was still dark") and place ("going to a deserted place to pray"), features that we recognize by now as editorial comments of the anonymous evangelist in order to provide a setting for the story that follows. The unit itself is quite general and probably a construction of the evangelist, not something he found in a written source.

When Simon and those who are with him finally find Jesus and try to take him back to Capernaum, Jesus has something quite different in mind: it is time to go into neighboring towns to preach because "for this purpose I have come forth."

Interestingly, as was the case in Capernaum, Jesus sets forth with his disciples ("Let us go") into their synagogues throughout Galilee, both to preach and to cast out demons, both signs of the imminent arrival of God's rule and the accompanying destruction of the powers of evil in the eschatological war that is gradually unfolding.

THE CLEANSING OF THE MAN WITH THE SCALY SKIN

> 1:40 And a man with a scaly skin disease came to him, imploring him, falling down on his knees, saying to him, "If you want, you are able to make me clean."
>
> 41 And moved with compassion, stretching out his hand he touched and said to him, "I do so want; be clean."
>
> 42 And immediately the scaly skin disease left him, and he was cleansed.

43 And he sternly warned him and immediately sent him away,

44 and said to him, "See that you say nothing to anyone; but go your way, show yourself to the priest, and offer for your cleansing those things that Moses commanded, for a proof to them."

45 But he who was going out began to proclaim loudly and to spread the word, so that he could no longer openly enter into a city, but was outside in deserted places; and they came to him from every direction.

This is the third miracle story in the gospel in addition to the general healings and exorcisms referred to in verses 34 and 39. This story contains the typical characteristics of a miracle story: (1) the man came to Jesus, (2) the request for a cleansing, (3) the manner of healing (by touch and verbal command), (4) the actual healing, (5) the command of silence (perhaps another example of the messianic secret), and (6) the command to go to the priest for an offering.

The nature of the man's disease is a matter of debate. Although the Greek says *lepros* (suggesting the English word leprosy), the word actually means a "scaly skin disease," ranging from psoriasis, lupus, ringworm, and favus to Hansen's disease (what we today call leprosy), which was not curable until the discovery of modern drug therapy.

The Greek verb *katharizo* (v. 40) usually refers to a religious or ritual purification or cleansing, not to a healing or cure. This detail may provide insight into the story. Jesus may have been saying to the man with the scaly skin disease that there is no such thing as ritual uncleanness and may, therefore, have declared the man *ritually* clean. In the retelling of the story over time, it is easy to see how such a story might evolve into a full-blown miracle story, proclaiming the physical healing of the man's disorder. The story in an earlier form might have meant that Jesus declared "with authority" an end to the discrimination between ritual cleanness and ritual uncleanness. Perhaps that was the message that the man was commanded to take to the priest, and there is merit to this detail. The man with the scaly skin disease was no longer ritually unclean simply by virtue of his disorder. It is, otherwise, puzzling and uncharacteristic that Jesus would command the man to uphold the Levitical law (Lev 13–14) by going to the priests and making an offering. In similar manner, Jesus drove out the "*unclean* spirit" from the man in the synagogue in Capernaum (v. 25 above). Supporting this interpretation of the story as evidence of Jesus' rejection of ritual uncleanness is the fact that Jesus stretched out his hand and touched the man (v. 41) in defiance of Jewish avoidance of people who were ritually unclean. A person who touched a ritually unclean person was also defiled and thus also ritually unclean.

Such defiance of the Jewish Law (Torah) by Jesus is evident elsewhere in this gospel. With regard to doing work on the Sabbath, Jesus says in 2:27: "The Sabbath came into being for the sake of man and not man for the sake of the Sabbath." And with regard to Jewish dietary laws, Jesus says in 7:18: "Do you not understand that whatever enters a human being from outside cannot defile him? . . . It is what comes out of a human being that defiles."

CONCLUSIONS AFTER CHAPTER 1

Our earliest gospel was apparently put together by using distinct units of tradition or pericopes, probably from one or more written sources, to which the evangelist had access. As such, there is likely no logical order to the stories after the story of John's baptism, which obviously needs to stand first. Neither are the references to time and place anything more than introductory phrases provided by the anonymous author.

At least one of the written sources of this gospel was probably a *testimonia* or collection of "testimonies" or "proof-texts" from the Old Testament, often in combination, to demonstrate that details in the life and ministry of Jesus occurred "in accordance with the Scriptures." Although there is only one such example in chapter 1, the passage combining elements of Exodus, Malachi, and Isaiah, mistakenly identified in verse 2 as coming from Isaiah, we shall see other examples of this later, most especially in the author's account of Jesus' crucifixion and death: an extremely elaborate example of such a *testimonia*. More likely, however, we shall see that the evangelist's written sources already had access to written *testimonia*.

The literary forms of the pericopes found in chapter 1 are legends and miracle stories and a single saying of Jesus, probably coming from different sources. Perhaps someone had already gathered into a written source available to our author a collection of miracle stories, inasmuch as we find three miracle stories in the latter part of this chapter: (1) The Healing of the Man with the Unclean Spirit (1:21–28), (2) The Healing of Peter's Mother-in-law (1:29–31), and (3) The Healing of the Man with the Scaly Skin (1:40–45).

There is also, even in the short space of these forty-five verses, evidence of some of the editorial characteristics of the evangelist:

1. The evangelist tends to begin an unusual number of sentences with the word "and" (Greek *kai*). He uses the word "and" eighty-four times in chapter 1 and often at the beginning of a sentence. This may be a Semitism, as it is quite common to begin sentences in Hebrew and Aramaic with the prefix *wē* (and) attached to the first word of the sentence.

2. The evangelist uses the word "immediately" (Greek *euthus*) quite frequently, eleven times in just forty-five verses in chapter 1. Of the fifty-four appearances of this word in the New Testament, forty-two (or 78%) occur in this gospel, eleven (or 20%) in the first chapter. Moreover, the author frequently misplaces the word "immediately" with the wrong verb in the sentence, reflecting the likelihood that Greek was not his mother language.

3. The evangelist appears to use throughout the gospel the theological theme of the Messianic Secret, which appears twice in this chapter. The Messianic Secret is a theory of biblical criticism first advanced in 1901 by Wilhelm Wrede (*The Messianic Secret in the Gospels*) to explain why, in this gospel, Jesus wants to hide his messiahship by commanding his disciples and demonic forces to keep silent about his identity. Wrede claimed Jesus made no messianic claims during his lifetime but that the anonymous author of this gospel (perhaps following the lead of Christians before him) *made* Jesus the Messiah from the outset of his ministry. The Messianic Secret was then a theme of the gospel created to provide a reason why Jesus was *not proclaimed* Messiah by his followers until *after* his death and resurrection.

4. The evangelist created some material of his own invention in addition to his use of written sources. The evangelist is probably responsible for composing some elements in this chapter: The Superscription or Title (1:1), Jesus Teaches in the Synagogue (1:21–22), The Healing and Exorcism of Many (1:32–34), and Jesus Departs on a Teaching Tour of Galilee (1:35–39). Not only does this material not conform to the literary forms identified above, but it is often quite general and sometimes serves merely to move Jesus from one place to the next.

Chapter 2

THE HEALING OF THE PARALYZED MAN AND JESUS HAS AUTHORITY TO FORGIVE SINS

2:1 And entering again into Capernaum after some days, it became known that he was at home.

2 And many people were gathered together, so that there was no longer room, not even near the door. And he spoke to them the word.

3 Then they came, carrying to him a paralyzed man, who was being carried by four [men].

4 And not being able to carry him (the man) to him (Jesus) because of the crowd, they removed the roof where he was. And when they had broken through the roof, they let down the pallet upon which the paralyzed man was lying.

— — —

2:5 And seeing their faith, Jesus said to the paralyzed man, "Child, your sins are forgiven."

6 Now there were some of the scribes sitting there and deliberating in their hearts,

7 "Why does this man speak like this? He is blaspheming! Who is able to forgive sins except one, God alone?"

8 And Jesus, immediately knowing in his spirit that they were deliberating about this among themselves, said to them, "Why are you deliberating these matters in your hearts?

9 What is easier, to say to the paralyzed man, 'Your sins are forgiven,' or to say, 'Get up, pick up your pallet and walk?'"

10a But in order that you may know that the Son of Man has authority to forgive sins on the earth"—

— — —

2:10b he said to the paralyzed man,

11 "I say to you, get up, pick up your pallet, and go to your house."

12 And he got up and immediately picking up the pallet went out ahead of them all, so that all were amazed and glorified God, saying, "We have never seen anything like this!"

WE ALREADY SAW IN the story of The Healing of the Man with the Unclean Spirit (1:21–28) that Jesus taught "with authority" and not like the scribes, the acknowledged experts in the Jewish Law (Torah). The evangelist takes up that theme once again in 2:1—3:6 with a series of similar stories relating to Jesus' authority. These stories all share the same literary form: what are called conflict stories or pronouncement stories. These pericopes set forth conflict between Jesus and his Jewish opponents. The cluster of these stories probably points to the author's use of still another written source for this conflict or pronouncement material.

In this periscope (2:1–12), the miracle story of The Healing of the Paralyzed Man (2:1–4, 10b–12) is set within the context of the pronouncement story of Jesus' Authority to Forgive Sin (2:5–10a). This is not simply one more miracle story.

Once again, the opening words of this pericope merely provide a setting and have no historical value as to when or where this incident took place. "Some days" after when? And Jesus is "at home" (or perhaps simply "in a house") in Capernaum, perhaps his home base in Peter's house or in Peter's mother-in-law's house. But such detail is irrelevant and probably a simple editorial detail of the evangelist.

After Jesus has, for a while, been teaching or preaching the word (presumably the good news about the imminent arrival of [the Son of Man and?] the kingdom of God), four men arrive carrying a paralyzed man on a pallet (2:3). There is no request for a healing here, because the healing is not the real purpose of this story.

There is no precedent in the Old Testament for a situation in which a man grants forgiveness of sins. That is reserved for God, or for the priests speaking with authority about God's forgiveness of sins. However, in a fragment from the *Prayer of Nabonidus* found in cave 4 of the Dead Sea Scrolls, a Jewish soothsayer or exorcist forgives Nabobidus's sins, showing the possibility that the Essenes, the people of the Dead Sea Scrolls, believed that a man could forgive sins.

It is understandable that the scribes would express consternation: "He is blaspheming!" (2:7), because only God can forgive sins. However, the author's point in the story is that Jesus can forgive sins because he is the anointed Messiah, the adopted Son of God, who speaks and acts with the authority of God, or with authority from God.

It is important to understand that in the ancient world there was generally thought to be a connection between disease and sin. A person is ill or afflicted because of something that person did. Hence, the significance of Jesus' forgiving the man's sin is clear. In some respect, the forgiving of the man's sin is the real cure. Just as sickness is connected to sin, so too is forgiveness connected to healing. Yet, for the observer and for people listening to the reading of this story decades later, perhaps in a house church on the occasion of a religious service, the physical cure of the paralyzed man served as the definitive proof of Jesus' authority.

The key to this story lies in the words of Jesus in verse 10: "In order that you may know that the Son of Man has authority to forgive sins on the earth . . . ." If this saying is genuine—and it may well be—about whom is Jesus speaking when he speaks of the Son of Man (Greek *ho huios tou anthropou*)? Jesus is obviously not referring to the coming eschatological Son of Man who will usher in God's rule. That would have no meaning in this context. But there is a clue later in this chapter in 2:27–28: "The Sabbath came into being for the sake of man, and not man for the sake of the Sabbath; so the Son of Man is master even of the Sabbath." Both 2:10 and 2:27–28 reflect the likelihood that the Greek phrase "Son of Man" is a translation of the Aramaic (the language Jesus and his disciples spoke) phrase *bar-nasha*, literally, a son of man, which often means simply "a man" or "humankind" (as correctly rendered twice in 2:27). So, although we have translated the Greek accurately into English, the phrase (if it was ever on Jesus' lips, or certainly early in the Aramaic evolution of the story) clearly meant "In order that you may know that man (humankind) has authority to forgive sins on earth, ..." Jesus is referring here to the authority of humankind (including himself) to forgive sins. We should also recall that John the Baptist preached a baptism of repentance leading to the forgiveness of sin. Although it is not clear that John actually forgave sin, he was at least the instrument through which sin was forgiven (by God?).

Like the story the Cleansing of The Man with the Scaly Skin Disease (1:40–45), the story of The Healing of the Paralyzed Man may be grounded in an historical event in which the issue was whether Jesus, or perhaps even humankind collectively, has the authority to declare people ritually clean or free from sin. If there is merit to this interpretation of the story, then Jesus may be shifting the focus of Judaism from being a theocentric (God-centered) religion to being an anthropocentric (humankind-centered) religion, a truly radical idea, and a clear threat to religious intermediaries such as the Pharisees, the scribes, and the Jerusalem priesthood—the establishment.

JESUS CALLS LEVI TO BE HIS DISCIPLE

> 2:13 And he went out again beside the sea; and all the crowd came to him, and he taught them.

> 14 And passing along, he saw Levi, the son of Alphaeus, sitting at the tax office. And he said to him, "Follow me." And getting up, he followed him.

The language of 2:13 is reminiscent of 1:16, where Jesus was also "beside the sea" when he called Simon (Peter), Andrew, James, and John. However, the call of Levi takes place not at the seaside but at the tax office, where Levi presumably worked collecting the tax on the transport of goods. The identity of Levi is unclear, although the author identifies him as the son of Alphaeus and as a tax collector. He is not mentioned anywhere else in this gospel, not even in the list of Jesus' twelve disciples just a few lines later in 3:16–19, although there is mention in 3:18 of a James, the son of Alphaeus, perhaps a brother of Levi.

This story and the list of disciples in chapter 3 may be drawn by the anonymous author from different sources. Consistency was not as much of an issue as one might assume.

As in the call of the original four disciples, Jesus calls out to Levi to follow him, and he gets up and immediately follows Jesus. This story should probably be classified as a legend or perhaps, more likely, as a construction of the evangelist.

JESUS EATS WITH SINNERS AND TAX COLLECTORS

> 2:15 And it happened that he was reclining in his (i.e., Levi's?) house, and many tax collectors and sinners reclined with Jesus and his disciples; for there were many, and they followed him.
>
> 16 And the scribes of the Pharisees seeing that he was eating with the sinners and tax collectors, said to his disciples, "Does he eat with tax collectors and sinners?"
>
> 17 And hearing [this], Jesus said to them, "Those who are well do not need a physician, but those who are sick. I did not come to call the righteous, but sinners."

This pericope seems to be linked to the call of Levi above, although that is not entirely clear. The connection seems to be the fact that there were tax collectors at the dinner in his (i.e., Levi's?) house (2:15). The scene suggests a festal dinner, because the guests were reclining on couches at the table, the usual arrangement for such celebrations.

The presence of tax collectors and sinners at the dinner was shocking to the scribes of the Pharisees, once again representing opponents of Jesus in what is clearly more of a fabricated story than an actual event. Tax collectors were despised because of their dishonest and corrupt abuse of the tax system by their overcharging for the transport of goods. The word "sinners" in this story may refer to none other than ritually unclean peasants or people in violation of the Jewish Law in the eyes of the Pharisees. The nature of their sin is not clear and is not relevant to the story.

What is important is that Jesus was associating with people who were ritually unclean, thereby rendering himself also ritually unclean. This pericope is another example of a conflict story or a pronouncement story, as it ends with a pronouncement by Jesus: "Those who are well do not need a physician, but those who are sick." The evangelist added the editorial comment that Jesus came to call sinners. He did not come to call those who were already in a right relationship with God. In fact, Jesus not only eats with tax collectors and sinners, he called Levi from among them to be a disciple.

The purpose of pronouncement stories was apparently to provide a context for Jesus' pronouncement, no more, no less. The words of Jesus or the "pronouncement" probably survived isolated from any literary context, and the context was probably provided later by someone in the church when the saying was being used for instructional purposes.

The context of this particular pericope seems unlikely on several scores. Did the host (Levi?) invite the scribes of the Pharisees to the dinner? An improbable guest list! And were the scribes of the Pharisees not just as guilty as Jesus by associating with tax collectors and sinners? Is Jesus the only one at the party in violation of the purity laws? These issues point clearly to the fictitious element of the story. But the point is clear: by his action, Jesus once again violated the Jewish Law and disavowed the Pharisaic distinction between ritual cleanness and uncleanness. Once again, Jesus' message is anthropocentric (humankind-centered) rather than theocentric (God-centered).

THE QUESTION ABOUT FASTING AND THE NEW AND THE OLD

2:18 And John's disciples and the Pharisees were fasting. And they came and said to him, "Why do John's disciples and the disciples of the Pharisees fast, but your disciples do not fast?"

19 And Jesus said to them, "Can the sons of the wedding hall (i.e., the wedding guests) fast while the bridegroom is with them? As long as they have the bridegroom with them, they cannot fast.

20 But days will come when the bridegroom is taken away from them, and then they will fast in that day.

— — —

2:21 No one sews a patch of new cloth on a tattered garment; otherwise, the new piece pulls away from the old, and a worse tear occurs.

CHAPTER 2 29

> 2:22 And no one pours new wine into old wineskins; otherwise the wine will break the wineskins, and the wine is ruined, and even the wineskins. But [one puts] new wine into new wineskins."

We have in this pericope still one more pronouncement story, although in a very complex form because the question posed to Jesus in verse 18 is followed by three parabolic sayings: the saying or sayings about the wedding guests (vv. 19–20), and two seemingly unrelated sayings about the new and the old (vv. 21–22). The summary seems to come in the pronouncement "new wine into new wineskins" (v. 22b), but I think the matter is even more complicated.

There is already a problem in verse 18: Who is asking Jesus this question? If it is John's disciples and the Pharisees, then why do they refer to themselves in the third person? Perhaps it is the scribes of the Pharisees from the previous story (vv. 16-17), but that is unlikely given the independence of the pericope. More likely, it is simply an oversight on the part of the evangelist. Verse 18 seems to be referring to an indefinite "they," a not-uncommon feature in this gospel.

Moreover, the phrase "disciples of the Pharisees" is peculiar, because followers of the Pharisees were never referred to as disciples. The word "disciples" usually implied followers of an individual charismatic leader. The reference to Jesus' disciples in this pericope is also somewhat unusual. Why do the indefinite "they" ask Jesus why his disciples do not fast rather than ask Jesus the question why he does not fast? The answer is that the story in its present form is probably referring to the early Christian community (Jesus' followers), Christians in the church for which the anonymous author is writing. The story may simply be addressing the question of whether it is appropriate for Christians to fast, even though Jesus himself did not fast.

The reference in verse 20 to the "days will come" probably has a deeper meaning, referring to Jesus' death and perhaps even to the eschatological time when the Son of Man arrives to usher in the kingdom of God. Perhaps this verse is the actual pronouncement for what precedes. Although it was not appropriate for Jesus' disciples to fast while Jesus was alive, it seems appropriate for Christians to fast now that he is dead.

Verses 21 and 22, although somewhat related to each other, seem unrelated to the earlier material (vv. 18–20). I doubt these verses belong to this pericope, except very loosely. Both verses contrast the new with the old: new cloth onto an old garment, and new wine into old wineskins. However, the metaphorical allusion to Jesus' proclamation of the good news *with authority* seems unmistakable, especially when compared to the old order represented by the scribes of the Pharisees. The new order that Jesus is proclaiming cannot and does not fit into the old order of the Jewish Law as represented by the Pharisees (or, as we will see later, the Jerusalem priesthood).

Perhaps the message to the Christian community for which the evangelist was writing was even more radical. It is not simply a question of whether the followers of Jesus should or should not fast (vv. 18–20). The issue is even more foundational: the Jesus movement can no longer be seen merely as a sect within Judaism. It is a new order that must detach itself from the old: "new wine into new wineskins." The words of Acts 11:26b may be relevant in this connection: " . . . and it was in Antioch that the disciples were first called 'Christians.'" Perhaps this reference provides a clue to the meaning of this pericope. It may even be a further indication that the earliest gospel was written in Antioch, the city where the word "Christians" was first used of followers of Jesus.

JESUS' PRONOUNCEMENT ABOUT THE SABBATH

> 2:23 And it happened that he was going on the Sabbath through the grain fields; and his disciples began to make their way, picking the ears of grain.
>
> 24 And the Pharisees said to him, "Look what they are doing on the Sabbath what is not permitted?"
>
> 25 And he said to them, "Have you never read what David did when he was in need and hungry, he and those with him:
>
> 26 how he entered into the house of God in the time of Abiathar the high priest, and ate the [sacred] bread of the presentation, which it is not permitted to eat, except for the priests, and also he gave [some] to those who were with him?"
>
> 27 And he said to them, "The Sabbath came into being for the sake of humankind and not humankind for the sake of the Sabbath.

— — —

CHAPTER 2

28 For this reason, the Son of Man is master even of the Sabbath."

This pronouncement story answers the question of the validity of the Jewish Sabbath Law with Jesus' pronouncement: "The Sabbath came into being for the sake of humankind, and not humankind for the sake of the Sabbath." The issue was apparently not whether one could eat on the Sabbath but whether it is lawful to pick grain on the Sabbath. The law in Deut 23:25 is relatively clear: "If you go into your neighbor's standing grain, you may pluck the ears with your hand, but you shall not put a sickle to your neighbor's standing grain." So, the nature of the violation of the Sabbath by Jesus' disciples is not entirely clear.

Jesus answers the Pharisees' question with a question of his own, citing the story of David and Abiathar. However, according to the account in 1 Sam 21:1, it was Ahimelech and not Abiathar who was the priest at Nob who gave David the sacred bread used in the rituals at the shrine of Nob, "the city of the priests" (1 Sam 21:2). Perhaps the evangelist is quoting from a *testimonia* passage, where a detail in the reference is once again inaccurate (as in 1:2–3). Or perhaps the story about David and the priest was simply corrupted at some point in the oral retelling. Few people at that time had access to the written Scriptures.

In any event, Jesus made it clear that God made the Sabbath for the benefit of humankind as part of his own rest after the six days of creation (Gen 2:2–3).

Verse 28 is probably an addition by the anonymous evangelist, coming as it does *after* Jesus' pronouncement. It is, in fact, reminiscent of 2:10 above: "the Son of Man has authority to forgive sins on the earth," in which the phrase "Son of Man" refers not to the eschatological Son of Man but to humankind in general, or to Jesus specifically.

In its present form (referring to the Son of Man), verse 28 seems to make no sense. What does make sense is: "Humankind is master even of the Sabbath" or "The man Jesus is master even of the Sabbath."

CONCLUSIONS AFTER CHAPTER 2

As already noted, the earliest gospel was apparently put together by using distinct units of tradition (pericopes), probably gathered into several written sources to which the anonymous evangelist had access. And to repeat, there is likely no logical order to the stories, nor are the references to time and place anything more than introductory phrases by the evangelist to afford a setting for the individual pericopes.

The literary form of the material in chapter 2 is almost always pronouncement stories: The Healing of the Paralyzed Man (2:1–12); Jesus Eats with Sinners and Tax Collectors (2:15–17); The Question about Fasting (2:18–20); and Jesus' pronouncement about the Sabbath (2:23–28). It is even more evident in chapter 2 that the anonymous author was probably drawing from a written collection, in this case a written collection of pronouncement stories.

As was mentioned above, the call of Levi (2:13–14) is somewhat problematic, as Levi appears nowhere else in the gospel, not even in the list of Jesus disciples just a few verses later in 3:16–19. Perhaps, verses 13–14 are simply a construction of the evangelist in an effort to afford context for the following pericope (vv. 15–17) that he found in a written source that was available to him. As evidence of this, the stories in this chapter are almost all of the same literary form (pronouncement stories), whereas for chapter 1 the source was primarily a cluster of miracle stories, likely from a different source.

In addition there is, even in the short space of these twenty-eight verses, clear evidence of some of the editorial characteristics of the anonymous evangelist:

1. A propensity for starting sentences with the word "and" (Greek *kai*). The author used the word "and" eighty-four times in the forty-three verses in chapter 1 and more often than not at the beginning of a sentence. In chapter 2 that number is forty-seven times in twenty-eight verses (about the same frequency as in chapter 1). As stated earlier, this may be an Aramaism, as it is common to begin sentences in Hebrew and Aramaic with the prefix "and" (*wē*).

2. The word "immediately" (Greek *euthus*), which appeared eleven times in just forty-five verses in chapter 1, appears only twice in chapter 2, suggesting that our author may be following more closely his written source and is adding less of his own editorial material into the writing of this chapter than he did in chapter 1.

3. The evangelist has once again created some material of his own invention in addition to his use of a written collection of pronouncement stories. The evangelist is probably responsible for composing Jesus Calls Levi to be his Disciple (2:13–14), as well as the introductory settings to some of the pericopes.

Chapter 3

THE MAN WITH THE PARALYZED HAND

3:1 And he entered again into the synagogue, and there was there a man having a paralyzed hand.

2 And they were watching him carefully, [to see] whether on the Sabbath he would heal him, so that they might bring charges against him.

3 And he said to the man who had the paralyzed hand, "Get up, [go] into the middle [of the room]."

4 And he said to them, "Is it permissible on the Sabbath to do good or to do evil, to save a life or to kill?" But they kept silent.

5 And looking around at them with anger, deeply grieved at the hardness of their hearts, he said to the man, "Hold out the hand." And he held out his hand, and his hand was restored.

6 And the Pharisees going out immediately together with the Herodians took counsel against him, so that they might destroy him.

This story is the fifth pronouncement story in the sequence beginning in 2:1. But it is also more clearly a miracle story than those that came before. The conflict in this story is more heated than in the previous pronouncement stories in this series. Moreover, Jesus' emotion is much more graphic ("looking around at them with anger" and "deeply grieved at their hardness of hearts" in v. 5). The author introduces the story by saying Jesus entered the synagogue (3:1, similar to 1:21).

This pericope does not identify the enemy until the final verse. One might assume at the outset that it is the Pharisees from the previous story, but each unit of tradition (pericope) is, as we have seen, independent, and one cannot assume the relationship of one story to the next with respect to historical or even logical or literary sequence.

In this story, there is a growing conspiracy among the Pharisees to bring charges against Jesus for his violation of the Sabbath Law. Working on the Sabbath was, according to Exod 31:14–15 and Num 15:32–36, a crime punishable by death.

After directing the man with the paralyzed hand to go to the middle of the room, Jesus asks the Pharisees a question about what is allowed on the Sabbath. The question is particularly poignant because if it is forbidden for Jesus to save a life (i.e. to heal the man), then it is also forbidden for the Pharisees to kill Jesus on the Sabbath, perhaps anticipating the planned collusion in verse 6.

Although Rabbinic tradition of the time allowed someone to break the Sabbath Law if it was a matter of life and death, clearly the man with the paralyzed hand is not in mortal danger. Jesus seems to be claiming that one may break the Sabbath Law anytime if it is "to do good" (v. 4). But by his question to the Pharisees, Jesus has publically embarrassed them, inasmuch as they remained silent with no clear answer to his question. Yet, by implication, Jesus has violated the Sabbath Law by deciding it is never wrong to do good on the Sabbath. Once again, Jesus' interpretation of the Law is seemingly anthropocentric (humankind-centered) rather than theocentric (God-centered).

Jesus' response, motivated by his anger at the Pharisees for their insensitivity, is to defy the Pharisees and heal the man's paralyzed hand, to which the Pharisees respond by going out to conspire with the Herodians (Jewish supporters of the dynasty of Herodian rulers) about how they can destroy Jesus (i.e., how they can put Jesus to death according to the requirements of the Law). Miracle stories in this gospel generally end with the amazement of the crowd or the command to remain silent. However, this pericope is more of a pronouncement story than a miracle story, and I would so classify it.

The plot is thickening, and the evangelist is already anticipating Jesus' death, leading Jesus to spread his message even farther in the pericope that follows.

CHAPTER 3

THE MULTITUDE AT THE SEASIDE

3:7 And Jesus with his disciples withdrew to the sea. And a great crowd from Galilee followed, and from Judea

8 and from Jerusalem and from Idumea and Transjordan; and from around Tyre and Sidon, a great crowd, hearing how many things he did, came to him.

9 And he told his disciples that a boat should stand ready for him because of the crowd, lest they should crush him.

10 For he had healed many, so that as many as had [bodily] afflictions pressed about him in order that they might touch [him].

11 And the unclean spirits, when they saw him, fell down before him and cried out saying, "You are the Son of God."

12 And he sternly warned them that they should not make him known.

This summary, following immediately upon the beginning of the plot against Jesus, seems designed to prepare the reader or listener for what follows by suggesting that Jesus' popularity, particularly as a faith-healer, grew rapidly throughout the entire region. At what seems to be a turning point in his ministry, not only do the crowds increase in number, but even the "unclean spirits" are forced to acknowledge that Jesus is God's Son.

Jesus' withdrawal to the Sea of Galilee seems to be a popular device of the anonymous evangelist. In fact, these six verses are likely a construction of the evangelist to bring to resolution the series of pronouncement stories in chapter 2 and in 3:1–6. The likelihood that Jesus was attracting such large crowds from all areas of Palestine and even beyond seems improbable at this early stage in his ministry, but it is a forceful literary device by the evangelist, mindful of the fact that the "good news about Jesus Christ" had spread into areas of the Gentile world by the time he was writing this gospel several decades later. Moreover, these verses set the stage for what follow, a series of pericopes set by the sea.

The command in verse 12 not to make Jesus known is an element of the Messianic Secret, a literary device of the evangelist to say that Jesus was trying to hide his true identity until after his crucifixion and resurrection, the time when his true identity was apparently first proclaimed by his disciples.

JESUS APPOINTS THE TWELVE

3:13 And he went up into the mountain and called to him those whom he himself wanted. And they went to him.

14 And he made twelve, that they might be with him and that he might send them out to preach,

15 and to have authority to cast out demons;

16 and he made the twelve: Simon, to whom he gave the name Peter;

17 and James the son of Zebedee and John the brother of James, and he added to them the name Boanerges, which is "Sons of Thunder";

18 and Andrew and Philip and Bartholomew and Matthew and Thomas and James the son of Alphaeus and Thaddaeus and Simon the Cananaean;

19 and Judas Iscariot, who also betrayed him.

This pericope, probably a construction of the evangelist, introduces Jesus' twelve disciples (although the word "disciples" does not appear in the story), names probably drawn from a list available to the anonymous evangelist. The Gospel of Matthew has the same twelve names (Matthew 10:1–4), but the Gospel of Luke (Luke 6:12-16) lacks Thaddaeus and has instead another Judas, the son of James. Not surprisingly, the list in Acts 1:12–14 agrees with the list in Luke, inasmuch as both books were presumably written by the same author. Although the Gospel of John mentions "the twelve" four times (John 6:67, 70, 71; and 20:24), there is no list of the twelve in John. John mentions individual disciples throughout the gospel, but there is no mention of Bartholomew or Matthew. There is, of course, no mention anywhere of the mystery disciple Levi (from 2:13–14) as being among the twelve.

The language of verses 13–15 is somewhat awkward and unclear, but it appears that Jesus initially called a large number of his followers to go into the mountain with him and that from this group he selected twelve, who are listed as:

CHAPTER 3

(1) Simon, who continues to stand first in the list. The name Simon (Hebrew Shimeon) was a common name; the nickname Peter (Greek *petros*) means "rock," in Aramaic *kepha* (rendered in Greek as *kephas*, or Cephas by which name Peter is sometimes called in Paul's letters). The anonymous evangelist consistently calls him by his nickname Peter (or "Rocky"), except in 14:37, where Jesus addresses him as Simon.

(2) James (the Greek equivalent of the Hebrew Jacob) and (3) his brother John (the Greek equivalent of the Hebrew Yohanan), sons of Zebedee, were fishermen and among the first disciples called by Jesus. Their nickname Boanerges may be Aramaic, meaning "sons of thunder" because of their volatile personalities, but that is by no means certain.

(4) Andrew was the brother of Peter and among the first group of disciples Jesus called from their work as fishermen to become fishermen of men (1:16–20). He is otherwise mentioned nowhere else in this gospel. The name Andrew [Andreas] is Greek. Interestingly, Andrew is not listed here together with his brother Simon.

(5) Philip (also a Greek name Philippos, meaning "lover of horses"), (6) Bartholomew (Aramaic Bar Thalmai, meaning "son of Thalmai"), (7) Matthew (Hebrew Mattai), (8) Thomas (the Aramaic word for "twin" and probably not a name at this time), (9) James the son of Alphaeus, (10) Thaddeus (perhaps a nickname for Aramaic *tadh* or Taddai, meaning "heart" or "courageous heart," thereby suggesting someone with a warm personality), and (11) Simon the Cananaean (perhaps from the Aramaic meaning "Simon the zealous one") are mentioned in this list but nowhere else in this gospel.

(12) Judas Iscariot is identified in this list as the disciple who betrayed Jesus. The meaning of Iscariot is probably from the Hebrew *ish kerioth* meaning "a man from Kerioth," a village about twelve miles south of Hebron in southern Judea.

Whether it was Jesus or the early church that was responsible for the designation of the twelve, the number is significant. It mimics, likely consciously, the twelve tribes of Israel. By this calling of the twelve, Jesus is perhaps establishing the basis for the new Israel, the core or the nucleus of a new order in anticipation of the imminent arrival of God's rule. If by this calling of the twelve, the anonymous author means the church—and that is certainly possible—then this designation of the twelve was clearly the work of the church, inasmuch as it was never Jesus' intention to establish a new religion. The listing of Judas Iscariot as a disciple points to the likelihood that at least something like this list may reach back to Jesus, as it would not serve the interest of the church to list a traitor among Jesus' inner circle if it were not true.

In any case, the function of the twelve, at least according to the evangelist, was "to preach," and with authority "to cast out demons." (3:14–15)

JESUS AND BEELZEBUL

3:20 And he went home. And the crowd came together again, so that they were not even able to eat bread.

21 And hearing about this, members of his family went out to take charge of him, for they said, "He has lost his mind."

22 And the scribes coming down from Jerusalem were saying, "He has Beelzebul," and, "By the prince of the demons he drives out the demons."

23 And calling them to himself he spoke to them in parables: "How can Satan drive out Satan?

24 And if a kingdom is divided against itself, that kingdom is not able to stand.

25 And if a household is divided against itself, that household will not be able to stand.

26 And if the Satan has risen up against himself and is divided, he is not able to stand, but is at an end.

— — —

3:27 But no one can enter the strong man's house to steal his possessions, unless he first ties up the strong man, and then he will rob his house.

— — —

3:28 "Truly, I say to you, all sins will be forgiven to the sons of men, and whatever blasphemies they may blaspheme;

29 but he who blasphemes against the Holy Spirit has no forgiveness for all eternity, but he is guilty of an eternal sin"

— — —

3:30 because they were saying, "He has an unclean spirit."

The author introduces this complex pericope by affording a familiar although somewhat ambiguous setting. Jesus went either into a house, or he went home (to Nazareth, or more likely to the place in Capernaum where he was staying). The Greek is ambiguous (*kai erxetai eis oikon*). It says literally, "He went into a house," but that phrase is often idiomatic for "going home." What is clear, however, is the author is emphasizing the crowd that has once again gathered, so much so that the people who were with Jesus did not even have enough room to eat a loaf of bread (3:20). The opening words provide the general setting that the evangelist provides for most of the pericopes that he draws into the gospel from his written sources.

Members of Jesus' family, literally "those who were with him," but once again a Greek idiom for "his family," went out to take charge of Jesus, because they thought that he was out of his mind (3:21).

The arrival of scribes from Jerusalem (v. 22) seems to be a device in the story for them to characterize Jesus as a simple exorcist, in fact as an exorcist who is under the power of Beelzebul, the prince of demons, or Satan. In contemporary Jewish thought Beelzebul was the chief of the demons. There is no question that Jesus, by referring to Satan in his reply, assumes the mythology of the time that evil was personified in individual spirits (or demons), chief among whom was Satan, who appears in verse 23 without the definite article (*the* Satan) that we found in the story of Jesus' Temptation (see 1:12) and again later in this pericope in verse 26.

Verses 24 and 25 give two examples (or "parables" or "comparisons") of the absurdity of the claim that Jesus could be possessed by Satan and then use his supernatural power to expel Satan from anyone whom Satan possessed. If a kingdom is divided against itself, it cannot stand (v. 24), and if a household is divided against itself, it will not stand (v. 25). So too Satan cannot be divided against himself (v. 26), or he will destroy himself. This verse appears to be the end of the pericope, both logically and syntactically. Verses 3:20–26 appear to be a pronouncement story.

What follows in verses 27–30 is very disjointed and does not seem to be an integral part of the original pericope. Verse 27 is clearly unrelated to what precedes. It may have been a familiar saying that the evangelist drew into the text to emphasize that Jesus is even stronger than the "strong man," Beelzebul or Satan. Satan has not rebelled against himself. Rather someone stronger than Satan (i.e., Jesus) has tied Satan up. But there is nothing except context to suggest that this is an appropriate reading of verse 27. This verse is a failed effort on the part of the evangelist to strengthen the original pericope, verses 20–26 or perhaps only verses 22–26.

So too verses 28–29 are likely a further addition of another unrelated saying or teaching, probably of the church. The phrase "sons of men" in verse 28 clearly means "men" or "humankind" and, therefore, supports our reading of the phrase "son of man" as meaning "humankind" in verses 2:10 and 2:28 above. According to this saying, all sins and all blasphemies are forgiven to humankind except the sin against the Holy Spirit. The saying about the sin against the Holy Spirit almost certainly originated in the church as a warning to Christians that the unforgivable sin against the Holy Spirit is when someone identifies acts of God as being acts of Beelzebul or Satan, i.e. calling the work of God (such as Jesus' healings, or healings within the church) diabolical, the work of Beelzebul or Satan.

Verse 30, clearly an editorial creation of the anonymous author, attempts to link these additional elements in verses 27–29 to the original pericope, albeit awkwardly. In its present form, this is clearly a composite pericope, the creation of the anonymous author drawing together a pronouncement story and individual unrelated sayings.

JESUS' TRUE FAMILY

3:31 And his mother and his brothers came, and standing outside they sent [someone] to him, calling him.

32 And a multitude was sitting around him; and they said to him, "Look, your mother and your brothers [and your sisters] are outside looking for you."

33 And answering them, he said "Who is my mother and my brothers?"

34 And looking around at those who were sitting in a circle around him, he said,

"See my mother and my brothers!"

35 For whoever does the will of God, that one is my brother and sister and mother."

This pericope follows immediately upon the story in 3:20–30. It is, however, a separate pronouncement story. The only connection is that both pericopes deal with Jesus' relationship to his immediate family. The point of this story is found in verse 35.

The setting of the story is unclear, and the evangelist provides no context. Strictly speaking, Jesus is probably not at his family home in Nazareth, and it is unlikely that his entire family is in Capernaum or wherever this incident is supposed to take place. The context is little more than a construct to afford a setting in which Jesus can comment on what constitutes the true family by contrast to familial kinship. The point of the story is clear: the bonds that connect people in their obedience to the will of God are stronger than the bonds of the biological family. This saying would have had powerful significance not only to Jesus' disciples but also to members of the church for which the gospel was written. Christians referred to fellow Christians as "brother" and "sister" (see Rom 1:13, 16:1; 1 Cor 16:20; 2 Cor 1:8, 13:11; Eph 6:21; Col 1:2; 1 Thess 5:26; see also Mark 10:28–31). These relationships among Christians are regarded by the church as stronger than blood relationships.

Most scholars agree that Jesus had biological brothers and sisters, presumably of the same mother and father, Mary and Joseph. Since the fourth century, the official position of the Roman Catholic Church and of some later Protestant denominations has been that Mary bore only Jesus and that the so-called brothers and sisters must, therefore, be either Joseph's children from a previous marriage, or Jesus' cousins. These views are based not on the text or on the meaning of the Greek word *adelphos* (brother), but on theological presuppositions that sometimes trump historical facts and, therefore, require a rewriting of history. Moreover, the power of this passage would be considerably diminished if the relatives in question were Jesus' cousins rather than his brothers and sisters.

CONCLUSIONS AFTER CHAPTER 3

As indicated above, 3:1–6 is the fifth in a series of pronouncement stories, four of which appear in chapter 2. That block of five pronouncement stories is concluded with the account of the multitude at the seaside in 3:7–12, probably a creation of the evangelist to indicate that Jesus' popularity as a teacher and faith healer grew rapidly throughout the entire region. Verses 3:13–19 report the appointment and commissioning of "The Twelve," as if that phrase was already a technical term in the church by the time of the composition of this gospel.

That story is then followed by the complex pericope of Jesus and Beelzebul in 3:20–26 (containing mention of Jesus' family) to which material the anonymous author attached seemingly unrelated sayings (3:27, 28–29, and 30). The final pericope in this chapter (3:31–35) deals with the issue of Jesus' true family. The structure and linkage in chapter 3 is less clear than in earlier chapters in this gospel, but we should remember that the author is probably drawing material from different sources and trying to create a cohesive narrative story, sometimes more and sometimes less successfully. Chapter 3 marks a significant turning point in the story, because the Pharisees and the Herodians are now clearly determined to destroy Jesus (3:6).

From a literary point of view, it is already clear that one of the editorial features of the evangelist is to begin a sentence with a dependent participial clause, followed by the subject and the main part of the sentence. For example in the first three chapters:

1:10	"And immediately, going up out of the water, he saw . . ."
1:16	"And while passing along beside the Sea of Galilee, he saw . . ."
1:18	"And immediately leaving the nets, they followed . . ."
1:19	"And going forward a little, he saw . . ."
1:29	"And immediately coming out of the synagogue, he went . . ."
1:31	"And approaching, he lifted . . ."
1:35	"And early in the morning when it was still quite dark, having risen, he went . . ."
1:41	"And moved with compassion, stretching out his hand, he touched . . ."
2:1	"And entering again into Capernaum after some days, it became known . . ."

2:4	"And not being able to carry him to him because of the crowd, they removed . . ."
2:5	"And seeing their faith, Jesus said . . ."
2:14	"And passing along, he saw . . ."
2:17	"And hearing this, Jesus said . . ."
3:5	"And looking around at them with anger, deeply grieved at the hardness of their hearts, he said . . ."
3:21	"And hearing about this, members of his family went out . . ."
3:23	"And calling them to himself, he spoke . . ."
3:33	"And answering them, he said . . ."
3:34	"And looking around at those who were sitting in the circle around him, he said . . ."

The Greek word *kai* ("and") continues to be our author's favorite word, beginning twenty-nine of the thirty-five verses in this chapter; but Greek *euthus* ("immediately") appears only once (3:6). I shall not continue to comment on the Greek word *kai* in future chapters, but its appearance is evident throughout the gospel and I urge the reader to take note.

Chapter 4

THE PARABLE OF THE SOWER

4:1 And again he began to teach beside the sea. And the largest crowd [until now] gathered to him, so that getting into a boat he sat on the sea; and the whole crowd was on the land [facing] toward the sea.

2 And he was teaching them many things in parables, and he said to them in his teaching:

3 "Listen! Behold, the sower went out to sow.

4 And it happened, as he was sowing, that one [part of the seed] fell beside the road; and the birds came and ate it.

5 And another [part] fell on rocky ground, where it did not have much earth; and immediately it sprang up because it did not have depth of earth.

6 And when the sun rose, it was scorched; and because it did not have root, it dried up.

7 And another [part] fell into the thorn plants; and the thorns went up and choked it, and it gave no fruit.

8 And other [parts] fell into the good earth and gave fruit that grew up and increased and produced thirtyfold and sixtyfold and a hundredfold."

9 And he said, "The one who has ears to hear, let him hear!"

CHAPTER 4

VERSES 4:1–2 PROVIDE AN introduction to the Parable of the Sower. As such, these verses betray the author's editorial hand: "and" (Greek *kai*, *passim*), "again" (Greek *palin*, see e.g., 2:1, 13; 3:1, 20; 5:21; 7:14, 31; etc.); "began" (Greek *arxo*, see e.g., 1:45; 2:23; 5:17, 20; 6:2, 7, 34, 55; etc.); "teach" (Greek *didasko*, see e.g., 1:21, 22; 2:13; 6:2, 6, 30, 34; etc.); "by the sea" (Greek *para ten thalassan*, see e.g., 1:16; 2:13; 5:21; etc,); and "a very large crowd" gathered (Greek *oxlos*, see e.g., 2:4, 13; 3:9, 20, 32; 4:36; 5:21, 24, 27, 30, 31; etc.).

The purpose of Jesus' parables (many of which begin with the phrase "The kingdom of God is like . . . ") was to explain something by comparison with everyday elements that would be familiar to the listener of the parable. The comparison was often to something agricultural, which would have been particularly meaningful to Jesus' listeners.

The difficulty with the Parable of the Sower is we do not know its situational context or exactly what it was that Jesus was trying to make clear to his listeners by telling them this story. This parable may have been composed by Jesus and delivered orally, and in its original context its meaning would presumably have been clear to his audience. Even in the oral retelling of the parable, its context may initially have been clear, but by the time the parable was included in what was apparently a written collection of parables, the original context of the story was lost and is impossible to reconstruct with any degree of certainty. The anonymous author of the gospel does, however, provide an explanation of parables in general in 4:10–12 and of this parable in particular in 4:13–20, material that immediately follows the parable itself. Whether this explanation is faithful to the original context and meaning of the parable is, of course, uncertain and probably even doubtful.

With regard to the context of the parable in this gospel, the fact that this is the largest crowd that has yet gathered to hear Jesus teach requires that he get into the boat mentioned in 3:9, so that he can speak to the crowd that is standing on the shore. This detail is surely the hand of the evangelist.

The author's command in verse 3 to both "listen" and "behold" reinforces the importance of the parable so that the audience would both listen with their ears and see with their eyes in order to better understand the message and the meaning of the parable.

The sower in the parable is presumably God, or perhaps in the retelling of the parable within the church the sower is Jesus, but the meaning of the parable is not self-evident. Assuming that it originally explained some element in Jesus' eschatological teaching as expressed originally by John the Baptist in 1:15 ("The time has been fulfilled, and the kingdom of God is at hand. Repent, and believe in the good news"), the parable likely contrasts the two orders: one that yields no fruit and one that yields great quantities of fruit. The message of the parable, therefore, may contrast this present order under Satan's dominion and the future order of God's rule, which is being inaugurated in Jesus' teaching and ministry. This interpretation may be confirmed in verse 11, when Jesus says to his disciples "To you the mystery of the kingdom of God has been given." This mystery of the kingdom of God is likely that the time of God's rule is imminent.

The language of the parable itself has none of the evangelist's idiosyncratic language and may actually go back to Jesus himself. The imagery, as in many of the parables, is drawn from agriculture. And in form, the four examples of the deposit and the growth of seed are parallel: the location of the seed, how the seed grows, and the final results of the growth of each seed. The yield of the seed in verse 8 (thirtyfold, sixtyfold, and a hundredfold) refers to the ratio of the amount of the yield to the amount of seed that was sown. Assuming that the parable relates to Jesus' eschatological teaching, it likely contrasts the two world orders: one which yields no fruit and one which yields great quantities of fruit—perhaps a contrast between this order under Satan's dominion and the future order of God's rule, which is already being inaugurated in Jesus' teaching and ministry.

Clearly, the period of God's rule has not yet arrived, but it is arriving gradually. The Parable of the Sower may be the first of what scholars refer to as "parables of growth." Through the teaching and ministry of Jesus, God's rule is growing gradually, is arriving slowly. We see other such "parables of growth" later in this chapter in 4:26–29 (The Parable of the Growing Seed) and in 4:30–32 (The Parable of the Mustard Seed).

For the church (in Antioch?) for which this gospel was written, the message of this parable is eminently clear: the old order has not yet passed away, but the new order has already arrived in the church, the community of believers in the good news of Jesus the Messiah. We need to be mindful that whether this or any of the parables attributed to Jesus came, in fact, from Jesus himself, this material survived in and served the needs of the Christian community for whom the gospel was written. It is to that community that this pericope in this form is addressed. Tradition about Jesus survived to the extent that it served the needs of the church, and it was often reworked to address more clearly and more specifically those needs.

The pericope closes as it opened with a command to hear, but this time the command is directed not to everyone as in the introduction but to the one who has ears to hear (i.e. to the one who is actually willing to listen). Apparently God does not expect everyone to respond to his call—an important message for the church.

CHAPTER 4

THE PURPOSE OF PARABLES

> 4:10 And when he was alone, those around him with the Twelve asked him [about] the parables.
>
> 11 And he said to them, "To you the mystery of the kingdom of God has been given; but to the ones outside, all things are in parables,
>
> 12 so that seeing they may see and not perceive, and hearing they may hear and not understand; lest they turn, and [their sins] be forgiven them."

Verses 10–12 pose a serious problem. Although there is no literary transition, Jesus is apparently now alone with his disciples and a small group of believers and, therefore, no longer in the boat addressing the very large crowd. Moreover, Jesus advances an understanding of the purpose of parables that is quite different from their original intent: to illustrate or explain an important truth. In fact, what Jesus says in these verses is quite the contrary. He now establishes a difference between the "inner circle," who alone can understand the mystery of the kingdom of God, and "those outside" the inner circle, for whom everything is in parables in order to confound the possibility of their perceiving and understanding, lest they repent and God forgive their sins. This does not sound like Jesus and certainly does not reflect the original purpose of parables, which was to clarify through metaphor, not to obscure.

In Paul's letters, "the ones outside" (Greek *hoi exo*) is a reference to non-Christians (1 Cor 5:12–13; 1 Thess 4:12; see also Col 4:5). This is clearly the meaning in this passage, suggesting therefore that it was the church and not Jesus that was referring to "those inside" and "those outside." Yet even then this is a harsh message: namely, that the church was teaching that it was God's intended purpose to make it impossible for those outside the church to perceive and understand the good news, lest they repent of their sins and be forgiven by God. Perhaps the reference in the immediate context of this gospel is to the scribes and the Pharisees and the Herodians, who earlier in this gospel were determined to bring Jesus down (3:6), but this interpretation is improbable as there is no direct link to this earlier pericope.

In spite of the efforts of some to soften the harsh message in these verses, they are actually reminiscent of a passage in Isa 6:10

> Make the mind of this people dull,

and stop their ears,
and shut their eyes,
so that they may not look with their eyes,
and listen with their ears,
and comprehend with their minds,
and turn and be healed.

The meaning of Isaiah's message is clear: God's word through the prophet will not lead to the people's repentance and, thereafter, to God's forgiveness. It is too late for that. The words of the prophet will actually harden the people's hearts and, therefore, prepare them for God's imminent judgment. Like Isaiah, the evangelist, writing sometime before 70 CE, may also believe it is too late, that the coming of God's kingdom is imminent. A harsh judgment indeed! However, the distinction between those who understand the word and those who do not understand is apparently God's will.

In any event, verses 10–12 come from a very different source with a very different message than parables would have had in the context of Jesus' own teaching. Yet the evangelist obviously believes these harsh words are relevant for the readers or listeners in his church.

THE INTERPRETATION OF THE PARABLE OF THE SOWER

4:13 And he said to them, "Do you not understand this parable? And how [then] will you comprehend all of the parables?

14 The sower sows the word.

15 And these are the ones who [are] along the road where the word is sown and who, when they hear [the word], Satan comes immediately and takes [away] the word that was sown in them.

16 And these are the ones sown on rocky ground who, when they hear the word, immediately receive it with joy;

17 and they do not have root in themselves but last only for a little while; when oppression comes, or when there is persecution because of the word, immediately they fall away.

18 And others are the ones sown among the thorn-plants. These are the ones who hear the word,

19 and the worries of the world and the seduction which comes from wealth and the desires for the other things going [into them] choke the word, and it becomes unfruitful.

20 And those are the ones sown on the good ground, who hear the word, and accept it, and they produce fruit thirtyfold and sixtyfold and a hundredfold."

This interpretation of the Parable of the Sower is apparently a later explanation by the church (in Antioch?) of what may originally have been an authentic parable of Jesus. There is no indication elsewhere in this gospel that Jesus explained his parables. In fact, parables were devices to explain something that was otherwise unclear, such as the meaning of Jesus' message regarding the imminent arrival of the kingdom of God.

Verse 13 seems unaware of the material in verses 10–12. Verses 10–12 are about parables in general; verse 13 addresses the meaning of this particular parable. Moreover, the interpretation of the Parable of the Sower is given only to those in the "inner circle," who presumably already understand its meaning (see vv. 11–12). Clearly verses 10–12 interrupt the transition from the Parable of the Sower to its interpretation and were likely introduced by the evangelist, perhaps from another source. Verse 13 once again has Jesus addressing the crowd with no transition from his meeting with the disciples and the inner circle.

Verse 14 makes it clear that the sower is sowing the word, presumably the word of God, or more specifically "the good news of Jesus Christ" (1:1; see also 2:2). Whoever the sower was in Jesus' original telling of the parable, the evangelist clearly understands the sower to be Jesus.

The subject of the original parable was the sower, presumably God, and the message that God was sowing was probably the word (4:14). In the interpretation, the subject matter has been shifted from God to various kinds of people who received the seed but responded differently. The four kinds of individuals who heard the word and received it differently represent a later allegorical interpretation of the original parable, an interpretation that probably reflects the position of the church to which the gospel was addressed.

The reference in verse 17 to tribulation or persecution because of the word may refer to the situations that many Christians were currently experiencing, and because of which some—probably even some in the home church of this gospel—had abandoned the faith.

A COLLECTION OF MISCELLANEOUS SAYINGS

4:21 And he said to them, "Does the lamp come in order to be put under the measuring container or under the bed? Is it not in order to be set on the lamp stand?

— — —

4:22 For there is nothing hidden that will not be revealed, and nothing has been kept secret that will not come to light.

— — —

4:23 If someone has ears to hear, let him hear!"

— — —

4:24 And he said to them, "Pay attention to what you hear! By the same measure you measure, it will be measured to you, and it will be added to you.

— — —

4:25 For whoever has, to him more will be given; but whoever does not have, even what he has will be taken away from him."

The meaning of these five sayings attributed to Jesus is difficult to unravel, because there is once again no context within which to interpret them. The "and" in verse 24 is likely an editorial addition of the author indicating perhaps that verses 21–23 and 24–25 were not linked in the author's source(s). These sayings are not parables, but they are similar enough in form to the ones in this chapter that they may originally have been part of a collection the author had access to. Moreover, verses 33–34 seem to imply this material is all parabolic.

If these sayings reach back to Jesus, at least in some form, perhaps the context was once again Jesus' teaching about the coming of the kingdom of God. If so, the sayings in verses 21–22 may indicate Jesus' teaching is not to be hidden or kept in secret, just as a lamp is not brought into the household only to be covered up. This message would then be in contrast or perhaps even contradictory to 4:10–12 in which Jesus states there is an esoteric teaching for the inner circle, but to others Jesus teaches in parables to prevent those outside from understanding, then repenting, and then being forgiven by God. Perhaps there is an element of the Messianic Secret in the saying in verse 22: Jesus' messiahship may be hidden now, but it will ultimately be revealed, inasmuch as anything that is hidden will eventually come to light. Christians believed that at Easter Jesus was exalted to the right hand of God where he was *made* Lord and Messiah. This proclamation, apparently hidden or secret during Jesus' lifetime, became the core of the good news proclaimed in Christian communities after his death.

The material in verses 24–25 is even more difficult to understand. The saying in verse 24 implies that one will get back what one gives out to other people. Verse 25 suggests one will get back even more than one gives out. This verse is particularly challenging, because it states the rich will get richer, and the poor will get poorer. Is this how a merciful God treats his people, or is this simply a comment on how human beings relate unjustly toward one another? Perhaps it is simply a statement of fact, however harsh it may sound! Or it may be a description of what life is like without the kingdom of God, when the powers of Satan are still largely in control of humankind.

As we struggle with the meaning of these verses, we must be mindful of the fact that consistency does not appear to have been a factor in the composition of the gospels. In fact, inconsistency may point to different sources that the evangelist used in composing the gospel. In any case, the transition within the gospel is not always smooth, because the author is apparently comfortable with incorporating different kinds of material into his narrative and because the context and the meaning of what the author is saying is often obscure to the modern reader.

THE PARABLE OF THE GROWING SEED

4:26 And he said, "The kingdom of God is as if a man would scatter seed on the ground,

27 and he would sleep and get up night and day, and the seed would sprout and grow, as even he does not understand how.

28 By itself the earth produces crops: first a stalk, then an ear, then full grain in the ear.

29 But when the grain ripens, immediately he puts in the sickle, because the harvest-time has come."

The Parable of the Growing Seed states its context clearly: it concerns and explains an aspect of Jesus' teaching about the kingdom of God or the period of God's rule. The kingdom of God is not compared to "a man [who] would scatter seed"; it is compared to the entire story. As is often the case, the comparison is agricultural, because such a comparison would be clear to Jesus' audience. This is one of several parables of growth in this gospel.

Verse 27 follows the Jewish order of the day, which begins at sunset and ends at the following sunset, hence "he would sleep and get up night and day."

The kingdom begins as something as small as a seed planted on the ground, but night and day it grows in ways we do not understand until it is fully ripe, at which time it is harvested. Perhaps the harvest in the parable is a metaphor for the eschatological, and perhaps even the *imminent* eschatological, coming of God's rule, a message that seems to have been central to Jesus' teaching and ministry from the very outset.

Within the context of the author's church, the man sowing the seed would probably have been understood as Jesus, but within the context of the teaching of Jesus, the man was probably just that: a man sowing seed. The emphasis in the parable is on the mystery of growth, not on the sower of the seed.

THE PARABLE OF THE MUSTARD SEED

4:30 And he said, "To what should we compare the kingdom of God, or in what parable should we put it?

> 31 [It is] like a mustard seed which, when it is sown upon the earth, is smaller than all the seeds that are on the earth;
>
> 32 and when it is sown, it grows up and becomes larger than all the shrubs, and it produces large branches, so that the birds of the heaven can nest in its shade."

The Parable of the Mustard Seed begins with a twofold question addressed to the audience, either Jesus' listeners, or the evangelist's church, or both. And like the previous parable, this too is a parable of growth about the kingdom of God, representing once again the gradual development or the in-breaking of God's rule in the teaching and ministry of Jesus. As in the Parable of the Growing Seed, the comparison here is also agricultural. And once again the comparison is not simply with a mustard seed, but with the entire story.

At the time the evangelist wrote, he was probably trying to say to his audience that the time of God's rule has already arrived in the life and ministry of Jesus, although the full rule of God will be consummated in the near future. Jesus may have also seen his own ministry as part of that process, so the parable may, in fact, be an authentic teaching of Jesus. That said, the members of the church to which this gospel was addressed may also have seen themselves as the smallest of seeds in a world in which they were only a very small minority, facing all kinds of adversity and even persecution. To such a community, the Parable of the Mustard Seed might afford reassurance and even hope.

CONCLUDING STATEMENT ABOUT JESUS' PARABLES

> 4:33 And with many such parables he spoke the word to them so far as they were able to understand.
>
> 34 But without a parable he did not speak to them. But in private, he explained all things to his own disciples.

This saying implies that Jesus had been speaking to the crowd and not merely to his disciples or the inner circle (4:34b). The move to the inner circle is, however, not clear in the transition from verse 9 to verse 10. There is also some tension between verse 33 and verses 11–12, which imply that Jesus spoke to the outer circle in parables with the clear intention that they would not be able to understand and repent and be forgiven their sins. Verse 34b seems more in accord with verses 11-12. Might the evangelist be drawing from two difference sources?

1. A written source containing a series of parables:

    The Parable of the Sower, verses 3-8
    The incomplete parabolic sayings in verses 21-25
    The Parable of the Growing Seed, verses 26-29
    The Parable of the Mustard Seed, verses 30-32
    Concluding statement about Jesus' parables, verses 33-34a

2. A written source containing other material about parables:

    The purpose of parables, verses 11-12
    The interpretation of the Parable of the Sower, verses 13-20

Moreover, the author's own editorial hand may be seen in:

1. The introduction, verses 1-2
2. The comments about hearing in verses 9 and 23
3. The transitional comments in verse 10, and the transitional introductions in verse 11 ("And he said to them"), verse 13 ("And he said to them"), verse 21 ("And he said to them"), verse 24 ("And he said to them"), verse 26 ("And he said"), and verse 30 (And he said")
4. The concluding comment in verse 34b ("But in private, he explained all things to his own disciples"), which appears to be a feeble attempt to tie the two contradictory sources together.

THE STILLING OF THE STORM

4:35 And he said to them on that day, when evening was coming, "Let us cross over to the other side."

36 And having dismissed the crowd, they took him with them, when he was back in the boat. And other boats were with him.

37 And a fierce gust of wind arose, and the waves beat upon the boat, so that the boat was already beginning to be filled with water.

CHAPTER 4   55

38 And he was in the stern, sleeping on the cushion. And they awoke him and said to him, "Teacher, do you not care that we are perishing?"

39 And waking up, he rebuked the wind, and said to the sea, "Make no sound; be silent." And the wind stopped, and there was a great calm.

40 And he said to them, "Why are you cowardly? Don't you have trust?"

41 And they were terribly frightened and said to one another, "So who is this that both the wind and the sea obey him!"

This pericope is a miracle story, the beginning of a series of four miracle stories extending from 4:35 to 5:43. These stories imply, perhaps, that Jesus' power as a miracle worker reinforces or validates the divine origin of his teaching. Stated differently, it might have been better if our predecessors had begun a new chapter with the material in 4:35–41.

The story of the Stilling of the Storm has similarities to passages in Virgil's *Aeneid*, Homer's *Odyssey*, the Dead Sea Scrolls, and the book of Jonah in the Old Testament. The implication of these similarities is that stories in one tradition give rise to similar stories elsewhere. Jesus could certainly do as much or more than others about whom such stories circulated. The Stilling of the Storm indicates Jesus had power even over nature, meaning perhaps this world order, which is otherwise under Satan's control. In this pericope Jesus also questions the fear and the trust of those with him in the boat. The word in verse 40 translated as "trust" (*pistis*) means both "trust" and "faith." There is no single English word that captures the double meaning of the original Greek. In the context of the story, Jesus asks those in the boat whether they trust God for their deliverance, but in the context of the author's church the question to his community is more likely whether they have placed their faith in Jesus as the Christ, the Messiah. Like the disciples in the boat, Jesus' followers in the church have the power of God with them in the person of Jesus or the risen Lord. In this miracle story they appear to have only questionable faith.

Verse 35 is a clear effort on the part of the anonymous author to link the Stilling of the Storm to the preceding pericope with his typical double setting of the time: "on that day," and "when evening was coming." "Them" in verse 35 obviously reaches back to "his own disciples" in verse 34. Moreover, this story is set in the evening of the same day as the preceding parable(s).

This setting is, of course, the editorial framework of the evangelist and has nothing to do with the actual chronology or location of events in the life and ministry of Jesus.

The mention of the boat in verse 36 is a reference to the boat in 4:1. Apparently Jesus is now leaving Galilee for the first time since he arrived there following the death of John the Baptist. He is now headed "to the district of the Gerasenes" (5:1), the people of Gerasa (in modern-day Jordan). In the time of Jesus this area was called the Decapolis (or the "ten [Greek] cities"), most of which were located east of the Jordan River and the Sea of Galilee and in a small area of northern Palestine.

Jesus' commands to the wind and the sea to "make no sound" and to "be silent" are words of exorcism (v. 39), as if it is demonic powers that are causing the severe storm and that, therefore, need to be rebuked. Verse 41 makes it clear that even Jesus' inner circle is amazed at Jesus' power over the wind and the sea. Who is this man that even the powers of nature obey him? Jesus' identity is being revealed slowly but surely.

CONCLUSIONS AFTER CHAPTER 4

We are beginning to see more clearly the material in the earliest gospel that reflects the evangelist's editing apart from the written sources from which he clearly drew. The use of certain words and phrases is increasingly evident as we move more deeply into the text of the gospel, and these words and phrases of the evangelist are more easily identified, as they are repeated frequently in the introductions to and even within individual stories or pericopes.

This chapter also marks the introduction of the parable as a teaching device, probably both for the historical Jesus and for the author of the gospel, who was speaking more directly to the church to which he was writing. As we have seen, a parable is a simple story (told by Jesus) to illustrate an important truth, often a message related to Jesus' teaching about the kingdom of God, or the impending arrival of the time of God's rule.

The parables regrettably do not always reveal their original historical context, so some parables are difficult to understand. That is particularly the case with the Parable of the Sower, for which an allegorical interpretation is subsequently provided, an interpretation that likely differs from the message Jesus intended, if in fact this parable reaches back to the historical Jesus.

Perhaps because the parables were not always understood, even within the Christian community, the evangelist provides an explanation or interpretation of the Parable of the Sower that reflects not the historical Jesus, but rather the teaching of the early church. According to the evangelist, Jesus spoke in parables so that those outside would not understand, and repent, and be forgiven. An interpretation that makes no sense in the context of the teaching of Jesus!

The Parable of the Growing Seed (vv. 26–29) and the Parable of the Mustard Seed (vv. 30–32) are easier to understand, because Jesus makes it clear in both instances that the parable is explaining something about the kingdom of God, whose growth is apparently already present in his teaching and ministry. The meaning of the miscellaneous sayings about the Lamp (v. 21), Nothing Hidden (v. 22), Ears to Hear (v. 23), With What Measure You Give (v. 24), and He Who Has (v. 25) are relatively clear and may at one time have been parables that now survive as isolated sayings.

This chapter ends with the miracle story of the Stilling of the Storm (verses 35–41), which focuses on Jesus' authority over the forces of nature. This story also raises the question of who Jesus really is without providing a clear answer. Obviously, Jesus has superhuman powers, a point already made in miracle stories in each of the first three chapters. This miracle story is, however, best understood as belonging to the next unit, a series of miracle stories in chapters 4–11.

After reviewing chapter 4, we are also beginning to see more clearly that the evangelist probably had access to several written sources, minimally one or more collections of miracle stories, at least one collection of parables, and perhaps one or more collections of isolated sayings of Jesus. The evangelist is apparently a collector and redactor of existing written sources and not the actual author of the material he is penning. The order of the pericopes and their specific geographical and historical settings are evidently the evangelist's work, inasmuch as the pericopes were simply at one time merely independent units in the evangelist's multiple written sources.

Why were these earlier written collections of stories made? That is not entirely clear; however, the individual pericopes may have served the early church as stories to read to the people when they assembled for worship or for the Lord's Supper. After the reading of a story, the meaning and application of that story to the life of the church might then serve as a topic of discussion, much as such readings today serve as the basis for the delivery of a sermon. Such an explanation may also account for why there were apparently separate collections for pronouncement stories, miracle stories, parables, etc. It is interesting that these stories were apparently saved in collections according to their literary forms: pronouncement stories, miracle stories, parables, etc.

Chapter 5

THE HEALING OF THE GERASENE DEMONIAC

5:1 And they came to the other side of the lake into the country of the Gerasenes.

2 And when he had come out of the boat, immediately there came out from the tombs to meet him a man with an unclean spirit,

3 who had the dwelling among the tombs; and no one was able to control him, not even with a chain,

4 because he had often been bound with shackles and chains. And the chains had been pulled apart by him, and the shackles broken in pieces; and no one could subdue him.

5 And always, night and day, he was in the tombs and in the hills, screaming and cutting himself with stones.

6 And seeing Jesus from afar, he ran up and threw himself down before him.

7 And crying out with a loud voice, he said, "What have I in common with you, Jesus, Son of the Most High God? I implore you by God that you not torment me."

8 For he said to him, "Let the unclean spirit come out of the man!"

9 And he asked him, "What is your name?" And he said to him, "My name is Legion, because we are many."

CHAPTER 5

10 And he implored him earnestly not to send them out of the region.

11 Now a large herd of pigs was feeding there near the hillside.

12 And the demons begged him, saying, "Send us into the pigs, so that we may enter into them."

13 And he gave them permission, and the unclean spirits came out and entered into the pigs (there were about two thousand); and the herd rushed down the steep bank into the lake, and they drowned in the lake.

14 And the herdsmen fled, and they told it in the city and in the country. And they went to see what had happened.

15 And they came to Jesus, and they saw the one who had been demon-possessed and who had the Legion, sitting and clothed and in his right mind. And they were afraid.

16 And those who saw it told them how it happened to him who had been demon-possessed, and about the pigs.

17 And they began to plead with him to depart from their region.

18 And when he was getting into the boat, he who had been demon-possessed begged him that he might be with him.

19 And he did not permit him, but said to him, "Go home to your own people, and proclaim to them what great things the Lord has done for you, and how he has shown mercy to you."

20 And he departed and began to proclaim in the Decapolis all that Jesus had done for him; and they were all amazed.

THE SETTING FOR THIS miracle story is the eastern side of the Sea of Galilee in Gentile territory. There is, however, a problem with the geography. The city of Gerasa is more than thirty-five miles from the Sea of Galilee into which the pigs are said to have plunged. Whether the error was in the evangelist's written source is, of course, impossible to determine. However, the name Gerasa appears in the introductory material (vv. 1–2a), which is probably the evangelist's editorial introduction to this pericope. Also in this introduction the evangelist indicates "they" came to the other side of the lake, implying that the disciples were with Jesus. Yet, the disciples appear nowhere in the story and were probably not included in the evangelist's original written source.

The miracle story itself seems to begin in verse 2b with the appearance of the demon-possessed man coming out from the tombs, which in Judaism were ritually unclean places where demons were generally thought to dwell. There are several Greek words found only in this pericope in the entire gospel, suggesting perhaps that they were in the evangelist's original written source: *katoikesis* ("dwelling" in v. 3), *halusis* ("chain" in v. 3), *pede* ("shackles" in v. 4), *diaspao* ("pulled apart" in v. 4), and *damazo* ("subdue" in v. 4).

Verse 6 introduces a contradiction: the demoniac sees Jesus from afar, whereas in verse 2 he "immediately" (Greek *euthus*, a favorite word of the evangelist) approached Jesus as he was getting out of the boat. This disagreement once again supports the separation between verses 1–2a (the evangelist's introduction) and the remainder of the pericope from a written source. Bowing before Jesus may be understood as a gesture of respect by the demons, as the demoniac seems otherwise totally out of control.

The demon cries out in verse 7, "What have I in common with you, Jesus, Son of the Most High God?," indicating that the demon, as a supernatural being, knows Jesus' true identity. In verse 8, Jesus commands the unclean spirit to come out of the man and then asks its name (v. 9), because knowing the name would give Jesus power over the demon. The demon replies with the Latin word "Legion" (v. 9), implying that thousands of Satan's armies had possessed the man.

The demons ask Jesus not to send them away into a foreign land (v. 10), and Jesus concedes to the demons' request by sending them into a herd of two thousand pigs, who in a panic then rushed down the hillside into the sea, where they drowned (v. 13). Jesus was clearly victorious over the demons.

The healing of the man is evident in verse 15, where he is described as being seated, clothed, and in his right mind. This dramatic change apparently led to fear of Jesus on the part of those who had witnessed the healing. They, therefore, requested that Jesus leave, as they were likely afraid to live in the presence of such power. The man who had been demon-possessed then asked Jesus if he might join him (v. 18). Instead, Jesus directed the man to go home and "tell the people what the Lord has done" (v. 19). This command to the man is in conflict with commands Jesus gave following miracle stories in 1:25, 44; 3:12; 5:43; and 7:36, verses that contain elements of the Messianic

CHAPTER 5

Secret motif. In verse 20, the man follows Jesus' directive and spreads the word about him throughout the ten cities of the Decapolis.

There is an interesting modification in the meaning of Jesus' words in verse 19, as "Go home to your own people, and proclaim to them what great things the Lord [i.e., God] has done for him" becomes in verse 20 ("all that *Jesus* had done for him"). The accomplishment of God is now credited to Jesus. The former demon-possessed man is now a missionary to the Gentiles of Gerasa, proclaiming the good news of Jesus Christ (verse 20).

It may be that the pericope originally ended in verse 16, which sounds like a reasonable ending to the story, and that verses 17–20 are editorial additions by the evangelist. In fact, we see in those final four verses some of the typical vocabulary of the evangelist, e.g., "began" (Greek *erxato*), verse 17; "to plead" (Greek *parakalein*), verse 17; "to depart" (Greek *apelthein*), verse 17; "getting into" (Greek *embainontos*), verse 18; "be with him" (Greek *hina met' autou*), verse 18; "permit" (Greek *apheken*), verse 19; and " to proclaim" (Greek *kerussein*), verse 20.

In addition, there are some similarities between this miracle story and the miracle story of the Healing of the Man with the Unclean Spirit in 1:21–28:

1. In both stories the demoniac appears suddenly (Greek *euthus*) (1:23 and 5:2).

2. In both stories the man is described as "a man with/in an unclean spirit" (1:23 and 5:2).

3. Both ask "What do we/I have in common with you, Jesus (Nazarene)?" (1:24 and 5:7).

4. In 1:24, "Have you come to destroy (Greek *apolesai*) us?" In 5:7, "I implore you by God that you not torment (Greek *basanises*) me." (Both phrases immediately after the question in #3)

5. In 1:25, Jesus said, "Be quiet and come out of him." In 5:8, Jesus said, "Let the unclean spirit come out of the man."

6. Both are the first miracle story narrative in Jesus' ministry in a different region: the first story takes place in the Jewish region of the Galilee, the second story in the Gentile region of the Decapolis on the "other side" of the Sea of Galilee.

Are these similarities coincidental, or are the two miracle stories variations of an earlier oral and/or written tradition? I am inclined to believe the latter. The more detailed variations of the story of the pigs in chapter 5 may be because Jesus was now in the Decapolis, where pigs were not ritually unclean animals, so the detail of the drowning of the pigs may be intentional for Jesus' first exorcism in a foreign land.

THE WOMAN HEALED OF THE FLOW OF BLOOD AND THE GIRL RESTORED TO LIFE

5:21 And when Jesus had crossed over again to the other side in the boat, a large crowd gathered toward him; and he was beside the lake.

22 And one of the synagogue officials, whose name was Jairus, came. And seeing him, he fell at his feet

23 and begged him earnestly, saying, "My daughter is at the point of death. Come and lay your hands on her, in order that she may be cured and live."

— — —

5:24 And he departed with him, and a large crowd followed him and was pressing upon him.

— — —

5:25 And a woman was suffering from a flow of blood for twelve years,

26 and was suffering very much under many doctors and had spent all that she had and was no better, but had rather grown worse.

27 Having heard about Jesus, she came behind him in the crowd and touched his clothing.

28 For she said, "If I touch even his clothing, I shall be saved."

29 And immediately the fountain of her blood dried up, and she knew in her body that she was healed of the affliction.

30 And immediately Jesus, knowing in himself that power had gone out from him, turning around in the crowd said, "Who touched my clothing?"

31 And his disciples said to him, "You see the crowd pressing upon you, and you say, 'Who touched me?' "

32 And he kept looking around to see the woman who had done this.

33 But the woman, frightened and trembling, knowing what had happened to her, came and fell down before him and told him the whole truth.

34 But he said to her, "Daughter, your trust has cured you. Go in peace, and be healed from your affliction."

— — —

5:35 While he was still speaking, some came from the synagogue official's house saying, "Your daughter has died. Why trouble the teacher any further?"

36 But Jesus, paying no attention to what was said, said to the synagogue official, "Do not be afraid; just trust."

37 And he permitted no one to follow him except Peter, James, and John, the brother of James.

38 And they went into the synagogue official's house, and he saw a disturbance and people who were weeping and wailing loudly.

39 And upon entering, he said to them, "Why are you making this commotion and weeping? The child has not died but is sleeping."

40 And they began to laugh at him. But when he had put them all outside, he took the father and the mother of the child, and those who were with him, and went into where the child was.

41 And taking the hand of the child, he said to her, "*Talitha koum*," which is translated, "Little girl, I say to you, arise!"

42 And immediately the girl arose and began to walk, for she was twelve years old. And they were immediately overcome with great amazement.

43 And he commanded them strictly that no one should know this, and he said that she should be given something to eat.

WE HAVE IN THIS pericope something unusual: a miracle story within a miracle story. The evangelist interweaves the two stories after taking Jesus back by boat to the west side of the Sea of Galilee (5:21), where a large crowd gathered around him, typical introductory features of the evangelist.

The miracle stories of the Woman with the Flow of Blood and of Jairus's Daughter Restored to Life were probably independent stories in a single written source, and the evangelist apparently wove them into their present form. Verses 22–23 and 35–42 are one coherent miracle story; so too are verses 25–34. Verse 24 is transitional and is the evangelist's effort to link the two miracle stories into a single literary unit. Verse 43 is almost certainly an addition by the evangelist, a feature of the Messianic Secret.

Looking first at the inserted story, according to Jewish law the woman with the flow of blood was ritually unclean. Anything that she touched was also ritually unclean. The woman is convinced, however, that by simply touching Jesus' clothing, his power (Greek *dynamis*) will be transmitted to her and will cure her of her illness (v. 28). Jesus is immediately aware that power has gone out from him and inquires who touched him (v. 30), and the woman admits what she has done (v. 33). The woman's cure is attributed in the story to her trust (Greek *pistis*) in God, (v. 34), although the evangelist would probably like his readers or listeners to believe it is her faith (also Greek *pistis*) in Jesus that has saved her. The Greek verb *sozo* in verse 34a means both "to cure" and "to save," and this double entendre, or use of a word with two meanings, is surely intentional. There is no way to capture in English the double meanings of both Greek words (*pistis*, meaning "trust" or "faith"; and *sozo*, meaning "to cure" and "to save"). No translation into English can convey the richness and the nuances of the original Greek.

The other miracle story begins by introducing a synagogue official, named Jairus (meaning in Hebrew "he enlightens" or "he awakens"). The name is probably symbolic in meaning (v. 22), as Jesus *enlightens* or *awakens* the child. Jairus came to Jesus and fell at his feet in obeisance, seeking Jesus' help because his daughter was close to death. Jairus pleads that if Jesus will only touch his daughter, she will live (v. 23). While he was still imploring Jesus, members of Jairus's household arrived to tell him his daughter had died (v. 35).

Jesus' inner circle of three—Peter, James, and John—are permitted to accompany Jesus to Jairus's house, where people are already mourning the girl's death (vv. 37–38). Jesus then takes Peter, James, John, and the girl's mother and father into the room where the girl lies and takes her hand and says to her in Aramaic *Talitha' koum* (vv. 40–41). The words of healing are a Greek transliteration of the Aramaic *talitha' qum* (meaning "Little girl, arise") and are reminiscent of incantations used in miracle stories in the ancient world. The use of such phrases in magic and healing stories (both here and again in 7:34, where Jesus says "*ephphatha*," meaning in Aramaic "be opened," when he healed the deaf man) imply the magical power of the words to produce a cure. Their translation into Greek suggests that the evangelist's readers or listeners did not all understand Aramaic.

The raising of the girl from the dead is reminiscent of similar miracle stories involving Elijah (1 Kgs 17:17–24) and Elisha (2 Kgs 4:18–37) in the Old Testament. If Elijah and Elisha were able to bring about resuscitations of dead children, then early Christians would surely have believed that Jesus was capable of comparable wonders. The Old Testament stories may, in fact, have been the inspiration for the miracle story of the Raising of Jairus's Daughter.

The twelve years of the woman's flow of blood (v. 25) and the twelve-year age of Jairus's daughter (v. 42) are probably the link that connects the two stories in the mind of the evangelist.

The witnesses to the girl's resuscitation were amazed (v. 42b), but Jesus ordered them to say nothing (v. 43), another example of the gospel's motif of the Messianic Secret. Jesus' messiahship would not become known until after his resurrection. Moreover, Jesus' final command to give the girl something to eat (5:43) comes almost as an afterthought and is probably intended by the evangelist to prove that she is really alive.

CONCLUSIONS AFTER CHAPTER 5

The three miracle stores in chapter 5 (The Healing of the Gerasene Demoniac and the combined stories the Woman Healed of the Flow of Blood and the Girl Restored to Life) are likely part of a larger collection of five miracle stories beginning with the Stilling of the Storm in 4:35–41 and including the Feeding of the Five Thousand Men in 6:30–44. The reason for including the Feeding of the Five Thousand in this grouping of five is that these five miracle stories are similar to five miracle stories in 6:45—8:26 (Jesus Walks on the Water [6:45–52], the Healing of the Sick in Gennesaret [6:53–56], the Syro-Phoenician Woman's Request for her Daughter [7:24–30], Jesus Cures the Deaf Man [7:31–37], and the Feeding of the Four Thousand [8:1–9]). In both groupings there is a miracle on the Sea of Galilee, followed by three healing miracles, followed by the feeding of a multitude. Although the stories are different in many ways, the repetition of the feeding of the thousands in 6:30–44 and 8:1–9 demands that we look closely at the surrounding stories. The parallelism of these two collections of five miracle stories suggests that they may have had a common background or source earlier in oral and/or written tradition. Mere coincidence seems an unlikely, although not an impossible, explanation.

In any event, the grouping of these miracle stories in chapters 4–6 suggests our author had access to a written source containing these miracle stories, to which he added the connective tissue necessary to incorporate the stories (or pericopes) into a meaningful narrative, an apparent sequence of events in the unfolding life and ministry of Jesus of Nazareth. The author's additions are evident, inasmuch as the introductions to these stories increasingly betray the vocabulary, literary style, and favorite physical settings of the evangelist.

Just as chapter 4 appears to have used a collection of parables, we now see a collection of miracle stories in this cluster of pericopes. It is becoming increasingly more apparent, as we move more deeply into the gospel, that the evangelist may have had access to several written sources that contained collections of pronouncement stories, miracle stories, parables, and perhaps other literary forms.

These written pericopes may have had their origin in the church in which the evangelist lived, perhaps as stories designed originally to illustrate aspects of Jesus' teaching and aspects of the teaching of the church about Jesus. Whether most or all of those stories had roots in the life and ministry of Jesus is another question, but there is little doubt that in their present form these stories were shaped by the church to serve the interests of the church, probably the very church in which and for which the evangelist was writing. The evangelist was apparently giving coherence to what were otherwise unconnected stories about Jesus. He was, therefore, proclaiming the good news about Jesus Christ, probably following the model of contemporary Greco-Roman or Hellenistic biographies. In fact, it is increasingly clear that the evangelist was not so much an author as he was a collector and editor of existing written material to which he had access in the church (in Antioch?), where he lived.

We are gradually but increasingly discovering the building blocks of the earliest gospel. Individual pericopes may have served originally as readings during church services at which they could have served as the basis for preaching the good news. Obviously we cannot know for sure, but it is helpful to speculate about how such stories and collections of stories came into existence for the evangelist to weave later into his gospel narrative.

We have seen once again that the stories in this chapter have introductions that often betray the hand of the evangelist in verses 1–2a and verse 21. Both introductions reflect the style and vocabulary of the evangelist. We have also observed that there are three distinct written miracle stories: the Healing of the Gerasene Demoniac (verses 2b–20), the Woman Healed of the Flow of Blood (verses 25–34), and the Resuscitation of Jairus's Daughter from the Dead (verses 22–23 and 35–42). In addition to the introductions, the hand of the author can be seen in the transition in verse 24 between the interwoven miracle stories and in the addition of the motif of the Messianic Secret in verse 43.

Verses 19 and 34 also reveal how the pericopes likely evolved in meaning within the church for which the evangelist wrote. "Go home to your own people, and proclaim to them what great things the Lord has done for you, and how he has shown mercy to you" in verse 19, and "Daughter, your trust (Greek *pistis*) has saved you" in verse 34 both probably referred to God in their original context. However, by the time the stories were incorporated into the gospel in both passages they were probably referring to Jesus: "what great things the Lord (Jesus) has done for you" in verse 19, and "faith" (Greek *pistis*) in Jesus, not "trust" (Greek *pistis*) in God, in verse 34.

All three miracle stories in this chapter revealed to the reader or the listener increasingly that Jesus was more than a prophet, more than a herald of the coming of God's rule. The author is building up to the final disclosure about who Jesus really is, a disclosure that will continue to unfold in future chapters.

It seems appropriate at this point to comment on the question of whether these miracle stories reflect actual events in the life and ministry of Jesus. Historians, as historians, are not able to verify miracle stories as reliable reports of actual events. There is no way to verify supernatural events.

Neither should we look for rational explanations of such events (e.g., Jairus's daughter was not really dead, but only in a coma). The best we can do is to speculate about how and why miracle stories about Jesus originated in the church's tradition. In doing so, we find that miracle stories were not uncommon, both in Judaism (witness the stories about Elijah and Elisha) and throughout the Hellenistic world. Christians simply developed such miracle stories about their own heroic figure, Jesus, in order to illustrate what a remarkable man he was and to confirm that he had been sent by God, for whom all things are possible. It is difficult to comment on whether there may be a historical kernel behind some of these stories. For example, did Jesus actually perform exorcisms? What is relevant is that the purpose of the miracle stories was clear and that such stories were familiar in that age in that part of the world.

Chapter 6

THE REJECTION OF JESUS AT NAZARETH

6:1 And he went out from there and came to his own country, and his disciples followed him.

2 And when the Sabbath had come, he began to teach in the synagogue. And many hearing him were astonished, saying, "Where did this man get these things? And what wisdom is this which is given to him, that such mighty works are performed by his hands!

3 Is this not the son of the carpenter and of Mary, and a brother of James, Joses, Judas, and Simon? And are not his sisters here with us?" And they were offended at him.

4 And Jesus said to them, "A prophet is not without honor except in his own country, among his own relatives, and in his own house."

5 Now he could do no mighty work there, except that he laid his hands on a few sick people and healed them.

6a And he marveled because of their unbelief.

THIS PERICOPE, PROBABLY A legend in its present form, is problematic for several reasons: (1) it reports the rejection of Jesus in his home town of Nazareth rather than the usual positive and enthusiastic reception of his teaching and healing proclaimed earlier in the gospel (1:27–28, 45; 2:12; 4:41; 5:20); (2) it introduces the problematic issue that Joseph was Jesus' biological father; and (3) it states that Jesus was unable to perform miracles in Nazareth because of the people's unbelief. These issues all point to the likelihood that we are dealing in these verses with a very early tradition, one that may reach back to the historical Jesus, because the story clearly does not serve the interests of the early church. Quite the contrary: it introduces issues that are dissimilar and embarrassing to the teaching of the early church.

The introduction to this pericope in 6:1 ("And he went out from there and came to his own country") attempts to link this story to what precedes, but it is a rather weak connection, as it says very little.

Moreover, the introductory phrase "when the Sabbath had come" (v. 2) uses the singular word for Sabbath (Greek *to sabbaton*) rather than the plural (Greek *ta sabbata*), which is found in 1:21; 2:23, 24; 3:2, 4. Only in the passage quoting the proverb "The Sabbath came into being for the sake of humankind, and not humankind for the sake of the Sabbath" (2:27) does the author elsewhere use the singular form *to sabbaton*, and in that instance he is likely quoting a popular saying.

The questions posed by the Nazarenes are minimally sarcastic, if not outright contemptuous:

"Where did this man get these things?"

"What wisdom is this which is given to him, that such mighty works are performed by his hands?"

"Is this not the son of the carpenter and of Mary, and a brother of James, Joses, Judas, and Simon? And are not his sisters here with us?"

The implication of these questions is that Jesus is nothing but an ordinary man incapable of such wise teaching and such mighty works, unless his power comes from (the) Satan, because it certainly does not come from God. This cold reception in Nazareth ("And they were offended at him" in v. 3) is quite different from the warm reception Jesus received in the synagogue in Capernaum on the Sabbath ("And they were astonished at his teaching, for he was teaching them as someone having authority, not as the scribes" in 1:21–22).

Also problematic is the identification of Jesus' family. Most English translations of verse 3 read something like: "*Is this not the carpenter, the son of Mary* and a brother of James and Joses and Judas and Simon? And are not his sisters here with us?" Textual critics, scholars who try to reconstruct the most nearly original text (or the autograph) of the books of the New Testament generally agree that the autograph likely read "Is this not the son of the carpenter and of Mary?" and that this phrase was later amended by a scribe to read "Is this not the carpenter, the son of Mary?" in order to conform to later Christian teaching regarding Jesus' birth from a virgin, a tradition not found in this gospel. The reading I have rendered is found in the earliest surviving fragment of this verse, in several ancient Greek manuscripts, and in several early translations of the gospel into Old Latin, Vulgate Latin, Boharic Coptic, and Ethiopic. It is virtually impossible to imagine why a scribal copyist would change the text to say that Joseph was Jesus' father, whereas it is very easy to imagine why a scribe would change the text to say that Joseph was *not* Jesus' father. Moreover, not only does this passage state that Joseph and Mary were Jesus' biological parents, but that they had at least six other children, four brothers named James, Joses, Judas, and Simon, and at least two unnamed sisters. Later efforts on the part of the church to identify these siblings as children of Joseph by a previous marriage or as cousins of Jesus are ostensibly Christian apologetic. The author of this gospel and the sources to which he had access were unaware of subsequent stories of the virgin birth of Jesus found in Matthew and Luke or of the late second-century teaching of the perpetual virginity of Mary in the apocryphal *Protevangelium of James*.

Another detail in this story is particularly interesting. Jesus seems to assume the title of "prophet" in this passage (v. 4). Moreover, he is referred to as prophet by others in two additional passages in this gospel, in 6:15 and 8:28. The criterion of dissimilarity or embarrassment once again suggests "prophet" may have been a title by which some called the historical Jesus. It is certainly not a title that early Christians would otherwise have used of him.

JESUS SENDS THE TWELVE OUT ON A MISSIONARY JOURNEY

6:6b And he went around the villages in a circle, teaching.

7 And he summoned the Twelve and began to send them out two by two, and he gave them authority over the unclean spirits.

8 And he directed them that they should not take anything for the journey, except a walking stick—no bread, no traveler's bag, no small change in their belts—

9 but to wear sandals, and not to wear two tunics.

10 And he said to them, "Into whatever house you enter, stay there until you depart from there.

> 11 And whenever a place does not welcome you or hear you, when you go out from there, shake off the dust from your feet as a testimony against them.
>
> 12 And going out, they proclaimed that they should repent.
>
> 13 And they cast out many demons, and they anointed with oil many who were sick and cured them.

Despite the rejection of Jesus in Nazareth, the mention of him going around in a circle (v. 6b) implies that starting somewhere (perhaps once again near the Sea of Galilee) Jesus traveled around to many villages in Galilee and ended up close to where he had started. The sentence is transitional and probably the construction of the evangelist.

The commissioning of the Twelve in 6:7–13 confirms the statement in 3:13–15:

> And he went up to the mountain and called to him those whom he himself wanted. And they went to him. And he made twelve, that they might be with him and that he might send them out to preach, and to have authority to cast out demons.

The Twelve begin their ministry and now have authority over unclean spirits, thereby sharing in Jesus' battle against Satan and in the struggle leading to the arrival of the period of God's rule.

Traveling in groups of two may reflect the practice of Jesus' apostles after his death and/or of the missionary activity of the early church. It is unlikely this practice reflects a command by the historical Jesus. It sounds more like a command to the church from the risen Lord. Moreover, directing the apostles to stay in just a single house in any community probably reflects the practice of Christian missionaries who stayed in the homes of other Christians, something Jesus would not have anticipated. The command to carry only a walking stick suggests an ascetic rigor for the missionaries. A walking stick was helpful for walking on uneven ground, but it might also afford protection from wild animals or a threatening person.

Does the evangelist understand that these instructions were only for the Twelve rather than for the church in general? Was Jesus really passing on his power concerning exorcisms and healings to the Twelve with the intention of setting up a small group of his followers to continue his work as a sort of "school?" Does this commission really reach back to Jesus, who apparently expected the imminent end of the world, or does it reflect rather the missionary work of the early church, which suffered rejection and even persecution? Probably the latter! Yet this pericope ends on a positive note with the success of the apostles' preaching and healing.

In addition to the transitional sentence in verse 6b, there is an additional literary feature of the evangelist in this passage: Jesus "began to" with an infinitive in verse 7 (see also 1:45; 4:1; 5:17, 20; 6:2, 7, 34, 55; 8:11, 31, 32; 10:28, 32, 41, 47; 11:15; 12:1; 13:5; 14:19, 33, 65, 69, 71; 15:8, 18).

Moreover, by way of clarification in verse 12, the indefinite "they" in "they proclaimed that they should repent" probably means "the disciples proclaimed that the people should repent." The use of a third-person-plural verb without a clear subject is also a common feature of the evangelist (see e.g., 1:22, 27, 29, 32, 45; 2:3, 12; 3:2, 30, 32; 5:14, 15; and see 6:14 below, etc.).

This pericope is probably best understood as a construction of the evangelist.

THE DEATH OF JOHN THE BAPTIST

> 6:14 And King Herod heard [about Jesus], for his name had become well known. And they were saying, "John the Baptist has been raised from the dead, and, because of this, special powers are at work in him."
>
> 15 But others were saying, "It is Elijah." But others said, "He is a prophet, like one of the prophets."
>
> 16 But when Herod heard [about this], he said, "The one whom I beheaded, John, has been raised!"
>
> 17 For Herod himself had ordered that John be apprehended and bound him in prison because of Herodias, the wife of his brother Philip; because he had married her.
>
> 18 For John had said to Herod, "It is not lawful for you to marry your brother's wife."
>
> 19 But Herodias held a grudge against him and wanted to kill him, and she was not able.

20 For Herod was afraid of John knowing that he was a righteous and holy man, and he protected him. And having heard him, he heard him gladly, though he was greatly perplexed.

21 And when an opportune day came, when Herod on his birthday gave a banquet for his courtiers, and military tribunes, and the most prominent men of Galilee,

22 and when his daughter Herodias came in and danced, she pleased Herod and his guests. The king said to the girl, "Ask of me whatever you want, and I will give it to you."

23 And he swore to her, "Whatever you ask of me, I will give you, even up to half of my kingdom."

24 And going out she said to her mother, "What shall I ask for?" And she said, "The head of John the Baptist!"

25 And immediately going in with haste to the king, she asked, saying, "I want you to give me immediately the head of John the Baptist on a platter."

26 And the king was deeply disturbed; but, because of the oaths and because of his guests, he did not want to refuse her.

27 And immediately the king sent a sentinel and commanded him to bring his head. And he went out and beheaded him in the prison,

28 and he brought his head on a platter and gave it to the girl, and the girl gave it to her mother.

29 And when his disciples heard about it, they came and took up his corpse and put it in a tomb.

This story, which I would classify as a legend, begins by introducing King Herod, who is actually Herod Antipas, the son of Herod the Great (who died in 4 BCE and whose kingdom was then divided among his sons). Herod Antipas was named tetrarch (ruler of a fourth part) of Galilee and Perea and ruled from 4 BCE until his exile in 39 CE. Antipas never had the title of king, although he tried unsuccessfully to secure the title from the Roman Emperor Gaius (Caligula). The designation "king" in verse 14 may reflect popular usage, or it is, more likely, a mistake of the evangelist or of his written source.

According to the evangelist, Jesus' popularity had spread widely throughout Galilee. Herod Antipas is credited in the text with thinking that Jesus might actually be John the Baptist *redivivus*. Others thought he might be Elijah, the expected precursor of the period of God's rule, or one of the many prophets who popped up during this period (vv. 14–15).

It was John's arrest (1:14–15) that ended his ministry in Judea and that likely led Jesus, who was probably a disciple of John, to begin "preaching the good news of God, and saying, 'The time has been fulfilled, and the kingdom of God is at hand. Repent and believe in the good news'" (1:15). Jesus' early ministry probably focused on the area of Galilee, not Judea, where John the Baptist had been preaching by the Jordan River. Jesus' ministry apparently did not include the continuation of John's baptism for the remission of sins. To the extent that we know anything about either John or Jesus, it is likely that both men understood that they were heralds or precursors of the imminent in-breaking of the period of God's rule. The evangelist would have us believe that John the Baptist was the precursor of Jesus, but that conviction is probably the result of a later effort on the part of the church to subordinate John to Jesus rather than to admit that Jesus might have been a disciple of and, therefore, at least initially, subordinate to John.

The story in this pericope is somewhat curious because its initial focus is on Jesus, who some thought was John the Baptist returned from the dead. Yet, John is not yet described as dead. That information comes later in the story in vv. 27–29.

According to the New Testament, John the Baptist criticized Herod Antipas, who had divorced his wife and married his half-brother Herod Philip's wife, Herodias (who was also Herod Philip's and Herod Antipas's half-niece). We learn more about the story from the Jewish historian Flavius Josephus: "Herod Antipas's first wife was King Aretas IV of Nabatea's daughter, who, upon learning of Herod Antipas's intention to divorce her, apparently fled to her father in Nabatea."[1] Moreover, Herod Philip's wife Herodias also apparently left her husband to marry his half-brother Herod Antipas. This scandalous marriage (condemned in Lev 18:16) resulted in the dissolution of the truce between Roman Galilee and Nabatea. According to Josephus, John the Baptist's popularity among the Jews and his outspoken criticism of Herod Antipas for this marital scandal lead to John's arrest and subsequent execution by Herod Antipas. In our gospel, it is not Herod

---

1. Josephus, *Antiquities of the Jews*, 18. 5. 1–2.

Antipas, but rather his wife Herodias, who is responsible for John the Baptist's death. According to the gospel, Herod Antipas rather liked John (6:20).

By way of further confusion, the text of 6:22 mistakenly identifies Herodias's daughter as Herodias after already identifying Herodias as Herod Antipas's wife just a few verses earlier (v. 17). Josephus identifies Herodias as Herod Philip's mother-in-law and Salome as Herod Antipas's daughter. Some manuscripts of our gospel try to correct the text of the gospel to read "the daughter of Herodias herself" instead of "his daughter Herodias," but the mistaken reading was probably in the original text of the gospel. Even more likely, the mistake appeared originally in a written source from which the evangelist copied. Josephus probably has the more reliable story. It is no wonder that the evangelist or, more likely, his written source was understandably wrong regarding the details of the genealogical nightmare of the Herod family.

We have no knowledge of the time frame between John's arrest and his execution. Neither can we place much credence in the details of the banquet at which Herodias's daughter supposedly danced for Herod Antipas's guests and thereby earned for her mother John the Baptist's head on a platter. The story in our gospel is highly improbable on several scores, most notably the tetrarch Herod Antipas offering half of his kingdom for a dance!

We should look at Malachi for belief in the return of Elijah (v. 15): "Lo, I will send you the prophet Elijah, before the great and terrible day of the LORD comes" (Mal 4:15, see also Mal 3:1). Apparently because the prophet Elijah did not die but was swept up in a whirlwind into heaven in a chariot of fire (2 Kgs 2:11), it was believed, at least in some Jewish circles, that he had not died and that he would, therefore, return to prepare the way for the coming of the time of God's rule.

THE FEEDING OF THE FIVE THOUSAND MEN

6:30 And the apostles gathered before Jesus and told him everything that they had done and taught.

31 And he said to them, "Come aside privately to a deserted place and rest a little while." For there were many coming and going, and they did not even have an opportunity to eat.

32 And they went away in a boat to a deserted place privately.

CHAPTER 6

33 And many saw them departing and recognized them and ran there on foot from all the cities and arrived there before them.

34 And when he disembarked, he saw a large crowd and was moved with pity for them, because they were like sheep not having a shepherd. And he began to teach them many things.

35 And as the hour was now late, his disciples came to him and said, "This place is deserted, and the hour is already late.

36 Send them away, so that they may go into the surrounding villages and towns and buy themselves something to eat."

37 But he answered and said to them, "You, give them something to eat." And they said to him, "Shall we go and buy two hundred denarii worth of bread and give it to them to eat?"

38 But he said to them, "How many loaves do you have? Go away and see." And when they found out, they said, "Five, and two fish."

39 And he ordered them to get them all to lie down in groups on the green grass.

40 And they sat down in groups of a hundred and in groups of fifty.

41 And taking the five loaves and the two fish, he looked up to heaven and gave thanks and praise and broke the loaves and gave them to his disciples so that they might set them before the people; and the two fish he distributed among them all.

42 And they all ate and were filled;

43 And they picked up twelve baskets of crumbs and of fish.

44 And those who had eaten the loaves were five thousand men.

The story of the Feeding of the Five Thousand Men in 6:30–44 probably belongs to a written collection of miracle stories that also contained the Stilling of the Storm (4:35–41), the Healing of the Gerasene Demoniac (5:1–20), the Woman Healed of the Flow of Blood (5:25–34), and the Girl Restored to

Life (5:21-23, 35-42). The miracle stories of Jesus in 6:45—8:9 may belong to a second written collection of miracle stories used as a source by the evangelist, an issue we shall consider later.

The introductory verses (6:30-34) are probably merely efforts on the part of the evangelist to reintroduce the apostles (v. 30) and then get them, together with a crowd of people (vv. 31, 33-34), to the other side of the lake (vv. 32 and 34). Obviously, a large crowd is essential to this miracle story, even as Jesus is apparently seeking solitude with his disciples (vv. 31-32).

The timing in this story is somewhat problematic. Verse 35 tells us twice that the hour is already late. Yet, there is still time to arrange the crowd of five thousand men (plus women and children?) into groups (vv. 39-40), to feed them the loaves of bread and the fish (v. 41), to collect the large amount of leftovers (v. 43), to send his disciples and the crowd away (v. 45), and to climb a mountain and pray (v. 46)—all before evening came (v. 47). Such difficulties point to the issues involved in collecting written stories and inserting them into what appears to be a chronological narrative.

The mention in verse 37 of two hundred denarii is also problematic, as a denarius was a laborer's average daily wage, enough money to feed an average family for one day. Two hundred denarii was more than half a year's average wage for a laborer. Where did the disciples expect to get such a large amount of money to go shopping for food at the last minute?

The mention of five loaves of bread (v. 38) may be symbolic, recalling the five books of the Torah, the Pentateuch, the books of Moses. The fish almost seem to be an afterthought; however, some of the disciples were fishermen, and the fish was an early Christian symbol of Christianity. In fact, the Greek word for fish (*IXTHUS*) was an acrostic for the Greek *Iesous Xristos THeou Uios Soter*, meaning "Jesus Christ Son of God Savior."

It is obvious that the story of the Feeding of the Five Thousand Men, which probably begins in verse 35, should be considered a eucharistic celebration in anticipation of the Last Supper on the eve of Jesus' death (see 14:22-25). The sequence of "taking the five loaves and the two fish" and "looking up to heaven" and "blessing" and "breaking" and "giving the bread" (v. 41) anticipates the events in 14:22: "And while they were eating, he took bread, gave thanks and praise, broke it, and gave it to them." This formula for the church's eucharistic celebration was apparently fixed relatively early in the history of the church, its earliest written reference being in a letter from Paul written from Ephesus in about 54 CE to the church at Corinth (1 Cor 11:23-24):

> For I received from the Lord what I also handed on to you, that the Lord Jesus on the

night when he was betrayed took a loaf of bread, and when he had given thanks, he broke

it and said, "This is my body that is for you. Do this in remembrance of me."

Paul, of course, was not at the Last Supper and never knew Jesus, so his claim that he received this information from the Lord probably means that he received it from the Risen Lord by way of the Church's liturgical tradition, which may go back to an early period after Jesus' death. There is little doubt that the audience reading or hearing this story would have understood its communal eucharistic significance in the church's liturgy.

The Feeding of the Five Thousand Men	The Last Supper
and as the hour was now late (6:35)	when it was evening (14:17)
and gave thanks and praise (*eulogesen*) (6:41)	and after blessing it (*eulogesas*) (14:22)
and broke the loaves (*artous*) (6:41)	taking bread (*arton*) (14:22)
and gave (*edidou*) them to his disciples (6:41)	he gave (*edoken*) it to them (14:22)
and they all ate (6:42)	and all of them drank (14:23)

Whether Jesus ever celebrated such a celebratory meal during the course of his ministry, not only once but three times (see also 8:1–10), is another matter that we will address later. That the story uses the word "apostles" in verse 30 (the only occurrence of the word "apostle" in this gospel) instead of "disciples," the author's usual term, may also indicate the relative lateness of the story. The Feeding of the Five Thousand Men is also quite different from the other miracle stories in the gospel, which usually involve healings or exorcisms of someone who is ill or possessed. This story is reminiscent of several stories in the Old Testament:

1. The story of Moses and the people of Israel in the wilderness eating the manna from heaven (Exod 16:4–8);

2. The story of Elijah making sufficient for many days for himself, the widow of Zarephath, and her children the scant food of a jar of meal and a flask of oil 1 Kgs 17:8–16);

3. The story of Elisha multiplying the oil for the wife of a member of the company of prophets and her children (2 Kgs 4:1–7); and

4. The story of Elisha taking twenty loaves of barley to provide food for one hundred men with some food left over (2 Kgs 4:42–44).

In all these stories the miracle worker multiplies food. It is almost certain the miracle story of Jesus multiplying the loaves to feed five thousand men was modeled on these earlier stories about Moses, Elijah, and Elisha. What they could do, surely Jesus could do—even better.

The twelve baskets left over may also be symbolic: the twelve tribes of Israel, the old order; and the twelve disciples (apostles), the New Israel in Christ, the church.

JESUS WALKS ON THE WATER

6:45 And immediately he made his disciples get into the boat and go before him to the other side, toward Bethsaida, while he himself dismissed the crowd.

46 And when he had taken leave of them, he went away to the mountain to pray.

47 And when evening had come, the boat was in the middle of the sea; and he himself was alone on the land.

48 And seeing them straining at the oars, for the wind was against them, at about the fourth watch of the night he came toward them, walking on the sea, and wanted to pass them by.

49 But seeing him walking on the sea, they supposed that it was a ghost, and they cried out;

50 for they all saw him and were terrified. But immediately he spoke with them and said to them, "Have courage! It is I; don't be afraid."

51 And he went up to them into the boat, and the wind ceased. And they were astonished within themselves,

52 for they did not understand about the loaves, but their heart was hardened.

This miracle story appears to be almost a doublet of 4:35–41, the Stilling of the Storm, or it is at least likely influenced by that story.

CHAPTER 6

Once again the disciples are going across the Sea of Galilee but this time they are headed to Bethsaida, a town on the northern tip of the lake on the eastern side of the Jordan River in what is today the Golan Heights. Although they set sail for Bethsaida (v. 45), they arrive in Gennesaret (v. 53), a plain on the northwest side of the lake. There is nothing in the story to suggest that they were blown off course, so it is difficult to explain the inconsistency. One theory is this pericope was followed in the author's source by the Healing of the Blind Man at Bethsaida (8:22–26), and that the evangelist rearranged the stories and created the error of heading to Bethsaida and winding up at Gennesaret. A difficulty with this theory is the geographic details of most stories and the introductions to the individual pericopes are generally considered the work of the evangelist and not material he found in his source(s).

The reference to "the mountain" to which Jesus retreated in verse 46 implies the author has a specific mountain in mind. Is the author comparing Jesus to Moses ,who went to Mount Sinai to commune with God (Exod 24:15, 18), implying thereby that Jesus is the new Moses or that he is replacing Moses? Such symbolic imagery is not unusual in the early church or in this gospel and suggests the authors who created these stories were creative writers, not reporters of actual historical events.

Romans customarily divided the dark time of night (about 6 p.m. to about 6 a.m.) into four periods, so the fourth watch would have been from about 3–6 a.m. That Jesus is able to see that the disciples are having difficulty rowing (v. 48) implies Jesus has supernatural perception, inasmuch as it was already dark and the boat was in the middle of the lake (v. 47) at some distance from Jesus probably about two or three miles.

Moreover, verse 48a implies Jesus was coming to the aid of the disciples, so verse 48b seems to make no sense: "and he wanted to pass them by." The thought that Jesus wanted to pass by the disciples at a time when they were having difficulty at sea is perplexing. Perhaps the author of this story is thinking about the tradition that when Moses asked Yahweh to show Moses his glory, Yahweh answered, "I will make all my goodness *pass before you*, and will proclaim before you the name 'Yahweh (the divine I AM)'" (Exod 33:18–19). See also 1 Kgs 19:11–13a:

> He (Yahweh) said [to Elijah], "Go out and stand on the mountain (Mount Horeb, i.e., Mount Sinai) before Yahweh, for Yahweh is about to pass by." Now there was a great wind, so strong that it was splitting mountains and breaking rocks in pieces before Yahweh, but Yahweh was not in the wind; and after the wind an earthquake, but Yahweh was not in the earthquake; and after the

earthquake a fire, but Yahweh was not in the fire; and after the fire a sound of sheer silence. When Elijah heard it, he wrapped his face in his mantle and went and stood at the entrance of the cave. (See also Isa 47:8, 10 for allusions to the divine I AM)

Jesus' words to the disciples in verse 50 are: "Have courage! It is I; don't be afraid." That could as well be translated: "Have courage; I AM (Greek *ego eimi*); don't be afraid." Jesus may be invoking the words of the divine I AM, an apparent play on words with a double entendre.

This suggestion implies the early church played a major role in shaping the stories about Jesus and minimizes the likelihood that the evangelist is reporting something that actually happened. The gospel is a proclamation of the good news of Jesus Christ. It is not a history book, as we understand the word "history." Just as Yahweh (the divine I AM) passed by Moses and Elijah in those theophanies, so too Jesus wanted to pass by the disciples but assures them of who he is, when the disciples think they have seen a ghost.

Miracle stories emphasize Jesus' divine power (*dynamis*) and his gradual disclosure of himself as embodying the divine I AM, although not necessarily in a metaphysical way. We are a long distance, both in terms of time and theology, from Christians thinking of Jesus as part of a Trinitarian Godhead.

Power of the sea is found in a number of stories in the Old Testament:

1. Yahweh gave Moses power to divide the Sea of Reeds so the Israelites could cross over on dry land, and then drowned their Egyptian pursuers (Exod 14:21–29);

2. Yahweh gave Joshua power to divide the waters of the Jordan River so the Israelites might cross from Transjordan and enter the Promised Land (Josh 3:7–17);

3. Elijah touched the Jordan River with his mantle to separate the water so he and Elisha could cross (2 Kgs 2:8); and

4. Elisha subsequently took Elijah's mantle and struck the water of the Jordan River enabling him to cross over (2 Kgs 2:13–14).

Moreover, in Greek and Roman mythology the gods Poseidon and Neptune respectively had power over the sea. Surely, in the minds of the early church, Jesus could exercise such power as well, a point that would not be lost on Gentile Christian members of the church.

Like these older stories, the miracle story of Jesus Walking on the Water was composed to honor Jesus and to win followers to Christianity. Jews in the evangelist's church would have understood this story in light of their

CHAPTER 6

Jewish background, and Greeks and Romans in light of their respective backgrounds. In any case, the theme of the story is clear: it portrays Jesus as a divine messenger of God; indeed, as the embodiment of the divine I AM of Exod 3:13-15:

> But Moses said to God, "If I come to the Israelites and say to them, 'The God of your ancestors has sent me to you,' and they ask me, 'What is his name?' what shall I say to them?" God said to Moses, "I AM WHO I AM." He said further, "Thus you shall say to the Israelites, "I AM has sent me to you." God also said to Moses, "This shall you say to the Israelites, 'Yahweh, the God of your ancestors, the God of Abraham, the God of Isaac, and the God of Jacob has sent me to you':
>
> This is my name forever,
>
> and this is my title for all generations.

It is by the power of God that Jesus is able to walk on the sea. Jesus possesses that divine power (*dynamis*) as a gift from God.

The miracle stories of the Feeding of the Five Thousand Men (6:30-44) and Jesus Walking on the Water (6:45-52) are linked in the final words of verse 52: "for they did not understand about the loaves, but their heart was hardened." These two pericopes are also linked in the Gospel of John (John 6:1-15 and 6:16-21). These two gospels otherwise have very little in common, so this connection almost certainly indicates the two stories were already linked in a written source to which our evangelist and the author of the Gospel of John both had access.

We now end where we began. The similarities between the miracle story of Jesus Walking on the Water (6:45-52) and the miracle story of the Stilling of the Storm (4:35-41) suggest the evangelist incorporated elements of the earlier story into this pericope to heighten the drama. The account of the Walking on the Water in the Gospel of John is much simpler and may, therefore, be closer to the original written source.

THE HEALING OF THE SICK IN GENNESARET

> 6:53 And when they had crossed over to the land, they came to Gennesaret and went into the harbor.

54 And when they came out of the boat, immediately recognizing him,

55 they ran around that whole region, and began to carry about on pallets those who were sick to wherever they heard that he was.

56 And wherever he entered into villages, or into cities, or into hamlets, they put the sick in the marketplaces, and begged him that they might just touch the fringe of his garment. And as many as touched him were cured.

The story of the Healing of the Sick in Gennesaret (probably a plain on the northwest side of the Sea of Galilee) is a general summary of Jesus' Galilean ministry. The story is apparently a construction of the evangelist (in the form of a collective miracle story), as Jesus moves around Galilee, pursued by large crowds, as he performs healings either willingly or simply by having people touch his clothing. There is no mention of Jesus' teaching in this story. The general healings in Gennesaret are somewhat reminiscent of the story of the Woman Healed of the Flow of Blood (5:25–34). Simply touching a part of Jesus' garment releases power that heals, apparently a popular belief of the time when the evangelist wrote.

CONCLUSIONS AFTER CHAPTER 6

This is a particularly interesting chapter because it addresses a number of issues that enable us to understand better both the historical Jesus and the development of the early Christian community. First of all, in the opening pericope (6:1–6a), we learn that Jesus was apparently not popular in his home town of Nazareth, that Joseph and Mary were his biological parents, that Jesus had four brothers and at least two sisters, and that both Jesus and others may at times have referred to him as a "prophet." It is because of the criterion of dissimilarity or embarrassment that we come to such conclusions. More specifically, a saying of Jesus or a tradition about Jesus has a greater claim to historical authenticity if it is dissimilar to the teaching or the theological bias of the early church. It is unlikely that the church would have fabricated sayings or traditions that clearly contradict the church's preaching or theological predisposition.

We see increasingly in this chapter that the evangelist was not a reliable historian, as we understand the writing of history. He was rather a storyteller who apparently made use of multiple written sources. As such, the accuracy of the stories in this chapter relies on the accuracy of the evangelist's written sources. Individual stories or pericopes obviously took shape initially in oral and/or in written form in the church primarily to serve the needs of the church. Some stories may have originated in events in the life and ministry of Jesus, such as the story of the Rejection of Jesus at Nazareth in 6:1–6a and at least some elements in the story of the Death of John the Baptist in 6:14–29, especially those details confirmed by the Jewish historian.

On the other hand, the story of Jesus Sending the Disciples on a Missionary Journey in 6:6–13 probably reflects missionary practices of Jesus' disciples or of missionaries of the early church. The story of the Feeding of the Five Thousand Men in 6:30–44 is heavily grounded in motifs found in the story of Moses and the Exodus in the Old Testament, and in the celebration of the church's eucharistic meal in 14:17–25. The story of Jesus Walking on the Water in 6:45–52 discloses the divine element in Jesus. The account of the Healing of the Sick in Gennesaret in 6:53–56 purports to summarize elements of Jesus' healing ministry in Galilee and is likely a construction of the evangelist. We are seeing increasingly in this gospel that even those stories that appear to be grounded in the life, ministry, and teaching of Jesus of Nazareth were shaped to serve the needs of the church.

The meaning of the words "The Good News of Jesus Messiah" in the title or superscription of the gospel (1:1) is ambiguous. They can refer either to the good news proclaimed *by* Jesus or to the good news proclaimed by the church *about* Jesus. Although it is increasingly clear that there is an element of both in this gospel, the balance appears to be tipping more toward the church's proclamation of the *kerygma*, the preaching of the good news *about* Jesus the Messiah, Jesus the Christ.

This chapter apparently contains material that was part of a collection of miracle stories, whose purpose was to heighten belief in Jesus as the Christ, the Messiah sent by God himself. Gradually the gospel is unfolding the story of Jesus as a divine messenger sent by God for a purpose that is not yet entirely clear but that is growing chapter by chapter. Jesus' teaching and preaching are increasingly taking a back seat, because Jesus' significance is of much greater importance than that of a mere teacher. Increasingly, the message is not what the messenger may have delivered; increasingly the messenger is the message. The conclusion of the Gospel of John in John 20:30–31 applies to the earliest gospel just as well as it applies to the Gospel of John:

> "Now Jesus did many other signs in the presence of his disciples, which are not written in this book. But these are written so that

you may come to believe that Jesus is the Messiah, the Son of God, and that through believing you may have life in his name."

The miracle story of the Feeding of the Five Thousand Men (6:30–44) seems to have been drawn from a written source of five miracle stories available to the evangelist: the Stilling of the Storm (4:35–41), the Healing of the Gerasene Demoniac (5:1–20), the Woman with the Flow of Blood (5:24–34), the Girl Restored to Life (5:21–23, 35–43), and the Feeding of the Five Thousand Men (6:30–44). For whatever reason, the evangelist broke open his written source of miracle stories to include before the fifth and final miracle story in the sequence the material in 6:1–29, including The Rejection of Jesus at Nazareth in 6:1–6a; Jesus Sends the Twelve on a Mission Journey in 6:6b–13; and the Death of John the Baptist in 6:14–29.

Beginning with Jesus Walks on the Water in 6:45–52, the evangelist is probably drawing from an additional written collection of miracle stories, an issue we will address in a future chapter.

One other feature in this chapter deserves passing comment. Once again the author's use of the third-personal-plural verb without a clear subject (the indefinite "they" meaning a group of unspecified people) occurs five times in this chapter: 6:14, 53, 54, 55, 56. We have seen this literary feature of our evangelist previously in this gospel.

Chapter 7

THE TRADITION OF THE ELDERS

7:1 And the Pharisees and some of the scribes came together before him, having come from Jerusalem.

2 And they saw some of his disciples eating bread with ritually impure (hands), that is, with unwashed hands.

3 For the Pharisees and all the Jews do not eat unless they wash with a cupped hand, adhering carefully to the tradition of the elders.

4 and if they are returning from the market, they do not eat unless they immerse themselves; and there are also many other things that they received to observe: the immersing of cups, and pitchers, and copper kettles, and beds.

5 And the Pharisees and the scribes asked him, "Why do your disciples not walk in accordance with the tradition of the elders but eat bread with ritually impure hands?"

6 But he said to them, "Well did Isaiah prophesy concerning you hypocrites, as it has been written:
　'This people honors me with their lips,
　but their heart is far from me.

7 They worship me in vain, teaching as divine instructions the commandments of human beings.'

8 Laying aside the commandment of God, you support the tradition of human beings.

THE MATERIAL IN 7:1–23 is the second major collection of sayings of Jesus in this gospel, the first being the collection of parables in 4:1–32. This unit appears to be a collection of sayings of Jesus concerning differences between the Jewish law as found primarily in the oral tradition of the elders (of the Pharisaic party) and human matters of necessity, seemingly embraced in the text by Jesus. We are, however, likely witnessing in this material the discussion of a critical issue in the early years of Jewish and Gentile Christianity rather than an issue that appeared during the ministry of the historical Jesus. The form of verses 1–8 is probably a pronouncement story.

The role of the Jewish Law was an issue that divided the early church, an issue that we read about in greater detail in the letters of Paul and in the Acts of the Apostles. Galatians 2 explains some of Paul's disagreements with the Jerusalem church, most especially with Peter, James, and John, who would more likely have known what Jesus taught than would Paul. Yet, Jesus' name is never invoked by Paul or the Jerusalem church in making their separate cases. Jesus' attitude toward the Jewish law would have been critical to the early church, and most especially to both Jewish Christians and Gentile Christians who had to deal on a regular basis with Jewish Christians, often in the same church community.

The question is whether any of the sayings in this section can be traced back to the historical Jesus, or whether this material simply reflects the debate within the early church, and most particularly the position of the church of the evangelist (presumably the church at Antioch of Syria?). I suggest this material probably reflects the latter. However, in the minds of early Christians, Jesus, or rather the risen Lord, continued to speak to the church through its prophets, hence the justification for reporting this material as if it reflects the actual words of Jesus.

The introduction in verse 1 is totally artificial and reflects the hand of the evangelist. Pharisees and scribes had come from Jerusalem, perhaps specifically to test the issue of Jesus' attitude toward the Jewish Law, although that is not entirely clear. We should remember that in 3:6 the Pharisees are reported to have conspired with the Herodians (Jewish supporters of the Herodian dynasty) about how they could destroy Jesus.

There is no credible introduction or setting to this pericope. The presumed setting is somewhere in Galilee and involves a confrontation between Jesus and Pharisees and scribes, who had come from Jerusalem. Some (but not all?) of the disciples of Jesus are eating their food with ritually impure hands (v. 2), which serves as an introduction to the material in verse 5. The parenthetical explanatory comment at the end of verse 2 ("that is, with unwashed hands") and all of verses 3–4 are editorial remarks, probably by the evangelist, to explain the context of the issue more clearly to his Gentile audience, who would likely not have understood the issue without such clarification.

The quotation from Isaiah in verses 6–7 differs from both the Septuagint (the ancient translation of the Hebrew Bible from Hebrew into Greek) and the Hebrew Masoretic Text of Isa 29:13, although it is closer to the Septuagint. This citation of Isaiah from a text close to the Greek Septuagint also suggests that this dialogue occurred within the early church at a time when Greek-speaking Christians were diligently searching through the Greek translation of the Jewish Scriptures in order to support their teachings.

MORE ON THE TRADITION OF THE ELDERS

> 7:9 And he said to them, "All too well you lay aside the commandment of God, in order to confirm your tradition.
>
> 10 For Moses said,
>
> 'Honor your father and your mother'; and,
>
> 'He who curses father or mother, let him be put to death.'
>
> 11 But you say, 'If a man says to his father or mother, "Whatever profit you might have received from me is *korban*' '—(which means a gift [consecrated to God])—,
>
> 12 then you no longer allow him to do anything for his father or his mother,
>
> 13 annulling the word of God by means of your tradition which you have handed down. And you do many such similar things."

Verses 9–13 are likely a separate pronouncement story, which the evangelist attached to verses 1–8 because of the similarity of the issue involved. The clue to the fact that this was originally a separate unit is probably to be found in the opening words of verse 9: "And he said to them," used here to introduce an additional pericope on a related subject, the practice of *korban* rather than the hand-washing in verses 1–8. If these words of transition are editorial additions of the evangelist, as I suspect they are, then he may have found the various components of the discussion in separate but related sources. In fact, the evangelist may have brought together five different collections of material: (1) verses 2a, 5–8; (2) verses 9b–13; (3) verse 15; (4) verses 18b–20; and (5) verses 21–23. The evangelist's own words may be found in:

1. the general introduction in verse 1;
2. the explanation in verses 2b–4 (beginning with "that is, with unwashed hands");
3. the transitional words in verse 9a "And he said to them";
4. the introductory words in verse 14 (see below) "And when he had called the multitude to himself again, he said to them";
5. the introductory words in verse 17; and
6. the introductory words in verse 24.

The command "Honor your father and your mother" in verse 10a follows the Greek Septuagint of Exod 20:12 and Deut 5:16, suggesting a setting for this story in the church rather than in the life and ministry of the historical Jesus. Likewise in verse 10b, "He who curses father or mother, let him be put to death" follows the Greek Septuagint of Exod 21:17 and Lev 20:9a, once again evidence of the likely development of this material in a Greek-speaking church rather than in the life and ministry of Jesus.

Verses 11–13 are confusing:

> If a man says to his father or mother, 'Whatever profit you might have received from me is *korban*'—(which means a gift [consecrated to God])—, then you no longer allow him to do anything for his father or his mother, annulling the word of God by means of your tradition which you have handed down.

Specifically, if a man tells one of his parents that a gift to them should count as if it were a gift to God, then he is not following the commandment to honor his father and his mother, as this commandment obliges the son to provide material support for his parents. One cannot devote to God a gift made for a parent's material well-being and expect to receive credit as if it were a gift to God.

CHAPTER 7

THE JEWISH LAW OF RITUALLY CLEAN AND UNCLEAN

7:14 And when he had called the multitude to himself again, he said to them, "Listen to me, all of you, and understand:

15 There is nothing outside the human being that going into him can make him ritually impure; but those things that come out of the human being is (sic) what makes the human being ritually impure.

[16 If anyone has ears to hear, let him hear!"]

The evangelist's hand is evident in the transitional words of verse 14, as he apparently introduces in verse 15 still another setting for another saying on the same general subject. This more comprehensive statement put into Jesus' mouth probably represented the position of the author's Gentile Christian community (in Antioch?). It is carefully crafted and was likely known to the evangelist from a written source or as a saying that was almost proverbial in his church. Although many scholars see in this saying an authentic saying of the historical Jesus, I find that unlikely. It runs counter to the position of the early Jerusalem church and its leaders, who were closest to Jesus during his lifetime. This material seems to have been addressed to the church in which and to which the evangelist was speaking, probably from already existing polemic. If the historical Jesus actually spoke to this issue, he may have said something similar to the biblical prophets of old, something like: "A person is not defiled so much by what goes into his body but by what comes out of his body." It is not clear that Jesus intended to overthrow the Jewish Law.

Verse 15 is a summary of everything that precedes in this chapter. Neither unwashed hands nor any food that enters a human being defiles that human being, because it passes through the body as human waste. Rather, it is what comes out of a human being that defiles him.

Verse 16 (printed above in brackets) is not found in our best manuscripts and was likely a later scribal addition (see also 4:9, 12, 18, 20, 23, 24, 33; and 8:18 for references in this gospel to "hear" in the sense of take seriously), perhaps to reinforce the command in verse 14a to both listen and understand.

Might verses 2, 5, and 15 be the original core of a story that reaches back to Jesus?:

7:2 And they saw some of his disciples eating bread with ritually impure (hands), that is, with unwashed hands.

5 And the Pharisees and the scribes asked him, "Why do your disciples not walk in accordance with the tradition of the elders but eat bread with ritually impure hands?

15 There is nothing outside the human being that going into him can make him ritually impure; but those things that come out of the human being is (sic) what make the human being ritually impure."

This cluster of verses makes some sense, even in the context of the life and ministry of Jesus. The intervening material, documented by scriptural arguments from the Greek Septuagint, sounds like the kind of early Christian polemic that might have arisen in a predominantly Gentile Christian church. It is possible such a conflated cluster of material might have already been available to the evangelist in a written source.

STILL ANOTHER SAYING ON THE SUBJECT OF RITUALLY CLEAN AND UNCLEAN

7:17 And when he had entered into a house away from the crowd, his disciples asked him about the parable.

18 And he said to them, "Are you thus also mindless? Do you not understand that whatever enters a human being from outside cannot defile him,

19 because it does not go into his heart but into his stomach, and passes into the latrine?" thus making all foods clean.

20 But he said, "What comes out of a human being is what defiles the human being.

Once again we see the evangelist's hand in verse 17, an effort to introduce still one more saying or cluster of sayings on the subject. In addressing the disciples in verse 18, Jesus asks them whether they are mindless or senseless, like the crowd he has been speaking to.

Interestingly, the author describes the material in verse 15 as a parable. In this case, an incomprehensible or puzzling saying that requires explanation rather than a full-blown comparison, the usual form of a parable in this gospel.

In Hebrew thought, the heart (Greek *kardia*) is the seat of spiritual life and moral conduct. This is what the evangelist means in verse 19. Rather the food goes instead into the stomach (Greek *koilia*), perhaps a play on words, and from there into a latrine. The participial phrase "thus making all food clean" is awkwardly attached to the saying of Jesus by way of explanation, clearly a comment of the evangelist intended to refer to Jesus as the one who declared all food clean.

Verse 19b is unequivocal: Jesus eliminated all food laws, or perhaps more accurately the church in which the evangelist lived and to which he wrote has eliminated all dietary laws for followers of Jesus, whether Jewish or Gentile Christian. It is likely this issue may still have been a matter of concern in the church to which the evangelist was writing. Yet the text is clear: the observance of Jewish dietary laws is unnecessary.

A LIST OF VICES THAT COME FROM WITHIN A HUMAN BEING

> 7:21 For from within, out of the heart of human beings come evil machinations: acts of sexual immorality, thefts, murders,

> 22 adulteries, acts of greed, acts of wickedness, deceit, licentiousness, an evil eye, blasphemy, arrogance, foolishness.

> 23 All these evil things come out from within and defile the human being."

The saying in verses 21–23 make it clear that out of an evil heart with evil intentions or machinations come evil deeds, followed by a list of vices the author provides from what were probably well-known lists of such vices in his church. The initial six evil deeds, all in the plural form, are:

- *porneia* (acts of disapproved forms of sexual intercourse, such as prostitution, unfaithfulness, unchastity, and fornication);
- *klopoi* (acts of theft or stealing);

- *phonoi* (acts of murder, slaughter, or killing);
- *moixeiai* (acts of adultery, an act probably also understood in *porneia* above, but now made even more explicit);
- *pleonexiai* (acts of greed both in terms of desire for power and possessions, insatiableness, avarice, covetousness, striving for wealth or power through devious means, arrogance);
- *poneriai* (acts of wickedness, baseness, maliciousness, sinfulness, intentionally practiced evil will);

The next six evil acts in this list, all in the singular form, are:

- *dolos* (deceit, cunning, treachery);
- *aselgeia* (licentiousness, indecency, voluptuousness, debauchery, sensuality);
- *ophthalmos poneros* (evil eye, usually referring to an act of jealousy, greed, or envy);
- *blasphemia* (blasphemy, slander, defamation, abusive speech);
- *hyperephania* (arrogance, haughtiness, pride, boasting);
- *aphrosyne* (foolishness, lack of both moral and intellectual sense, lack of practical wisdom).

This more detailed explanation of the nuanced meanings of these Greek words makes it clear how difficult it is to translate any of these terms with a single English word. There are a subtlety and a range of meaning that are unfortunately often lost in translation.

This list of vices (vv. 21–23) certainly circulated independently within the early church and was perhaps known if not derived from contemporary Jewish and/or Hellenistic lists. The fact that there are six vices in the plural followed by six vices in the singular suggests we are dealing with a written list from which the evangelist drew. There is nothing specifically Christian about this list of vices, which complements the material in verses 17–20.

Verses 14–23 represent a change: Jesus turns his attention from the Pharisees and scribes (vv. 1 and 5) to address the multitude, laying out his own teaching on the subject of what is ritually clean and unclean, first to the multitude (vv. 14–15), then to his disciples (vv. 17–23).

Many scholars think verse 15 may be an authentic saying of Jesus, as it does not reflect the kind of dialogue going on within contemporary Judaism at that time. My concern is that I would expect Jesus' inner circle in the Jerusalem church (Peter, James, and John) to have embraced this teaching wholeheartedly if Jesus had ever said something like this in their presence. Quite the contrary, Peter, James, and John appear to have advocated in favor of having Jewish Christians follow the precepts of the Jewish law (Torah). The words in verse 19b "thus making all foods clean," are obviously from the evangelist. Nevertheless, Jesus' saying effectively nullifies the concept of ritual uncleanness, which is found not only in Judaism but in many religions. There is an element of this radical position in some of Israel's prophets, especially in the prophet Amos's attack on cultic practices, and in Mic 6:8, which reduces Judaism to doing justice, loving mercy, and walking humbly with God. Clearly moral principles are more important than narrow legalism.

THE SYRO-PHOENICIAN WOMAN'S REQUEST FOR HER DAUGHTER

7:24 Then he got up from there and went away into the region of Tyre. And he entered into a house and wanted no one to know, but he could not escape notice.

25 But immediately a woman, whose daughter had an unclean spirit, heard about him and came and fell at his feet.

26 Now the woman was Greek, Syro-Phoenician by race, and she asked him to drive the demon out of her daughter.

27 But he said to her, "Let the children be fed first, for it is not good to take the children's bread and throw it to the dogs."

28 Then she answered and said to him, "Sir, even the dogs under the table eat from the children's crumbs."

29 And he said to her, "Because of this saying go on your way; the demon has gone out of your daughter."

30 And when she went into her house, she found the child lying on the bed and the demon gone out.

Jesus is apparently seeking escape from the crowds and enters the territory of Tyre, the area of Phoenicia (modern Lebanon), northwest of Galilee, hoping not to be recognized. But his reputation has apparently preceded him. Even outside his native Galilee, Jesus could not hide from recognition. The purpose of this miracle story is apparently to include the Gentiles in Jesus' ministry. There are, however, serious issues with the geographic location of this story and with Jesus' change of heart in the story.

The identification of the woman as Greek (meaning she was a Gentile and not a Jew), and more specifically as Syro-Phoenician, is a bit strange if the story unfolds in Phoenicia. That detail would be obvious, as Syro–Phoenicia was a Gentile area. Moreover, the reference to feeding the children first and then leaving the crumbs from the table for the dogs sounds like a reference to Jesus delivering his message first to Jews, then to Gentiles (presumably after his resurrection). However, it is questionable, even doubtful, whether the historical Jesus ever went to the Gentiles to preach his message or perform healings.

If this interpretation of feeding the children is correct, the story probably makes better sense in the context of Galilee. In this case, the evangelist's written source probably began with the words "And he entered into a house and wanted no one to know, but he could not escape notice" in verse 24b–c. The opening words of verse 24a, "Then he got up from there and went away into the region of Tyre," would then be an editorial addition of the evangelist. We have already seen that the evangelist is generally responsible for the opening words in most of the pericopes in the gospel. Without a clear geographical context in his source, the evangelist might have thought the story of the Syro-Phoenician woman could appropriately serve as the beginning of Jesus' mission to the Gentiles.

The identification of the woman as Syro-Phoenician has sometimes been considered as a clue to the origin of the gospel. Some have argued the term "Syro–Phoenicia" was first used by Roman writers in the second century BCE, hence an indication that the gospel was written in Rome. Others have argued the term originated in the east to distinguish between Syria Coele in northern Syria and Syro–Phoenicia in southern Syria, hence an indication that the gospel was written somewhere in Syria.

When the woman asks Jesus to cure her demon–possessed daughter, Jesus refuses and rebuffs her by saying the children (Jews) must be fed first. It is not right to take the children's food (Jews' food) and feed it to the dogs (Gentiles). Jews of this period did not keep dogs as household pets, so calling Gentiles dogs was an insult, reflecting the attitude of many Jews and Jewish Christians toward Gentiles and Gentile sympathizers within the early church. The identification of the woman as Greek (*Hellenis*), implies she is a polytheist, a pagan, a member of a people unworthy of receiving the good news.

The indication that the children (i.e., Jews) must be fed first likely indicates God's message first came to the Jews, but subsequently some of Jesus' disciples, probably not Jesus himself, took the good news to the Gentile community, probably the audience to which the evangelist was writing.

Through her persistence, the woman convinces Jesus to change his mind and perform an exorcism on her daughter. This is an important moment, because it marks a transition from a mission to the Jews to a mission to the Gentiles, an issue that caused considerable controversy in the early church.

The miracle story is also an instance of Jesus' cure at a distance. There is no encounter with the daughter. Not only does Jesus cure at a distance, he knows the girl has been cured and sends the woman home to see her daughter.

Perhaps most important, this story implies that God's original mission, and until now Jesus' mission, was to the Jews, the chosen people of God, but now the message also goes out to include the Gentiles, the dogs who initially received only the scraps that fell from the table. It is clear the evangelist stood on the side of Gentile Christianity.

In verse 28, the woman addresses Jesus as *kyrie*, a word that means both "Sir" and "Lord." The ambiguity in the address to Jesus may be intentional; however, there is no single word in English that conveys that ambiguity. So if we translate the word as "Sir," do we diminish the woman's greeting? And if we translate it as "Lord," do we overstate her greeting?

JESUS CURES A DEAF MAN

7:31 And again, departing from the region of Tyre, he went through the midst of the region of Sidon to the Sea of Galilee, passing through the territory of the Decapolis.

32 And they brought to him a man who was deaf and had a speech impediment, and they begged him to put his hand on him.

33 And he took him aside from the crowd, and put his fingers in his ears, and he spat and touched his tongue.

34 And looking up to heaven, he sighed and said to him, "*Ephphatha*," which means, "Be opened."

35 And his ears were opened, and the impediment of his tongue was loosened, and he spoke correctly.

36 And he ordered them that they should tell no one; but the more he ordered them, the more widely they proclaimed it.

37 And they were completely astonished, saying, "He has done all things well. He makes both the deaf to hear and the mute to speak."

Verse 31 is clearly a transitional sentence from the evangelist, and it is somewhat problematic. Jesus is headed from Tyre to the Sea of Galilee, which is about forty miles southeast of Tyre. Yet he heads north about twenty-five miles to Sidon, and then about sixty miles southeast into the Decapolis on the eastern shore of the Sea of Galilee. This appears to be a major detour with no stated reason or purpose. Either the evangelist did not understand the geography of the area, or he had something specific in his mind but offers no explanation. The pericope itself, a miracle story, begins in verse 32.

For reasons that are not clear, the gospels of Matthew and Luke, whose authors used the earliest gospel as a source, do not have this miracle story. Either this story was not in the copies of the gospel to which both Matthew and Luke had access, or they both chose independently to omit the story from their gospels. Was this story perhaps added to our earliest gospel later, after copies of the gospel had already been made and circulated to other churches? Did the authors of both Matthew and Luke find something offensive in this story and independently choose to omit it from their gospels? These appear to be the choices, but we will, of course, never know.

The request for Jesus to put his hands on the afflicted man (v. 32) is consistent with earlier healings (the Healing of Peter's Mother-in-law in 1:31; the Cleansing of the Man with the Scaly Skin in 1:41; the Girl Restored to Life in 5:23, 41; and Multiple Healings in 6:2, 5). There are also several such references later in this gospel in 8:23, 25; 9:27; and in 16:18 (in a secondary ending to this gospel written not earlier than the end of the second century CE).

The healing itself, however, takes place not simply through Jesus' touching the man with his hands but, after taking him aside, by putting his fingers in the man's ears and by putting his saliva on the man's tongue (v. 33) and by looking up to heaven and crying out in Aramaic *ephphatha*, which means "be opened" (v. 34). At this point the man was cured and was now able both to hear and to speak normally. This use of Aramaic in a healing also appeared in the miracle story of the Girl Restored to Life (5:41, *talitha cum*," "Little girl, I say to you, arise"), perhaps implying the magical power of the words in their original language to bring about the cure.

This pericope likely has Isa 35:5–6a in mind:

> Then the eyes of the blind shall be opened,
> and the ears of the deaf unstopped;
> then the lame shall leap like a deer,
> and the tongue of the speechless sing for joy.

Verse 36 may be another element of the Messianic Secret in this gospel. In any event, verses 36–37 are probably an addition by the evangelist. However much Jesus commands the people's secrecy, word of his miraculous power spreads even more widely.

CONCLUSIONS AFTER CHAPTER 7

Chapter 7 marks an important turning point in the gospel and in the history of Christianity. The first part of the chapter addresses some regulations of Jewish exclusivism, as reflected in both the Jewish Scriptures and in the oral tradition associated especially with the Pharisees. More particularly, verses 1–23 address questions posed in opposition to scriptural requirements regarding observance of the Jewish law (the Torah) and the opinions of contemporary Pharisaic oral tradition. Specifically, these verses address the ceremonial cleansing of hands before eating and the ceremonial washing of food from the market, and of cups, pitchers, copper kettles, and beds. In several verses (vv. 15, 18, 19, 20, and 23), Jesus repeats that what goes into someone is not what defiles him, but what comes out of him, thereby overturning both written and oral regulations regarding ritual cleanness.

In verses 24–30 there is a clear and unequivocal reaching out to the Gentile community and presumably the evangelist's own church by having Jesus enter Gentile territory. There he first refuses to address the request of the Syro-Phoenician woman, but he then changes his mind. The text makes clear that although God first chose the Jews as his special people, he is now reaching beyond Judaism to the Gentile world to include Gentiles among the people of God. Jesus changed his mind and consciously reached beyond Jewish exclusivism.

The healing of the man with the speaking and hearing impediment (vv. 31–37) also takes place in the Gentile world in the region of the Decapolis, east of the Sea of Galilee.

There is no doubt that the evangelist is making very important points in this chapter. Judaism as represented by the Pharisees and the scribes and even in its scriptural roots in the Jewish Bible is something of the past. Although God elected the Jews as his chosen people, he is now moving on. The evangelist is, of course, looking backward probably from the beginning of the Jewish War against Rome (66–73 CE) at a time when Gentile Christianity was already more successful than Jewish Christianity in terms of growth and development. And so the evangelist (and probably his written source), puts into Jesus' mouth the change of mind and heart to take his message not only to the Jews, but also to the Gentiles. What is not clear is that this change of mind reaches back to the historical Jesus, but by the late sixties CE, when this gospel was probably written, the church made no distinction between the teaching of the historical Jesus and what was revealed to them by the risen Lord through their prophets and teachers.

Chapter 8

THE FEEDING OF THE FOUR THOUSAND

8:1 In those days, when the crowd was again very big and had nothing to eat, he called his disciples to him and said to them,

2 "I have pity on the crowd, because they have now remained with me for three days; and they have nothing to eat.

3 And if I send them away hungry to their own homes, they will faint on the way; and some of them have come from a great distance."

4 And his disciples answered him, "From where can anyone provide bread for these people here in the wilderness?"

5 And he asked them, "How many loaves do you have?" And they replied, "Seven."

6 And he commanded the crowd to sit down on the ground. And taking the seven loaves and giving thanks, he broke [them] and gave [them] to his disciples to distribute; and they distributed them to the crowd.

7 And they had a few small fish. And having blessed them, he said to distribute also these things.

8 And they ate and were filled, and they took up seven large baskets of leftover scraps.

9 And they were about four thousand [people]. And he sent them away.

THE GOSPEL HAS TWO accounts of the feeding of a crowd of people: here and in 6:35–44. Is this pericope a duplicate version of the earlier story? Probably, but this is a feeding not of five thousand Jewish men, but of a crowd of four thousand Gentile people (presumably both men and women and perhaps even children) in the Decapolis by the Sea of Galilee.

The opening words of verse 1 ("in those days") are an eschatological formula to provide a setting for the ensuing story (see Jer 31:33; Joel 3:1; Zech 8:23; and later in this gospel 13:17, 19, 24; and perhaps also 1:9).

The two feeding stories seem to come at the end of two written collections of miracle stories available to the evangelist:

First Collection:
The Stilling of the Storm (4:35–41)
The Healing of the Gerasene Demoniac (5:1–20)
The Girl Restored to Life (5:21–23, 35–43)
The Woman Healed of the Flow of Blood (5:24–34)
The Feeding of the Five Thousand Men (6:30–44)

Second Collection:
Jesus Walks on the Water (6:45–52)
The Healing of the Sick in Gennesaret (6:53–56)
The Syro-Phoenician Woman's Request for Her Daughter (7:24–30)
Jesus Cures a Deaf Man (7:31–37)
The Feeding of the Four Thousand (8:1–9)

The form of the Healing of the Sick in Gennessaret (6:53–56) is not that of a traditional miracle story and may be a construction of the evangelist to create the balance of five stories in each section.

Interestingly both of these collections begin with a miracle story on the Sea of Galilee; both contain three additional healing miracles; and both end with a feeding of a multitude. Is this simply coincidental? Probably not! But what, then, is the purpose of this pattern in both collections? The first collection contains miracle stories that are set in Galilee and ends with a feeding for Jews. The story has clear eucharistic overtones and also recalls the story of Moses and the Israelites eating manna from heaven in the Sinai wilderness (Exod 16). The second collection also begins with a miracle story on the Sea of Galilee. There follow three miracle stories transitioning from Galilee into the Gentile world. The second unit then ends with a feeding for Gentiles. The second feeding story also has clear eucharistic overtones and also recalls the story of Moses and the Israelites eating manna from heaven in the Sinai wilderness (Exod 16). In fact, Moses' typology is evident throughout the gospel, which is replete with themes from the Jewish Scriptures.

It appears there is significance to the organization of these two collections of miracle stories, although the significance is not self-evident. Did these feeding stories play a role in the eucharistic celebration of the evangelist's church? Were they perhaps read at ritual meals in which the assembled church believed the risen Christ was present? Of course we cannot know with certainty, but it is useful to speculate about the situation in the life of the church that might have led to the creation of such presumably written "collections."

In any case, the account of taking the bread, giving thanks, and then breaking the bread and distributing it in 6:41 and in 8:6 is remarkably similar and certainly intentional. Like the Feeding of the Five Thousand Men, the Feeding of the Four Thousand should be considered a eucharistic celebration in anticipation of the Last Supper on the eve of Jesus' death (see 14:17–23). But this time it is not Jews but Gentiles who are participating in this eucharistic meal. The good news of Jesus Christ is now intended for both Jews and Gentiles in seemingly equal measure, although perhaps slightly different in detail.

In the miracle story of the Feeding of the Five Thousand Jewish Men in chapter 6, Jesus' disciples took the initiative to inquire about feeding the crowd (6:35–36). In the account of the Feeding of the Four Thousand, it is Jesus who assumes the initiative, perhaps to reinforce the theme in the previous chapter (beginning already in verse 2) that it was Jesus' idea to take his message to the Gentiles. The parallels between the two stories suggest the evangelist may have drawn these two collections from different, although probably related, written sources.

It is possible, perhaps even likely, that the phrase "three days" in verse 2 has special significance. Three days in Jewish writings usually indicates a short period of time. But it is, of course, more importantly the time between Jesus' death and resurrection. By mentioning the passing of three days, is the evangelist or his source acknowledging that, despite Jesus' taking his message to the Gentiles, it was only after the resurrection that the message went into the Gentile world?

The question to Jesus from the disciples in verse 4 ("From where can anyone provide bread for these people here in the wilderness?") seems ingenuous, inasmuch as the disciples have already witnessed the feeding of the five thousand Jewish men.

Jesus' question to the disciples in 8:5 ("How many loaves do you have?") is the same as the question in 6:38 in a slightly different word order (Greek *posous artous exete* in 6:38; Greek *posous exete artous* in 8:5). The answers in both stories mention the special number seven (five loaves and two fish in 6:38; and seven loaves in 8:5, plus an additional mention in 8:7 of a few small fish).

The account of taking the bread, giving thanks, and then breaking the bread and distributing it in 6:41 and in 8:6 is remarkably similar and certainly intentional. Like the Feeding of the Five Thousand Jewish Men, the Feeding of the Four Thousand Gentiles should be considered a eucharistic celebration in anticipation of the Last Supper on the eve of Jesus' death (see 14:22-25). The good news of Jesus Christ is now clearly intended for both Jews and Gentiles in seemingly equal measure.

THE DEMAND FOR A SIGN

> 8:10 And he immediately got into the boat with his disciples, and came to the region of Dalmanutha.
>
> 11 And the Pharisees came out and began to argue with him, seeking from him a sign from heaven, putting him to the test.
>
> 12 And he sighed deeply in his spirit, and said, "Why does this generation seek a sign? Truly, I say to you, no sign shall be given to this generation."
>
> 13 And he left them and, getting into the boat again, went across to the other side.

Following the Feeding of the Four Thousand, the evangelist indicates that Jesus and his disciples got into a boat and set out for the region of Dalmanutha (8:10), a place unknown to us, presumably on the western side of the Sea of Galilee.

The Pharisees almost seem to be there waiting for Jesus to disembark, their first appearance since their controversy in 7:1-13. Now they ask Jesus for a sign from heaven, not just another miracle, to prove that Jesus' power to perform miracles comes from God and not from Satan. Jesus was last tested in the desert by Satan following his baptism by John, suggesting perhaps that in the evangelist's mind Satan and the Pharisees are both opponents of Jesus, and hence opponents of God.

Jesus repudiates the Pharisees by saying no sign will be given and then leaves them, gets into the boat, and departs for the other side of the Sea of Galilee. It is almost as if Jesus wants nothing more to do with the Pharisees. His stay in Dalmanutha is very brief. This pericope is probably best classified as a legend.

THE YEAST OF THE PHARISEES AND OF HEROD

> 8:14 And they had forgotten to take bread, and they had only one loaf with them in the boat.
>
> 15 And he ordered them, saying, "Take heed! Beware of the leaven of the Pharisees and the leaven of Herod."
>
> 16 And they were discussing among themselves that they did not have bread.
>
> 17 And being aware of it, he said to them, "Why are you discussing that you do not have bread? Do you still not yet know or understand? Are your hearts still hardened?
>
> 18 Having eyes, do you not see; and having ears, do you not hear? And do you not remember?
>
> 19 When I broke the five loaves for the five thousand, how many baskets full of leftover scraps did you pick up?" They said to him, "Twelve."
>
> 20 "When [I broke] the seven [loaves] for the four thousand, how many large baskets of leftover scraps did you pick up?" And they said to him, "Seven."
>
> 21 And he said to them, "How is it you do not yet understand?"

It is possible that this pericope is a construction of the evangelist built around the alleged saying of Jesus in verse 15. It may have been inserted by the evangelist into the context of the feedings of the five thousand and the four thousand in order to reprimand the disciples for their failure to understand what they had personally witnessed. It is interesting that with all of the miracles attributed to Jesus in this gospel, it is the two feedings that are singled out to illustrate the disciples' lack of understanding.

The setting for this pericope is apparently in the boat with Jesus and his disciples en route from Dalmanutha (8:10) to Bethsaida (8:22). However, the story may have been created by the evangelist to afford understanding for his own Christian followers, who, like Jesus' disciples in the story, occasionally suffered from doubt or disbelief. It would be comforting to questioning Christians that even Jesus' disciples, who personally witnessed his miracles, also suffered occasionally from doubt or disbelief. The call for a "sign" in verse 11 still goes unheeded.

The introductory words in verse 14 that they had forgotten to take bread with them into the boat seem to have no significance for this pericope. Likewise, the mention of the leaven of the Pharisees and of Herod is puzzling. However, leaven is a metaphor for malice and evil in Paul's letters (1 Cor 5:8 and Gal 5:7–10) and probably here in verse 15 as well. The leaven of the Pharisees, therefore, does have significance as the Pharisees' evil or malicious misunderstanding of the Torah or their evil or malicious demand for a sign from heaven in verse 11. The leaven of Herod (Antipas) may signify his evil or malicious rule and, more specifically, his killing of John the Baptist (6:17–28).

The comment about the disciples' "hardness of heart" in verse 17 is reminiscent of the charge Jesus made to them in 6:52 ("for they did not understand about the loaves, but their heart was hardened"). Jesus' rebuke of the disciples in verse 18 is also reminiscent of the Septuagint translation of

Isa 6:9:
> And he [the Lord] said [to Isaiah], "Go and say to this people,
> 'Keep listening, but do not comprehend;
> keep looking, but do not understand.'

Jer 5:21:
> Hear this, O foolish and senseless people,
> who have eyes, but do not see,
> who have ears but do not hear,

Ezek 12:2:
> Mortal, you are living in the midst of a rebellious house,
> who have eyes to see but do not see,
> who have ears to hear but do not hear.

The implication of verse 18 is the disciples are both blind and deaf to the significance of Jesus' miraculous feedings. In both narratives, the disciples do not "understand" or "comprehend" the significance of Jesus' mission and message (see also 4:13; and 8:31–33 below). Neither do they yet understand who Jesus really is, perhaps still one more example of the theme of the Messianic Secret in this gospel.

We should probably also note the similarity of verses 17–18, in particular, to Deut 29:2–4:

> Moses summoned all Israel and said to them: "You have seen all that the LORD did before your eyes in the land of Egypt, to Pharaoh and to all his servants and to all his land, the great trials that your eyes saw, the signs, and those great wonders. But to this day the LORD has not given you a mind to understand, or eyes to see, or ears to hear."

As we have seen previously, there is significant evidence of Exodus typology in the gospel.

The anonymous evangelist appears to have had a fascination with numbers. In fact, numerology was common in the ancient world. The numbers twelve and seven were particularly important in Judaism. Twelve represented the tribes of Israel and subsequently the number of Jesus' disciples and hence the church. Seven represented the number of days of creation. In this context, both numbers likely had eschatological significance, reflecting the fact that Christians believed Jesus was already bringing the new age, the period of God's rule, into existence in his ministry, his message, and his person. The concern in this passage is that Christians, and even Jesus' disciples, may be blind and deaf regarding what is happening in their very presence. The ending is particularly relevant: "How is it you (within the church?) do not yet understand?"

JESUS CURES A BLIND MAN AT BETHSAIDA

8:22 And they went to Bethsaida. And they brought to him a blind man, and they begged him to touch him.

23 And he took the blind man by the hand and led him out of the village. And having spat on his eyes and put his hands on him, he asked him, "Do you see anything?"

24 And having regained his sight, he said, "I see men; they look like trees walking."

25 Then he put his hands on his eyes again and made him look up. And he was restored and saw everything clearly.

26 And he sent him home, saying, "Do not go into the village."

The miracle story Jesus Cures a Blind Man at Bethsaida resembles in form the miracle story Jesus Cures a Deaf Man in 7:31–37. Both stories are surprisingly found only in this gospel, and the wording of the two stories is remarkably similar. The chart below contains only relevant portions of each pericope:

Jesus Cures a Deaf Man (7:32–35)	Jesus Cures a Blind Man (8:22–26)
And they brought to him	And they brought to him
a man who was deaf . . .	a blind man,
and they begged him	and they begged him
to put his hand on him.	to touch him.
And he took him aside . . .	And he took the blind man . . . and led him out of the village.
and put his fingers in his ears,	And having spat on his eyes
and he put his fingers in his ears	and put his hands on him . . . .
And looking up to heaven . . . he said *Ephphatha* . . .	
And his ears were opened	And having regained his sight, he said . . .
And he ordered them that they should tell no one	Do not go into the village.

This miracle story was perhaps motivated by the question to the disciples in verse 18:

Having eyes, do you not see;

and having ears, do you not hear? And do you not remember?

Perhaps the evangelist or his written source deliberately rewrote the miracle story, Jesus Cures the Deaf Man, in 7:31–37 in order to address, in addition, the matter of people's blindness. Of course, the deafness and the blindness in both of these stories are figurative (see also 7:18), but the transition from figurative to literal is a simple move for the evangelist, who is mindful of the expectation that the miracles of Jesus accompany the arrival of the new age of God's rule. We already indicated in 1:40–45 that the origin of the miracle story, the Healing of the Man with the Scaly Skin, may also have had its origin in a figurative story in which Jesus pronounced a leper ritually clean, thereby prompting the physical healing of his skin disorder. The major differences between the healing of the deaf man and the healing of the blind man are the lack of a magic Aramaic word in the latter story and the healing in two steps in the story of healing of the blind man. It is likely that these two stories were motivated by Isa 29:18 and 35:5–6a:

> On that day the deaf shall hear the words of a scroll,
>> and out of their gloom and darkness the eyes of the blind shall see (29:18).
>
>> and
>
> Then the eyes of the blind shall be opened,
>> and the ears of the deaf unstopped;
> then shall the lame man leap like a deer,
>> and the tongue of the speechless sing for joy (35:5–6a).

It is also possible, perhaps even likely, that in the author's written source, the pericope Jesus Cures the Blind Man in Bethsaida (8:22–26) followed immediately upon Jesus Walks on the Water (6:45–52), because of the words in 6:45: "And immediately he made his disciples get into the boat and go before him to the other side, toward Bethsaida, while he himself dismissed the crowd."

PETER'S DECLARATION ABOUT JESUS

> 8:27 And Jesus and his disciples went out to the villages of Caesarea Philippi; and on the way he asked his disciples, saying to them, "Who do they say that I am?"
>
> 28 So they spoke to him saying, "John the Baptist; but some say, Elijah; but others, one of the prophets."
>
> 29 And he said to them, "But who then do you say that I am?" Answering, Peter said to him, "You are the Messiah."
>
> 30 And he strictly ordered them that they should tell no one about him.

This story, clearly a legend, marks a significant change in the gospel: Peter's formal acknowledgement that Jesus is the Christ, the Messiah. The story takes place at Caesarea Philippi, a city about thirty-three miles north of Bethsaida and the Sea of Galilee.

Jesus begins by addressing the disciples as a whole with the question once again about the indefinite "they": "Who do *they* say that I am?" The question is clearly a literary device of the evangelist (or of his source), inasmuch as Jesus presumably already knew who he was. The identity of Jesus was addressed previously many times in this gospel:

1:11   And a voice came from heaven, "You are my Son, the Beloved (or "You are my Beloved Son"); in you I take delight."

1:24   And [the unclean spirit] cried out, "What do we have to do with you, Jesus Nazarene? Have you come to destroy us? I know who you are—the Holy One of God."

1:34   And he healed many who were sick with various diseases, and he cast out many demons. And he did not allow the demons to speak because they knew him.

4:41   And [the disciples] were terribly frightened and said to one another, "So who is this that both the wind and the sea obey him?

6:3   "Is this not the son of the carpenter and of Mary and a brother of James, Joses, Judas, and Simon? And are not his sisters here with us?" [To which Jesus replied] "A Prophet is not without honor except in his own country, among his own relatives, and in their own house" (implying, perhaps, that Jesus was admitting that he was a prophet).

6:14–16   indicates that some (including Herod Antipas) thought Jesus was John the Baptist *redivivus*; others thought he was Elijah or a prophet.

However, apparently in none of these passages (except perhaps 1:11 where Jesus was alone) is the matter of Jesus' identity clearly resolved.

The answers of the apostles to Jesus' question are threefold, mimicking some of what has been said previously: John the Baptist *redivivus* (once again alive after being killed by Herod Antipas); Elijah (whose coming would precede the arrival of the time of God's rule according to Mal 4:5 ["Lo, I will send you the prophet Elijah before the great and terrible day of the LORD comes"]); and one of the prophets (like the prophets of old in Israel and Judah).

The resolution of the matter comes in Peter's declaration about Jesus, which appears mdiway through this gospel. Enough has unfolded in the first half of the gospel for the reader to understand that Jesus is a special person with a special relationship to God. But exactly who is he? What is his relationship to God? And where is the story headed? In this pericope, the matter is made clear by the words of Peter, but only to the inner circle of Jesus' own disciples: Jesus is the Christ, the Messiah.

According to the testimony of Paul in 1 Cor 15:3–5, Peter was the first person to whom the risen Christ appeared, a detail that may be the inspiration for the role of Peter in this story. The passage in Paul's letter to the church at Corinth reads:

> For I handed on to you as of first importance what I in turn had received:
> that Christ died for our sins in accordance with the Scriptures; and
> that he was buried, and
> that he was raised on the third day in accordance with the Scriptures, and
> that *he appeared to Cephas* (Peter), then to the twelve (italics mine).

Paul identifies this statement as the church's most important claim and perhaps its oldest tradition, which Paul had received from some nameless source or sources.

It is Peter (Cephas, Aramaic *kepha*, meaning "rock") alone who answers Jesus' question by saying, "You are the Messiah" (Greek *christos*). The Greek word *christos* in the Septuagint Greek translates the Hebrew word "*messiah*" (meaning "anointed"), a title used in the Jewish Scriptures of the patriarchs, kings of Israel and Judah, prophets, priests, the Persian king Cyrus, and the future ideal Davidic king. What exactly the evangelist understood by this term is not explained in the text.

Moreover, Acts 2:36 states: "Therefore, let the entire house of Israel know with certainty that God *has made him both Lord and Messiah*, this Jesus whom you crucified" (italics mine). The passage in Acts makes it clear that the titles of Lord (*kyrios*) and Messiah (*christos*) were bestowed upon Jesus by God *following* Jesus' death and exaltation to God's right hand, the position of honor (Acts 2:33). Even earlier than Acts, Paul in Rom 1:4 states that Jesus "*was declared to be Son of God* by power according to the spirit of holiness *by resurrection from the dead*, Jesus Christ our Lord" (italics mine). It appears these titles ("Lord," "Messiah," "Son of God") were bestowed upon Jesus only after his death. However, in the passage in 8:29, the evangelist intentionally traces the title of Messiah (*christos*) to Peter during the period of Jesus' ministry, just as Jesus is about to embark on a journey to his final days in Jerusalem.

Jesus appears to consent to Peter's declaration and immediately commands his disciples to silence, probably a redaction or editorial addition of the evangelist, a further indication of the Messianic Secret. Now the disciples—but only the disciples—know who Jesus really is: "the anointed of God."

Of course, the evangelist and the reader (or listener) of this gospel already know who Jesus is. The evangelist acknowledges as much in the opening words of the gospel: "The beginning of the good news of Jesus Christ." Moreover, at his baptism by John, Jesus was adopted as God's "Beloved Son."

JESUS FORETELLS HIS DEATH AND RESURRECTION

> 8:31 And he began to teach them that it was necessary that the Son of Man suffer much, and be rejected by the elders and the chief priests and the scribes, and be killed, and after three days rise again.
>
> 32 And he was speaking the word openly. And Peter took him aside and began to admonish him.
>
> 33 But turning around and seeing his disciples, he admonished Peter and said, "Get out of my sight, Satan, because you do not set your mind on the things of God, but on the things of men."

There are three predictions by Jesus of his own passion, death and resurrection in this gospel (8:31; 9:31; and 10:33–34). The predictions are similar but not identical in detail:

8:31	9:31	10:33–34
The Son of Man	The Son of Man	The Son of Man
must suffer much	is to be betrayed	will be handed over to
be rejected by the elders,		
the chief priests,		the chief priests
and the scribes		and the scribes
		they will condemn him to death
		and mock him
		and spit upon him
		and flog him

8:31	9:31	10:33–34
and be killed	and be killed	and kill him
and he will rise	and he will rise	and he will rise
after three days	after three days	after three days

The similarities among the three passages are striking, but even more striking is Jesus' use in all three passages of the title Son of Man to refer to himself with regard to his forthcoming suffering and death.

As we have seen, the phrase Son of Man is sometimes best understood in this gospel as an Aramaism for "man" or "humankind" (2:10, 28). It is also used in this gospel by Jesus to refer to the eschatological figure known as the Son of Man, who will come soon to usher in the age of God's rule (see below 8:38; 13:26; see also 14:62; and Ps 110:1 and Dan 7:13–14).

In verse 31, the phrase Son of Man is used by Jesus quite differently with reference to himself as the Suffering Messiah, a role unknown in Judaism of that period. It was, in fact, the early church that proclaimed that Jesus had been made Lord and Messiah by virtue of his resurrection (Acts 2:32–36; see also Rom 1:4 for a similar conferral of the title "Son of God" on Jesus by virtue of his resurrection). Most evident in all three passages in this gospel (8:31; 9:31; 10:33–34) is mention of Jesus' resurrection *after three days*, a belief of the church likely grounded in the church's discovery of the passage in Hos 6:2 well after Jesus' death:

> After two days he will revive us;
> on the third day he will raise us up,
> that we may live before him.

"Son of Man," especially a suffering Son of Man, is not a term the historical Jesus would have used of himself, especially in the context of his future passion and death. In these three passages Jesus appears to have known beforehand and in detail what lay ahead of him in Jerusalem. The hands of the church and the evangelist are especially evident in these three passages, in what are called *vaticinia ex eventu* or "prophecies *out of*, or *after*, the event." This pericope is obviously a legend. The other two may be, by way of imitation, constructions of the evangelist.

Like John the Baptist before him, the historical Jesus appears to have seen himself as a precursor and prophetic herald of the Son of Man. This supernatural angelic figure is mentioned in the *Similitudes of Enoch* (1 En. 37–71) and in 2 Esd 13 as a heavenly eschatological protagonist, who will serve as God's agent in the final judgment that will usher in the period of God's rule. The dates of the *Similitudes of Enoch* and 2 Esdras are difficult to establish, but the former is probably from the first century BCE or the first century CE, and the latter from sometime in the first century CE. In other words, both works are contemporaneous with John the Baptist, Jesus, and the early church, reflecting the fact that there was likely an expectation, at least in some Jewish circles, of the imminent arrival of the eschatological Son of Man at the time of the life and ministry of both John the Baptist and Jesus.

Looking back on Jesus' passion, death, and resurrection, it was clear the church modified the role of the Son of Man into a suffering Messiah (modeled on passages found in Isa 52:13—53:12), who would presumably return sometime soon as the eschatological Son of Man (1 Thess 1:10; 2:19; 3:13; 4:15; 5:1–2). Accordingly, the church came to believe Jesus must suffer, be rejected, die, and rise again as part of the divine plan (i.e., "according to the Scriptures"). And as part of that same divine plan, Jesus will come again very soon as the eschatological Son of Man.

Jesus is now disclosing to his disciples some of the details of this divine plan in 8:31; 9:31; and 10:33–34 as part of the unfolding of the Messianic Secret as the events of Jesus' final days grow closer. From the perspective of the early church, Jesus must have known in advance what was about to happen to him. His presumed disclosure of this to his disciples is, therefore, a necessary confirmation that Jesus knew in advance what was about to happen to him. To suggest Jesus did not know and understand what was about to happen to him in Jerusalem seemed unthinkable to the early church. A careful reading of the Jewish Scriptures enabled the church to understand retrospectively the significance of what had already unfolded in Jerusalem in those final difficult days of Jesus' suffering and death. As stated above, this pericope is clearly a legend.

A CLUSTER OF ESCHATOLOGICAL SAYINGS OF JESUS

8:34 And when he had summoned the crowd with his disciples, he said to them, "If someone wants to follow me, let him deny himself and take up his cross and follow me.

— — —

8:35 For whoever wants to save his life will lose it, but whoever loses his life for the sake of me and the gospel will save it.

— — —

8:36 For what will it profit a man to gain the whole world and lose his life?

37 For what can a man give in exchange for his life?

— — —

8:38 For whoever is ashamed of me and of my words in this adulterous and sinful generation, the Son of Man will also be ashamed of him when he comes in the glory of his Father with the holy angels."

— — —

9:1 And he said to them, "Truly I say to you that there are some standing here who will not taste death until they see that the kingdom of God has come with power.

It appears that mention of the Son of Man in 8:31 may be the link for the anonymous evangelist to introduce this cluster of five or perhaps six distinct eschatological sayings of Jesus that relate to commitments of personal sacrifice and loyalty to Jesus. The opening words of verse 34a are typical of the evangelist as he introduces these sayings, which he probably already found grouped in a written source.

Scholars have identified several criteria in an effort to determine what traditions about Jesus and which sayings of Jesus in the gospels are likely reliable traditions and genuine sayings of Jesus and what are likely traditions about Jesus and sayings that arose within the church and were later merely attributed to Jesus. The following criteria have proved helpful:

1. The Criterion of Dissimilarity or Embarrassment

    A saying of Jesus or a tradition about Jesus that does not reflect the beliefs and confessional claims of the church about Jesus has a greater likelihood of being genuine than a saying or tradition that reflects the church's preaching or theological bias. Why would the early Christian community create a story about Jesus or attribute a saying to Jesus that contradicts the church's own preaching or teaching?

2. The Criterion of Multiple Attestation

A saying that is attested by two or more *independent* witnesses has a greater likelihood of reflecting the teaching of the historical Jesus. This criterion is not helpful to us, as we are not considering in this book other early Christian writings in addition to the earliest gospel.

3. The Criterion of Contextual Credibility

A tradition or saying that reflects the historical, political, social, and religious environment of first-century Roman Palestine has a greater claim to authenticity than a tradition or saying that appears to be grounded in the Greco–Roman Hellenistic environment. Jesus was a first-century Galilean Jew, who lived and taught in Roman Palestine and must be so understood.

4. The Criterion of Aramaism or Semitism

Jesus, his disciples, and the earliest Christians were presumably Aramaic speaking. Therefore, a tradition or a saying that betrays Aramaic or Semitic qualities has a greater clam to authenticity than a tradition or saying that is linguistically more Greek or Hellenistic in quality.

5. The Criterion of Coherence

A tradition or a saying that is similar to material that has been established by one or more of the above criteria has a greater claim to authenticity because of its consistency with or coherence to more likely authentic material.

In verse 34 the words "and take up his cross" are clearly not words of Jesus. They obviously refer very specifically to Jesus' crucifixion from the vantage point of the early church and are either additions that appeared in the evangelist's source or that the evangelist added to what may otherwise be an authentic saying of Jesus. The saying reflects Jesus' call to deny the material values of this world in anticipation of the imminent arrival of the eschatological Son of Man and the inauguration of God's rule. When the

CHAPTER 8

added words are removed, the remaining words reflect the poetic parallelism familiar in the Jewish Scriptures and may be an authentic saying of Jesus:

> If someone wants to follow me,
> let him deny himself and follow me.

In this amended form, the saying meets the criterion of Aramaism or Semitism and the criterion of contextual credibility. Jesus may actually have spoken these words in Aramaic.

In verse 35 the words "for the sake of me and the gospel" are also obviously not words of Jesus. They refer clearly to the christocentric (Christ-centered) message of the church and are either additions that appeared in the evangelist's source or that the evangelist added to what may also be an authentic saying of Jesus. This saying also reflects the issue of attachment to this world rather than to the future age of God's rule. When the added words are removed, the remaining words reflect the poetic parallelism familiar in the Jewish Scriptures and may also be an authentic saying of Jesus:

> Whoever wants to save his life will lose it,
> but whoever loses his life will save it.

In this amended form, the saying meets the criterion of Aramaism or Semitism and the criterion of contextual credibility. Jesus may actually have spoken these words in Aramaic.

It is not clear whether verses 36 and 37 are a single saying or two distinct sayings:

> 36 For what will it profit a man to gain the whole world and forfeit his life?

> 37 For what can a man give in return for his life?

These sayings seem similar to those that precede them. It is, however, not clear whether verse 37 is part of verse 36 or a gloss by the evangelist that adds little to the content or meaning of verse 36. In any event, these two sayings meet the criterion of Aramaism or Semitism and the criterion of contextual credibility.

It is doubtful all of these sayings (vv. 34–38) were delivered by Jesus in sequence on a single occasion. The grouping does, however, suggest a similarity of subject matter that may point to a single written source. Verse 38 is particularly interesting:

> For whoever is ashamed of me and of my words in this adulterous and sinful generation,

> The Son of Man will be ashamed of him when he comes in the glory of his Father with the holy angels.

This saying is important because Jesus is speaking of the coming of the Son of Man in the third person. Jesus is clearly referring to the imminent arrival of the eschatological Son of Man known to us from contemporary Jewish literature—someone who may also have been a figure in John the Baptist's preaching. This saying meets the criterion of dissimilarity or embarrassment, the criterion of Aramaism or Semitism, and the criterion of contextual credibility and has a strong claim to authenticity.

The saying in 9:1 is obviously part of the same cluster of sayings, although it appears in chapter 9 in our text. The introductory words ("And he said to them") clearly come from the evangelist and are followed by another eschatological saying:

> Truly I say to you that there are some standing here who will not taste death

> until they see that the kingdom of God has come with power.

The imminent arrival of God's rule will take place during the lifetime of some who are listening to Jesus. The fact that the end did not come by the time the evangelist wrote this gospel is testimony to the authenticity of this as a genuine saying of Jesus. The saying clearly meets the criterion of contextual credibility and the criterion of dissimilarity or embarrassment. It is similar to the saying in 8:38, and it is clearly dissimilar with the church's teaching at the time the gospel was written. The kingdom of God had not yet come with power by the time the evangelist wrote the gospel.

CONCLUSIONS AFTER CHAPTER 8

This chapter marks the transition from a collection of pericopes that are primarily pronouncement stories, miracle stories, parables, sayings, legends, and constructions of the evangelist, to the beginning of, or perhaps the prelude to, the Passion Narrative, which deals with the story of Jesus' suffering, death, and resurrection.

CHAPTER 8

This chapter opens with the miracle story of the Feeding of the Four Thousand (8:1-9), the fifth and final miracle story in what appears to have been a second collection of five miracle stories available to the evangelist in one or more written sources. This final miracle story in the second collection probably served the evangelist's church as a eucharistic story addressed to Gentile men, women, and children with overtones of the story of Moses and the Hebrews surviving in the wilderness following the exodus from Egypt by eating the manna (bread) miraculously provided by God. This story also anticipates the eucharistic events of the Last Supper later in the gospel.

There follows the legend of the Pharisees' Demand for a Sign (8:10-13), which leads into Jesus addressing the deafness and the blindness of his disciples and of members of the evangelist's own church (8:14-21) and culminates in the miracle story, Jesus Cures the Blind Man at Bethsaida (8:22-26).

The actual turning point in this chapter follows in the legend of Peter's Declaration about Jesus (8:27-30), in which Peter proclaims Jesus is the Messiah (the anointed) of God, a story that probably reflects the fact that Peter was apparently the first disciple of Jesus to proclaim that Jesus was Messiah, but only following Jesus' death when the risen Jesus appeared to Peter, perhaps in a dream.

There then follows a story that is essential to both the evangelist and the church: the first of three accounts in which Jesus indicates foreknowledge of his suffering, rejection, death, and resurrection in his role as the Suffering Messiah (8:31-34), obviously a postmortem belief of the church in the fulfillment of the story of the Suffering Servant in Deutero-Isaiah—an example of *vaticinium ex eventu*, prophecy *out of* or *after* the event.

The chapter closes with A Cluster of Eschatological sayings of Jesus (8:34—9:1), that when stripped of later glosses by either the evangelist or the written source available to the evangelist likely contain authentic sayings of Jesus dealing with rejection of the values of this world in anticipation of the imminent coming of the eschatological Son of Man, who will inaugurate the arrival of the period of God's rule.

One additional observation: chapters 6 and 8 of this gospel share an interesting phenomenon with John 6, the same sequence of three stories:

A Miraculous Feeding	6:30-44	8:1-9	John 6:1-15
A Sea Crossing	6:45-52	8:10	John 6:16-21
An Allusion to Bread	6:52	8:14-21	John 6:22-59

Such similarity requires an explanation, and the most reasonable explanation is these three passages likely shared, either directly or indirectly, dependence on a pre–gospel written source.

Chapter 9

9:1 And he said to them, "Truly I say to you that there are some standing here who will not taste death until they see that the kingdom of God has come with power.

THIS VERSE WAS DISCUSSED at the end of Chapter 8, with which material it clearly belongs.

THE TRANSFIGURATION OF JESUS

9:2 And after six days Jesus took Peter and James and John and led them up into a high mountain alone by themselves, and he was transformed before them.

3 And his clothes became gleaming, exceedingly white, such as no cleaner on earth could so whiten them.

4 And Elijah appeared to them with Moses, and they were talking with Jesus.

5 And Peter answered and said to Jesus, "Rabbi, it is good for us to be here; and let us make three shelters: one for you, and one for Moses, and one for Elijah."

6 For he did not know what to say, for they were terrified.

> 7 And a cloud appeared and overshadowed them; and a voice came from out of the cloud, "This is my Son, the Beloved. Listen to him!"
>
> 8 And suddenly looking around, they saw no one, but only Jesus with them.

The story of the transformation (Greek *metemorphothe* = he was transformed) or the transfiguration (as it is usually called) is clearly a legend, a story about Jesus, linking the human with the divine. The three most important of Jesus' disciples, Peter, James, and John (3:16–17; 5:37; 9:2; and 14:33) are for a moment provided insight into who Jesus really is. Mention of Peter, James, and John by name may reflect their leadership position in the early church in Jerusalem.

The presence of Moses and Elijah is significant, because the early Christian community believed both the Law (personified by Moses) and the Prophets (personified by Elijah) bore witness to Jesus in the Jewish Scriptures. Here they bear witness at Jesus' transfiguration. Moreover, the appearance of Elijah is important because he was the precursor of the Messiah in Malachi 4:4–6:

> ^{4}Remember the teaching of my servant Moses, the statutes and ordinances that I commanded him at Horeb for all Israel. ^{5}Lo, I will send you the prophet Elijah before the great and terrible day of the LORD comes. ^{6}He will turn the hearts of parents to their children and the hearts of children to their parents, so that I will not come and strike the land with a curse.

Some scholars have looked at the story of Jesus' transfiguration and have seen it as a misplaced resurrection appearance story. However, this gospel has no resurrection appearance stories, and the story of the transfiguration functions intentionally at the beginning of the author's extended Passion Narrative as a hint, in the middle of the gospel, of what is to come. Indeed, this story makes it clear once more that Jesus is the Beloved Son of God already anticipated at the time of his baptism by John the Baptist in 1:11:

> And a voice came from the heavens, "You are my Son, the Beloved; in you I take delight."

At the time of Jesus' baptism, the address in 1:11 is to Jesus alone from a voice from heaven speaking in the second person "*You are* my Son, the Beloved" (italics mine). Here in the context of the transfiguration in 9:7, a voice from the cloud addresses Peter, James, and John in the third person:

"*This is* my Son, the Beloved" (italics mine). Clearly, these two passages and these two stories should be looked at together. Interestingly, in both passages the source of the voice is not specified, but it is clearly God. As stated in the context of the baptism story, the evangelist of this gospel embraced an adoptionist theology. Jesus was adopted as God's Son at his baptism and lived this role during his brief ministry. What is especially important in the story of the transfiguration is that Jesus' Sonship is now known not only to Jesus, as in the baptism story, but to three others: Peter, James, and John. However, Jesus' Sonship still remains a secret to everyone else, including the remaining nine disciples.

The significance of the introductory phrase "and after six days" is not entirely clear. There is, however, mention of six days in the story of God's revelation to Moses on Mt. Sinai in Exod 24:15–18, a story that our author or his source may have had in mind. The evangelist, otherwise, rarely provides such precise detail in his editorial introductions.

Moreover, the evangelist uses similar elements in the stories of the transfiguration and the resurrection:

1. *to be here* in 9:5, and *he is not here* in 16:6; and
2. *he (Peter) did not know what to say, for they were terrified* in 9:6, and *they (the women) said nothing to anyone, for they were afraid* in 16:8.

The evangelist clearly sees the story of Jesus' transfiguration in light of both the story of Jesus' baptism at the very beginning of his gospel and as an anticipation of the story of the resurrection at the very end of his gospel.

The fact that the legend of the Transfiguration of Jesus occurs almost immediately after Peter's confession serves also to confirm Peter's acknowledgment that Jesus is the anointed, the Messiah, and now the chosen, beloved Son of God. Verse 8 marks the end of the theophany, as everything is restored to normal.

THE COMING OF ELIJAH

9:9 And as they were coming down from the mountain, he ordered them to tell no one the things they had seen until the Son of Man had risen from the dead.

10 And they kept the saying to themselves, questioning what the rising from the dead was.

11 And they asked him, saying, "Why do the scribes say that Elijah must come first?"

12 But he said to them, "Indeed, Elijah is coming first and restores all things; and how it is written about the Son of Man, that he suffers many things and is treated with contempt.

13 But I say to you that Elijah has indeed come, and they did to him whatever they wished, just as it is written about him."

These verses are closely connected to what precedes. In fact, verse 9 and perhaps even verse 10 reflect the evangelist's theme of the Messianic Secret: Peter, James, and John are to tell no one what they have seen, even as they keep discussing the matter among themselves. Verses 9 and 10 are, therefore, likely the work of the evangelist.

Verses 11–13 introduce a new theme that defies categorical classification and that may reflect the kind of discussion that went on in the early church, as the Christian community wrestled with the question of Jesus' death. How could Jesus be Messiah if Elijah had not already returned as his precursor? The answer: Elijah has already come in the person of John the Baptist, who is not actually mentioned by name. The reference to John is, however, evident, inasmuch as the passage alludes to John's death at the hand of Herod Antipas, already reported in 6:14–29.

This passage illustrates the gospel's theme of the Messianic Secret. In reality, Jesus' life and ministry were apparently not messianic. Neither he nor his disciples nor anyone else regarded Jesus as Messiah during his lifetime. The belief that Jesus was Messiah came only after Jesus' death and the belief of Peter and others that God had raised Jesus from the dead and *made* him Lord and Messiah. Jesus' order to Peter, James, and John to say nothing *until the Son of Man had risen from the dead* confirms the likelihood that Jesus' followers believed Jesus was Messiah only *after* his death. The story of the Transfiguration of Jesus provides to the inner circle (and to the reader) and to them only a foretaste of Jesus in his resurrected glory. They, and only they, now know what Jesus knew at his baptism: that he is God's chosen Son—something that has now been revealed to Peter, James, and John and that will be revealed to all after Jesus' death.

The use of the term "Son of Man" in this context recalls, of course, Jesus' use of the term Son of Man in 8:31 as the suffering Son of Man. This understanding of the Son of Man is, of course, in defiance of the meaning it likely had when spoken by Jesus in his probable role as the precursor of the eschatological Son of Man. This pericope is probably best classified as a construction of the evangelist.

THE EXORCISM OF THE EPILEPTIC BOY

9:14 And when they came to the disciples, they saw a large crowd around them and scribes debating with them.

15 And immediately, when they saw him, the crowd was overcome with surprise, and running to him, they greeted him.

16 And he asked them, "What are you debating with them?"

17 And someone in the crowd answered him, "Teacher, I brought you my son, who has a spirit that makes him unable to speak.

18 And wherever it seizes him, it throws him down; and he foams at the mouth, and grinds his teeth, and becomes completely exhausted. And I spoke to your disciples, that they might drive it out, and they were not able."

19 But he answered them and said, "O unbelieving generation, how much longer shall I be with you? How long shall I put up with you? Bring him to me."

20 And they brought him to him. And when he saw him, the spirit immediately threw him into convulsions, and falling on the ground he rolled around, foaming at the mouth.

21 And he asked his father, "How long has this been happening to him?" And he said, "From childhood.

22 And often he threw him both into fire and into water in order to destroy him. But if you can do anything, have compassion on us and help us."

23 But Jesus said to him, "If you are able, all things are possible to the one who believes."

24 Immediately crying out, the father of the child said, "I believe; help my unbelief!"

25 When Jesus saw that the crowd came running together, he rebuked the unclean spirit saying to it, "Dumb and deaf spirit, I command you, come out of him and never enter him again!"

26 And crying out and convulsing him greatly, the spirit came out. And he was as one who is dead, so that many of them said, "He died."

27 But Jesus taking hold of his hand, lifted him up, and he stood up.

28 And when he had entered into a house, his disciples asked him privately, "Why were we not able to cast it out?"

29 And he said to them, "This kind can come out by nothing except by prayer."

The opening verse of this pericope may suggest that Jesus was still with Peter, James, and John as they approached the other nine disciples and a large crowd, with the disciples and scribes debating. But the language is not sufficiently clear to draw a detailed picture. Neither is it entirely clear that the evangelist intends the opening words to connect this miracle story to what precedes. Chronology is not a serious concern of the evangelist, so verses 14–15 (or 14–16) may be no more than an editorial link to introduce the next pericope: the Exorcism of the Epileptic Boy, which probably begins in verse 17.

The reaction of the crowd upon seeing Jesus reflects their prior knowledge of his authoritative teaching and especially of his healing power. The stage is set for the father who then approaches Jesus with his afflicted son. The symptoms described in this story suggest the boy was suffering from epilepsy, although the evangelist assumes that the disorder is caused by demon possession.

The man tells Jesus he had originally approached Jesus' disciples, who were unable to drive out the demon (v. 18). Jesus replies by rebuking the faithless generation with whom he is clearly impatient (v. 19), and demands they bring the boy to him. When the boy sees Jesus, the demon immediately throws the boy into convulsions (v. 20). Jesus asks the father how long the boy has been suffering, and the father answers "from childhood" (v. 21).

The father then describes further symptoms and the clear intention of the demon to kill the boy. The father begs Jesus in desperation to intervene and cure the boy, if he can, perhaps expressing the father's doubt about Jesus' power (v. 22).

Jesus turns the matter of the healing back to the father, saying "If you are able, all things are possible to the one who believes" (v. 23). The father tentatively expresses his belief (v. 24) at which point Jesus commands the demonic spirit to come out. The spirit does come out but only after first convulsing the boy (v. 25), who is apparently so exhausted that people think he is dead (v. 26). Jesus then took the boy's hand, and lifted him up, and the boy was able to stand (v. 27).

The setting shifts (vv. 28–29), and Jesus is alone with his disciples who ask Jesus why they were not able to drive out the demonic spirit. The simple answer is that this kind of spirit can be driven out only by prayer.

FOR A SECOND TIME JESUS FORETELLS HIS DEATH AND RESURRECTION

9:30 And departing from there, they passed along through Galilee. And he did not want anyone to know,

31 because he was teaching his disciples and was saying to them, "The Son of Man is being delivered up into the hands of men, and they will kill him. And after he is killed, after three days he will rise."

32 But they did not understand the saying, and they were afraid to ask him.

The phrase in 9:30 that Jesus "did not want anyone to know" may be a comment by the evangelist in support of the theme of the Messianic Secret. Jesus apparently did not want anyone to know who he was, because he was now about to offer his disciples the second prediction of his suffering, death, and resurrection.

In both 8:31 (Greek *didaskein*) and in 9:31 (Greek *edidasken*), Jesus' prediction is referred to by the evangelist, somewhat curiously, as "teaching." The verb "is being delivered up" in verse 31 is in the present tense, although the reference is clearly to the future, suggesting perhaps that the process has already begun.

The use of the term "Son of Man" here (and in 8:31 and again in 10:33) is not to the eschatological Son of Man who will usher in the age to come. Jesus is the Suffering Son of Man rooted in Second Isaiah (Isa 52:13–53:12), implying—indeed making it clear—the early Christian community created the entire theology that the Son of Man was the Suffering Servant and then attributed that teaching to Jesus himself. The evangelist (or his source) was not writing a modern biography of Jesus. He was interpreting the life and ministry of Jesus in light of the post-resurrection beliefs of the early church. The gospel is *kerygma* (preaching), not history.

Once again we are told the disciples did not understand (6:52; 7:18; 8:17), likely still further development of the evangelist's theme of the Messianic Secret. Interestingly, the disciples are represented by the evangelist as being afraid to ask Jesus about the meaning of what he had just said to them.

WHICH DISCIPLE IS THE GREATEST?

9:33 And they went to Capernaum. And when they were in the house, he asked them "What were you discussing on the road?"

34 But they kept silent, because on the road they had discussed among themselves who was the greatest.

35 And he sat down and called the Twelve and said to them, "If anyone wants to be first, he will be last of all and servant of all."

— — —

9:36 And he took a little child and set him in the midst of them. And when he had taken him in his arms, he said to them,

37 "Whoever receives one of these children in my name receives me; and whoever receives me, receives not me but the one who sent me."

The material in 9:33–50 appears to be a relatively large collection of several unrelated sayings of Jesus linked by catchwords or common phrases, as we will see later. Although this is likely a single block of material drawn from a written source, I will, in the remainder of this chapter, discuss this material in individual units that appear somewhat coherent.

At the outset of this collection of sayings, Jesus and the disciples return to Capernaum, where Jesus' ministry began in this gospel (1:21). The return to Capernaum seems appropriate to the evangelist, who is probably responsible for creating the introductory verses 33–34. The return to Capernaum marks, in fact, a new beginning of Jesus' ministry, but this time it is the beginning of the end.

Verse 35 almost sounds as if it stands at the end of a pronouncement story, but there is no preceding discussion or debate as there is in typical pronouncement stories, so the saying stands alone. Perhaps the debate should be seen in the discussion among Jesus' disciples, although that is not entirely clear.

Verses 36–37 are not strongly connected to what proceeds. The connection seems superficial. The child in the story is conveniently present, apparently to enable Jesus to make his point about who is the greatest of Jesus' followers. The verb Greek *dexomai*, translated in verse 35 as "receive," also means "welcome," suggesting a connection or reference to new believers in the evangelist's church. If that connection is appropriate, then, Jesus' intention in verse 37 was likely the same: namely, whoever welcomes one of these new believers into the church also welcomes me and him who sent me. Newer members of the community needed support and assurance that they were fully welcome. If the reference is literally to children, then the passage may suggest the question was whether children should be welcome to the church or even to meetings of the Christian community.

ANOTHER EXORCIST, FOLLOWED BY A SERIES OF UNRELATED MAXIMS

> 9:38 John said to him, "Teacher, we saw someone who does not follow us casting out demons in your name, and we tried to stop him because he was not following us."
>
> 39 But Jesus said, "Do not stop him, for no one who performs a work of power in my name can soon afterward speak evil of me.

> 9:40 For whoever is not against us is for us

— — —

> 9:41 For whoever gives you a cup of water to drink because you are in the name of Christ, I tell you truly that he will not lose his reward.

These verses are interesting because they report that non-Christian exorcists were driving out demons in the name of Jesus. Apparently it is the "name" that results in the healing. Acts 3:16; 4:10; and 16:18 make it clear that the "name of Jesus" has healing power, whoever employs it. That early Christian elders performed such healings of the sick "in the name of the Lord" is confirmed in James 5:14–15a:

> Are any among you sick? They should call for the elders of the church and have them pray over them with oil in the name of the Lord. The prayer of faith will save the sick.

See also 1 Cor 12:27–31:

> Now you are the body of Christ and individually members of it. And God has appointed in the church first apostles, second prophets, third teachers; then deeds of power, then gifts of healing, forms of assistance, forms of leadership, various kinds of tongues. Are all apostles? Are all prophets? Are all teachers? Do all work miracles? Do all possess gifts of healing? Do all speak in tongues? Do all interpret? But strive for the greater gifts. And I will show you a still more excellent way.

In Acts 9:13–17, exorcists, identified as seven sons of a Jewish high priest named Serva, tried unsuccessfully to use "the name of the Lord Jesus over those who had evil spirits," implying that only Christians could perform exorcisms in the name of Jesus. However, here in 9:39, Jesus apparently indicates it is all right for people who are not his followers to perform exorcisms in his name.

— — —

> 9:42 "And whoever causes one of these little ones who believes [in me] to sin, it would be better for him if a large millstone were hung around his neck, and he were thrown into the sea.

9:43 And if your hand causes you to sin, cut it off. It is better for you to enter into life maimed than, having two hands, to go to hell into the unquenchable fire

[44 where their worm does not die, and the fire is not quenched.]

9:45 And if your foot causes you to sin, cut it off. It is better for you to enter into life lame than, having two feet, to be thrown into hell, [into the unquenchable fire]

[46 where their worm does not die, and the fire is not quenched.]

9:47 And if your eye causes you to sin, tear it out. It is better for you to enter into the kingdom of God with one eye than, having two eyes, to be thrown into hell,

48 where their worm does not die, and the fire is not quenched.

9:49 For everyone will be salted with fire, [and every sacrifice will be salted with salt.]

9:50 Salt is good, but if the salt loses its saltness, with what will you season it? Have salt within yourselves, and be at peace with one another."

This is a passage that is especially interesting in helping us to understand better the evangelist's redactional method, because these eighteen verses (vv. 9:33–50) appear to be primarily a collection of loosely connected sayings attributed to Jesus.

Recovering the original text of these verses is itself problematic, as the ancient manuscript evidence likely supports the view that:

> V. 38: The words "because he does not follow us" may be a later addition and not original to the saying.

> V. 41: Some manuscripts not surprisingly read "my name" instead of the rather troublesome "because you are in the name of Christ."

> VV. 44 and 46: These verses in their entirety are probably later additions and not original, which is why they are printed in brackets. They simply repeat v. 48 and are not found in the best manuscripts.

> V. 49b is also not found in what scholars consider the best manuscripts and is bracketed.

The material in vv. 37–50 is especially problematic. Nothing holds them together. These sayings may have been part of a written source available to the evangelist in a catechism that was to be memorized by initiates as part of their formal introduction to their new religion. The use of catchwords or phrases may be the only real connection among these sayings:

1. "in my name" (vv. 37, 39), "in your name" (v. 38), "the name of Christ" (v. 41)
2. "cause to sin" (Greek *skandalizo*) (vv. 42, 43, 45, 47)
3. "it would be better" (Greek *kalos* followed by *mallon*) (vv. 42, 43, 45, 47)
4. "throw" or "cast" (Greek *ballo*) (vv. 38, 42, 45, 47)
5. "enter into life" or "enter into the kingdom of God" (Greek *eiselthein eis ten zoen*, or its equivalent, *eiselthein eis ten basileian tou theou*) (vv. 43, 45, 47)
6. "go to hell" or "be cast into hell" (Greek *apelthein eis ten geennan*, or *ballo eis ten geennan*) (vv. 43, 45, 47)
7. fire (Greek *pur*) (vv. 43, 48, 49)
8. salt (Greek *alas*) (vv. 49, 50)

CHAPTER 9

Moreover, verse 42 does not follow naturally on verse 41, but it does follow naturally on verse 37.

> 37 "Whoever receives one of these children in my name receives me; and whoever receives me, receives not me but the one who sent me."

> 42 "And whoever causes one of these little (or insignificant) ones who believes [in me] to sin, it would be better for him if a large millstone were hung around his neck, and he were thrown into the sea."

Perhaps these two alleged sayings of Jesus followed each other in the evangelist's written source, and he inserted the material in verses 38–41 between the two sayings. The sayings in verses 37 and 42 are not only similar, but they likely refer to the newest members of the Christian community. Verse 42 makes it clear that the evangelist is referring to believers ("one of these little ones *who believe in me*") and not simply to little children.

The three related sayings in verses 43 (hand), 45 (foot), and 47 (eye) make it clear it is better to enter "into life" or "into the kingdom of God" (a place of reward after death) with a disability rather than "to go to hell" or "be cast into hell" with one's body intact. Christians may have understood this saying quite seriously, or perhaps they formulated it during the period of the persecution of Christians by the Roman Emperor Nero in 64 CE in order to strengthen the community's belief.

The phrase "to go to hell" in verses 43, 45, and 47 says literally "to go to Gehenna," a valley southeast of Jerusalem where Jehoahaz (or Ahaz) (735–715 BCE) and Manasseh (687/686–642 BCE), both kings of Judah, sacrificed their sons to the Ammonite god, Molech. Gehenna is described in these verses as a place of torment, of unquenchable fire and an immortal consuming worm. Moreover, there is also another word for hell in Greek (Hades, the Hebrew *sheol*). I translate the word *Gehenna* as "hell," because it is described in this passage quite explicitly as a place of eternal suffering and punishment, a meaning more Gentile than Jewish.

Verse 48 (reproduced in some manuscripts of vv. 44 and 46) echoes Isa 66:24:

> And they shall go out and look at the dead bodies of the people who have rebelled against me; for *their worm shall not die, their fire shall not be quenched,* and they shall be an abhorrence to all flesh.

Verse 49 is unclear, and it is difficult to settle on its meaning, either in this context or in isolation. The connection between verses 48 and 49 is probably no more than their use of the word "fire," as the transition otherwise makes no sense. Whatever the author's intention, the meaning appears to suggest suffering or punishment as everyone's final lot.

The meaning of verse 50 is no clearer and appears to have no relationship to verse 49, except the mention of "salt." Verse 50 states the obvious: if salt loses its saltness, it is of no use. But what does this mean in the context of the teaching of Jesus or of the evangelist's church? The final command in verse 50c may provide a clue. For as long as you preserve your identity as Christians, you will have peace among you. It appears that embracing Christianity may be their saltiness. The collection of these seemingly unrelated sayings concludes with the command to "be at peace with one another," perhaps an answer to the opening question as to who among the apostles is the greatest.

CONCLUSIONS AFTER CHAPTER 9

This chapter marks another turning point in the earliest gospel. Midway through the gospel there is the legend of the Transfiguration of Jesus, a story in which Peter, James, John, and the reader learn who Jesus really is: the beloved Son of God. This pericope echoes Jesus' call as the adopted Son of God at his baptism by John and anticipates Jesus in his full glory at his resurrection at the very end of the gospel.

The transfiguration story (9:2–8) concludes with an element of the Messianic Secret: Jesus commands his inner circle of disciples to tell no one what they have seen until the Son of Man has risen from the dead. The revelation of Jesus as Messiah apparently raised a question in the eyes of many following Jesus' death: How could Jesus be Messiah until Elijah first returned as his herald? The next pericope (9:9–13) addresses that question when Jesus himself proclaims that Elijah has, in fact, already come in the person of John the Baptist.

The drama is about to unfold; but before it begins, the anonymous author introduces another miracle story, the Exorcism of the Epileptic Boy (9:14–29). The boy's father had first approached Jesus' disciples, but they were unable to heal the boy. The father then approached Jesus, who says that everything is possible to the one who believes. Once the father expresses his belief, although hesitantly, Jesus exorcizes the demon, and the boy is healed.

The disciples ask Jesus why they were unable to heal the boy, to which Jesus answers that this kind of demon can be exorcised only by prayer.

There then follows Jesus' second prediction to his disciples of his death and resurrection (9:30–32), but his disciples still seem unable to understand what is about to happen. This pericope, too, reflects the theme of the Messianic Secret. The understanding of Jesus as Messiah does not come to the disciples until after Jesus' death in spite of Peter's confession, in spite of the Transfiguration. The evangelist apparently had to deal with this historical reality by means of this ongoing theological theme: Jesus' messiahship was a secret during his lifetime.

The remainder of the chapter (vv. 33–50) contains a collection of generally unrelated sayings of Jesus that may have served a catechetical purpose in the evangelist's church. These sayings appear to be linked by nothing more than eight distinct catch words or phrases and likely came to the evangelist from a written, probably catechetical, source to which he had access. These sayings deal with the questions of which disciple is the greatest, whether a non-Christian can perform an exorcism in the name of Jesus, how Christians should deal with new members of the community, how to deal with sins committed by the body (hand, foot, eye), and somewhat puzzling sayings regarding fire and salt.

What is especially important in this chapter is that we have come to the turning point in Jesus' ministry. There is a new beginning, characterized by Jesus' return to Capernaum, where he first taught, but this beginning is the beginning of the end. It marks the beginning of the events leading up to the Passion Narrative, events on which Jesus is now focused and which he alone seems to understand.

We also gain insight in this chapter into the editorial or redactional features of the evangelist. He begins with a story of the Transfiguration, probably known to him from a written source. This leads him into the proclamation of John the Baptist as Jesus' precursor, Elijah returned to prepare the way for Jesus' life and ministry.

The evangelist then adds a rather long miracle story in the Exorcism of the Epileptic Boy, which leads him to the story of Jesus' Second Prediction of His Death and Resurrection. The chapter ends with a collection of almost random sayings attributed to Jesus that the evangelist likely found in a written source.

We are increasingly able to see the anonymous evangelist's hand primarily in the opening words of most pericopes; however, the bodies of most of the stories are almost certainly taken from written sources, which the author seems to modify freely to adapt them to his own agenda.

Chapter 10

JESUS' TEACHING ABOUT DIVORCE

10:1 And he arose from there and went into the region of Judea and beyond the Jordan. And crowds gathered to him again, and as he was accustomed, he taught them again.

2 And [the Pharisees approached and] they asked him if it is lawful for a man to divorce his wife—testing him.

3 But he answered and said to them, "What did Moses command you?"

4 But they said, "Moses permitted to write a certificate of divorce and to divorce."

5 But Jesus said to them, "Because of your hardness of heart, he wrote this commandment for you.

6 But from the beginning of creation, he made them male and female.

7 For this reason a man shall leave his father and mother and cling to his wife,

8 and the two will become one flesh, so they are no longer two, but one flesh.

9 Therefore, what God has joined together, humankind shall not separate."

CHAPTER 10

10:10 And when they were in the house again, his disciples asked him again about this.

11 And he said to them, "Whoever divorces his wife and marries another woman commits adultery against her.

12 And if she divorces her husband and marries another man, she commits adultery."

THE EVANGELIST'S SETTING FOR the pronouncement story in verses 1–9 is unclear, if not confusing: "And he arose from there and went into the region of Judea and beyond the Jordan (i.e., into Transjordan?). The most recent reference to location (9:33) shows that Jesus was in Capernaum at the northwest corner of the Sea of Galilee. We previously observed that the evangelist's editorial introductions to individual pericopes are not reliable with regard to history, geography, or sequence. However, in this introduction Jesus seems to be headed south from Galilee into Judea. Therefore, the reference to "beyond the Jordan" (or Transjordan) makes no sense geographically and may be an editorial gloss by a later scribe unaware of the geography of the area.

In verse 2, the opening phrase "the Pharisees approached and" is omitted in many ancient manuscripts. Hence, the original text likely read, "And they (the evangelist's indefinite 'they') asked him (Jesus) if it is lawful for a man to divorce his wife." Mention of the Pharisees was likely a later scribal addition to the text, reinforcing the Pharisees' earlier confrontations with Jesus.

The pericope (vv. 2–9) makes it eminently clear that Jesus did not allow divorce for any reason. The pronouncement itself is in verse 9: "Therefore, what God has joined together (in marriage), humankind shall not separate (by divorce)." The question to Jesus in verse 2 is viewed by the evangelist as hostile, as a test of Jesus. There were at the time two principal rabbinic schools in contemporary Judaism. The more conservative school of Rabbi Shammai allowed a husband to divorce his wife in the event of her sexual misconduct. The more liberal school of Rabbi Hillel permitted divorce for any reasonable cause. It should be noted that, to the best of our knowledge, no Jewish sect in the first century CE completely forbade divorce, so Jesus' position is remarkable, if, indeed, this is an authentic teaching of the historical Jesus.

Interestingly, Mosaic law in Deut 22:22 regards adultery as justification for the death of both parties to the infidelity, so divorce would not be an issue in such a situation:

> If a man is caught lying with the wife of another man, both of them shall die, the man who lay with the woman, as well as the woman.

So too Lev 20:10:

> If a man commits adultery with the wife of his neighbor, both the adulterer and the adulteress shall be put to death.

And compare Mal 2:10a:

> For I hate divorce, says the LORD, the God of Israel . . . .

However, the Greek Septuagint "translation" of this verse reads something quite different: "If you hate her (your wife), divorce her, says the LORD, the God of Israel."

At that time, marriage was a contract between two families to secure the interests of both families with regard to status, children, and property. The contract was made not by those getting married, but by the two families. Hence, divorce represented a break or dissolution of the two families' contract. Jesus' answer to the question skirts the disagreement between the two rabbinic schools by emphasizing the permanence of marriage through the pronouncement in verse 9: "What God has joined together, humankind shall not separate."

Verse 5 is particularly interesting because Jesus states that Moses wrote the commandment allowing divorce because of the people's adamant obstinacy. The implication of Jesus' comment is eminently clear: the law of divorce (Deut 24:1–4, where divorce is left to a husband's discretion) was a creation of Moses and not the will of God. This observation poses a serious problem: To what extent is the Torah the word of God, and to what extent is it the word of Moses?

Verses 10–12 are obviously an addition to the pronouncement story. The evangelist apparently added these related sayings to the pronouncement story as if Jesus were now teaching privately to the disciples inside the house. Whether the evangelist added them to the pronouncement story from a separate source or by way of personal editorial clarification is not evident.

Verse 12 is contrary to Jewish law, inasmuch as a woman could not divorce her husband. The fact that women could divorce their husbands under Greek and Roman law may indicate that this comment is a later addition of a Hellenistic church and does not reach back to Jesus.

Although the setting for this added teaching may be in the evangelist's church, the teaching about divorce may reach back to Jesus. In 1 Cor 7:10–11, Paul wrote in about 54 CE:

> To the married I give this command—not I but the Lord—that the wife should not separate from her husband (but if she does separate, let her remain unmarried or else be reconciled to her husband), and that the husband should not divorce his wife.

JESUS BLESSES THE CHILDREN

10:13 And they were bringing children to him, so that he might touch them; but the disciples reprimanded them.

14 But when Jesus saw this, he was angry and said to them, "Allow the children to come to me; do not prevent them, because the kingdom of God belongs to such as these.

15 Truly, I say to you, whoever does not receive the kingdom of God as a child will surely not enter into it."

16 And he took them up in his arms, blessed them, putting his hands upon them.

This pronouncement story has no introduction other than the connective opening word "and," so typical of the evangelist. The impersonal third-person-plural verb is also characteristic of the evangelist: and an unidentified "they" were bringing children to Jesus. The disciples try to stop the people, but Jesus is indignant and rebukes the nameless "them" (v. 14), one of the few passages in the gospel in which Jesus expresses anything like anger, acrimony, or grief (see also 3:5; 8:12; and 14:33–34).

In the ancient world, children were generally not held in high regard, so the disciples are trying to save Jesus from having to deal with them. Jesus expressed anger with the disciples and said that "the kingdom of God belongs to such as these."

The point of the pericope comes in verse 15: in order to enter the kingdom of God, one must receive or accept it as a gift from God with the receptiveness and innocence of a child. Perhaps Jesus' command to let the children approach him is even meant to imply that Jesus himself *is* or *reflects* the kingdom of God. The story ends with the blessing of the children.

The pronouncement in verse 15 may express an authentic teaching of the historical Jesus.

THE RICH MAN, TRUE RICHES, AND THE KINGDOM OF GOD

10:17 And as he was going out on the road, someone came running, and falling on his knees before him, asked him, "Good Teacher, what should I do so that I may inherit eternal life?"

18 But Jesus said to him, "Why do you call me good? No one is good except one—God.

19 You know the commandments: you shall not murder; you shall not commit adultery; you shall not steal; you shall not bear false witness; you shall not defraud; honor your father and mother."

20 But he said to him, "Teacher, all these things I have observed from my youth."

21 But Jesus, fixed his gaze on him, loved him, and said to him, "You lack one thing: go, sell whatever you have and give to the poor, and you will have treasure in heaven; and come, follow me."

22 But he was shocked at the saying, and went away heavy-hearted, for he had many possessions.

— — —

10:23 And Jesus looked around and said to his disciples, "How hard it is for those who have possessions to enter into the kingdom of God!"

CHAPTER 10   141

24 But the disciples were astonished at his words. But Jesus answered again and said to them, "Children, how difficult it is to enter the kingdom of God!

25 It is easier for a camel to go through the eye of a needle than for a rich man to enter into the kingdom of God."

26 But they were exceedingly amazed, saying to one another, "And who can be saved?"

27 Jesus fixed his gaze on them and said, "For human beings it is impossible, but not for God; for all things are possible for God."

— — —

10:28 Peter began to say to him, "See, we have left everything and have followed you."

29 Jesus said, "Truly I say to you, there is no one who has left house or brothers or sisters or mother or father or children or farms [on account of me or on account of the good news],

30 who will not receive a hundred times as much now in this time—houses and brothers and sisters and mothers and children and farms with persecutions—and in the age to come, eternal life.

— — —

10:31 But many who are first will be last, and the last first."

Verses 10:17–30 are a pronouncement story in three related parts, or perhaps distinct but related pronouncement stories. The separation is indicated by the spacing in the text above: 10:17–22, 10:23–27, 10:28–30, and 10:31. I shall comment on each unit individually.

10:17–22: The first part of verse 17 is obviously an editorial transition of the evangelist: "And as he was going out on the road . . . ," introductory language typical of this gospel.

The man kneels before Jesus and addresses him as "good teacher." Jesus asks the man why he refers to him as "good," inasmuch as only God is good.

The reference to "eternal life" in the man's question to Jesus in verse 17 is eschatological and may reflect a genuine teaching of the historical Jesus: What can the man do to earn from God the inheritance of everlasting life in the age to come? "Eternal life" is a life that is "entered into" as an "inheritance" from God at the resurrection of the dead in the age to come, the age of God's rule.

Jesus reminds the man of the requirements of the Law as contained (rather loosely but not literally) in the Ten Commandments that Moses received on Mount Sinai (v. 19): "you shall not murder; you shall not commit adultery; you shall not steal; you shall not bear false witness; you shall not defraud; honor your father and mother." The order and the list of commandments differs in the ancient manuscript tradition of this verse, making it difficult to know what was in the earliest text of the gospel, the autograph. The phrase "you shall not defraud" is not among the original Ten Commandments and is, probably for that reason, omitted in some ancient manuscripts. It may have been known in the oral tradition of the Pharisees.

The man replies to Jesus, this time addressing him as "Teacher" (without the adjective "Good") by telling Jesus he has observed all of the commandments since his youth. Jesus then says the man lacks one thing: that he should sell all of his worldly goods, give everything to the poor, and then follow Jesus. Unlike Jesus' disciples, the man did not respond to Jesus' call and went away heavy-hearted, because he was very rich and was not prepared to make the sacrifices required to become a disciple of Jesus.

— — —

10:23–27: Verse 23a ("And Jesus looked around and said to his disciples") connects the story of the rich man to what follows, and is almost certainly a device of the evangelist. Verse 23b makes it clear it is very difficult for anyone with great possessions to enter the kingdom of God. The demands of the kingdom are too great for someone who is very rich.

After the disciples express surprise at Jesus' words (v. 24a), Jesus repeats the message in a separate saying (vv. 24b–25): "Children, how difficult it is to enter the kingdom of God! It is easier for a camel to go through the eye of a needle than for a rich man to enter into the kingdom of God." Jesus addresses the disciples affectionately as "children" and then reminds them it is especially difficult for a rich man to enter into the kingdom of God. In fact, it is actually difficult for anyone. This saying is, of course, an exaggeration, to express Jesus' view that it is almost impossible for a rich man to enter the kingdom of God. The personal sacrifice is enormous.

The disciples answer in disbelief (v. 26): if the rich cannot enter the kingdom, then who can? Their question is based on the assumption of the time that wealth was an indication of God's approval of someone. Jesus' answer or pronouncement "For human beings it is impossible, but not for God; for all things are possible for God" (v. 27) makes it clear it is God who is in control. The evangelist's community, likely made up of both rich and poor, was not in a position to judge who would and who would not enter God's kingdom. The message of the evangelist for his church was clear: wealth can be a serious hindrance to entering the kingdom of God, but no one knows for sure.

The similarity of verse 27 ("for all things are possible for God") and 9:23 ("all things are possible to the one who believes") suggests this verse may be an editorial addition of the evangelist.

— — —

Verses 28–30 seem to be a separate unit of tradition added onto verses 17–27 by the evangelist. The introduction of Peter into the story otherwise comes as a surprise. It is likely nothing more than the evangelist's editorial introduction to the next block of material that he wants to include in this section and should probably be classified as a legend.

Unlike the rich man, Peter uses this occasion to remind Jesus that he and the other disciples had left everything behind to follow Jesus. Peter and Andrew left their fishing nets (1:18), and Peter also apparently left his wife and mother-in-law (1:30). James and John left their father Zebedee (1:20). Levi left his work (2:14). Jesus does not require all of his followers to leave everyone and everything behind, but true discipleship required more than simple membership in the early Christian community. Families were sometimes broken when some members of the family became Christians and others did not. Yet, the church itself was the family of God, and the gain from that community outweighed by "a hundred times" anything lost or left behind (v. 30).

The words "on account of me or on account of the good news" (v. 29) are not found in several important manuscripts and are probably a later scribal addition. Jesus would not likely have referred to his own message as good news, and certainly the even later meaning of the good news *about* Jesus the Messiah (i.e., the Gospel) would be a theme of the church, not of the historical Jesus.

Likewise the reference to "persecutions" in verse 30 certainly reflects the hand of the later church at a time when Christians were being persecuted, perhaps beginning with the persecutions under Emperor Nero in 64–68 CE.

— — —

10:31: "But many who are first will be last, and the last first" may simply be an isolated saying, an appendage, attached by the evangelist to the story in 28–30. It is found also in other contexts in both the gospels of Matthew and Luke:

> Matt 20:16—So the last will be first, and the first will be last.

> Luke 13:30—And indeed, some are last who will be first, and some are first who will be last.

The order in the earliest gospel (first, last, last, first) is the opposite of the order in both Matthew and Luke (last, first, first last). Furthermore, although the saying appears in a different context in all three gospels, in both the earliest gospel and in the Gospel of Matthew it appears immediately before Jesus' Third Prediction of his Death and Resurrection.

The meaning of the saying in the context of the earliest gospel is clear: many who are rich and in positions of authority will not enter the kingdom of God; but many who are poor and even homeless will enter the kingdom of God, likely a teaching of both Jesus and the church.

FOR A THIRD TIME JESUS FORETELLS HIS DEATH AND RESURRECTION

> 10:32 But they were on the road, going up to Jerusalem, and Jesus was walking ahead of them, and they were amazed; but those who followed behind were afraid. And he took the Twelve aside again and began to tell them the things that would happen to him:

> 33 "See, we are going up into Jerusalem, and the Son of Man will be handed over to the chief priests and the scribes; and they will condemn him to death; and they will hand him over to the pagans;

> 34 and they will mock him and spit at him, and whip him, and kill him. And after three days he will rise again."

The material in 8:27—10:45 is represented by the evangelist as a journey from Galilee to Jerusalem, the last stage of Jesus' ministry. Jesus and his disciples are approaching their final destination, as they are now "going up to Jerusalem." Inasmuch as Jerusalem was a walled city on a hill, it is appropriate that they are headed "up" toward or into the city.

The opening words of verse 32 are presumably the editorial introduction of the evangelist, but there is something puzzling in this introduction. Who are the "they" who were walking on the road and the "them" in front of whom Jesus was walking and who "were amazed," but "those who followed behind were afraid?" The phrase "those who followed behind were afraid" is omitted by some ancient manuscripts, suggesting the confusion was already evident to early scribes. One proposed suggestion is that the verb in the first part of the sentence should be singular and not plural, meaning Jesus was "surprised" or "amazed"; but those who followed him "were afraid." Unfortunately, not every problem in the text has an obvious solution. I suspect this verse is just one more example of the evangelist's indefinite "they."

In any event, Jesus then took his disciples aside to share some confidential information: Jesus' third prediction of his death and resurrection. Whereas the two earlier predictions (8:31 and 9:31) are introduced as "teaching," this one is introduced by the simple phrase "to tell." Moreover, this prediction contains much greater detail than the previous two predictions. Once again Jesus refers to himself here as the Son of Man, a phrase that is inspired by the suffering servant of Deutero-Isaiah (Isa 52:13—53:12).

This third prediction of the death and resurrection reflects much more closely than the previous predictions (8:31 and 9:31) what will actually unfold later in the gospel in the evangelist's version of the Passion Narrative:

Event	Third Prediction	Passion Narrative
handing over to the chief priests and scribes	10:33	14:53
condemnation by the chief priests	10:33	14:64b
handing over to the Gentiles	10:33	15:1
mocking	10:34	15:20
spitting	10:34	14:65
whipping	10:34	15:15
killing	10:34	15:24, 37
resurrection on the third day	10:34	16:1–8

There can be little doubt that we are dealing in all three predictions, and most especially in the third, with a *vaticinium ex eventu*. A *vaticinium ex eventu* (Latin for "prophecy out of the event") is a technical term for an author's prophecy or prediction of an event when the author already has information about the event he is presumably predicting. The detailed parallelism of the Third Prediction and the Passion Narrative should probably be credited to the evangelist. This third prediction (as well as the second) is evidently a construction of the evangelist.

JAMES AND JOHN ASK JESUS FOR PRECEDENCE

10:35 And James and John, the sons of Zebedee, approached him and said to him, "Teacher, we want you to do for us whatever we ask of you."

36 But he said to them, "What do you want me to do for you?"

37 But they said to him, "Grant us that we may sit, one at your right and one at your left,—in your glorious manifestation."

38 But Jesus said to them, "You do not know what you are asking. Can you drink the cup that I am about to drink, or be baptized with the baptism with which I am about to be baptized?"

39 But they said to him, "We can." But Jesus said to them, "You will drink the cup that I am about to drink, and be baptized with the baptism with which I am about to be baptized,

40 but to sit at my right or at my left is not mine to grant, but it is for those for whom it has been prepared."

41 And when the ten heard (this), they began to be incensed with James and John.

— — —

10:42 And Jesus called them to him and said to them, "You know that those who are recognized as rulers among the pagans are masters over them, and their leaders exercise authority over them.

43 But it is not so among you; but whoever wants to become great among you will be your servant.

44 And whoever among you wants to be first will be a slave of all.

— — —

10:45 For, indeed, the Son of Man did not come to be served, but to serve, and to give his life as a ransom in behalf of many."

Verses 35–45 are a composite work, probably put together by the evangelist from several written sources. Verses 35–41 are a legend about Jesus in his future heavenly glory—in his "glorious manifestation," perhaps the time of his anticipated second coming. Hence, these verses are obviously a composition of the early church and do not go back to Jesus himself. Verses 42–44 are sayings about rank in the early Christian community (presumably the church in Antioch?) to which this gospel was written, hence they address the composition of the church. Verse 45 is a confessional statement of the early church, a proclamation of the church's primitive preaching, the apostolic *kerygma*. It appears here as a saying of Jesus. We will examine these subunits separately.

The evangelist or his written source presumably created the setting for James and John, the sons of Zebedee, to ask Jesus to provide places of honor for them at the time of his future glorification, likely the time of Jesus' second coming as the eschatological Son of Man. They wanted to be assured that they would have positions of honor when Jesus is enthroned as God's agent at the dawning of the kingdom of God, the age of God's rule. The evangelist or his church may have created this legend to address rivalries within their own community.

Jesus answers their request by asking James and John whether they are prepared to endure the suffering he is about to endure, the events laid out in Jesus' third and most detailed prediction of his suffering, death, and resurrection (10:33–34). Verses 38–39 indicate it is Jesus' suffering that should be emulated in the church, not his glorious manifestation. James and John agree they are prepared to endure such a cup of suffering and such a baptism unto death. Jesus' suffering and death are a substitute for others, a point made clear in verse 45.

James was, in fact, executed by Julius Agrippa I sometime before 44 CE, an event perhaps known to the evangelist. Even though James and John agree to Jesus' request, precedence is not something Jesus can grant. He does not have final authority in that matter. That decision presumably rests with God, who has already made those preparations. Asking for such precedence is inappropriate for even the closest of Jesus' followers.

Verses 42–44 are a collection of three separate but related sayings attached to this pericope, much like what we saw earlier in 9:42–50 and 10:17–31. The cluster in verses 42–44 contrasts leadership in the pagan world, whose tyrants have mastery over their people, with leadership in the Christian community, which involves imitating Jesus in his service to others.

Verse 42 seems to be ironic, although it is difficult to render the subtleties of the Greek into English: "those who are recognized as rulers among the pagans" may imply something like "those so-called rulers among the pagans" or "those who are supposed to be rulers among the pagans." The pagans' would-be leaders "exercise authority over them," which probably means "impose total control over them."

Verse 43 continues, by mentioning that in contrast to the pagans (or Gentiles, or surrounding societies), Christians should operate differently. This is not the time to be involved in discussions about precedence. This is not the time for Christians to exercise power over one another, but to serve one another and the community as a whole.

Verse 45 is particularly interesting. The saying has Semitic qualities, which suggests it is relatively early although not necessarily from Jesus himself. It reflects the kind of parallelism found in Old Testament poetry, in which a second element either repeats or states the opposite of the first element (so-called synthetic and antithetical parallelism):

> The Son of Man did not come to be served
>
> > but to   serve
> >
> > and to give his life as a ransom for many.

The second line states the opposite of the first line (antithetical parallelism), and the third line restates or expands upon line two (synonymous parallelism).

The opening words of verse 45, "for even" or "for indeed," strengthen the meaning of the saying. Jesus is looking back at the whole of his ministry until the present, and he is also looking forward to his own death, another example of *vaticinium ex eventu* (prophecy *out of* or *after* the event). The central theme of the church's preaching is expressed in this single verse, which is likely an early confessional statement of the church, placed, however, on Jesus' lips. The Greek word *lutron* (ransom) is found only here (and in the parallel passage in Matt 20:28) in the entire New Testament. The word means "ransom," "the price of ransom," "the price paid for the return of a prisoner of war," "for the manumission of a slave," "payment of money in lieu of the execution of a guilty person," "a discharge from a debt or obligation," or "redemption or deliverance by purchase or the payment of a price." In verse 45, *lutron* refers to Jesus' death as an act of redemption, perhaps the central teaching of the early church.

The Greek word *anti* can mean "in behalf of," "instead of," or "in place of." "The many" is, of course, "the Christian community." The words of Isa 53:11b–12 are certainly in the mind of whoever composed the poetic confession of faith in verse 45:

> 53:11b The righteous one, my servant, shall make many righteous,
>   and he shall bear their iniquities.
> 12 Therefore, I will allot him a portion with the great,
>   and he shall divide the spoil with the strong;
> because he poured out himself to death,
>   and was numbered with the transgressors;
> yet he bore the sins of many,
>   and made intercession for the transgressors.

Like a sacrificial offering, the suffering of the servant will bring forgiveness to many. In this act of deliverance, the many not only benefit from but receive righteousness that they could never earn or accomplish themselves. The personal sacrifice of one man brings about the righteousness of many.

Many scholars question the antiquity and originality of verse 45 and trace its theology to the influence of Paul. The entire life and work of Jesus are seen in retrospect. It is, of course, doubtful that Jesus would have seen his own death as sacrificial, but it is not clear that the evangelist has borrowed the concept of redemption from Paul or from followers of Paul. This belief was at the core of the apostolic preaching soon after Jesus' crucifixion, once Jesus' disciples had come to grips with what appeared to be the end of Jesus' teaching and ministry. This proclamation is the church's answer to those responsible for Jesus' death. Almost from the outset, Christianity was a religion of expiation and redemption brought about by Jesus' death. The word *lutron* (ransom) is, of course, used metaphorically. This single verse lies at the center of the evangelist's theology.

JESUS HEALS THE BLIND MAN BARTIMAEUS IN JERICHO

10:46 And they went into Jericho. And as he and his disciples and a considerable crowd went out from Jericho, a blind beggar, Bartimaeus, the son of Timaeus, was sitting by the road.

47 And when he heard that it was Jesus of Nazareth, he began to shout out and to say, "Son of David, Jesus, have pity on me!"

48 And many rebuked him that he should be quiet; but he shouted even more loudly, "Son of David, have pity on me!"

49 And Jesus stood still and said, "Call him." And they called the blind man, saying to him, "Take courage. Stand up. He is calling you."

50 But throwing aside his outer garment, he jumped up and went to Jesus.

51 And Jesus answered and said to him, "What do you want me to do for you?" But the blind man said to him, "Rabboni, that I may recover my sight."

52 And Jesus said to him, "Go, your faith has saved you." And immediately he recovered his sight and followed him on the road.

The introduction to this miracle story is quite awkward. Jesus and his disciples appear to arrive in Jericho and to leave immediately, together with a large crowd. They are presumably all pilgrims headed to Jerusalem, about fifteen miles southeast of Jericho, for the Passover festival.

Just outside the city gates of Jericho, the blind man Bartimaeus (which actually means the son of Timaeus in Aramaic, hence redundant) sat begging. Learning that Jesus was there, Bartimaeus called out to Jesus as Son of David, a title found only in this pericope in the earliest gospel. What the evangelist intended by using this nationalistic title is unclear. Son of David usually referred to a political Messiah, who would restore Israel's independence and assume the Davidic throne.

Bartimaeus's recognition of Jesus as Son of David (i.e., Messiah) recalls Peter's recognition of Jesus as the Christ (i.e., Messiah) in 8:29. In this pericope, it is interestingly a blind man who ironically "sees" who Jesus really is. Bartimaeus's repeat of the title "Son of David" in verse 48 may be the evangelist's way of reinforcing Jesus' messianic identity in preparation for his triumphal entry into Jerusalem, the pericope that immediately follows.

The crowd tries to silence Bartimaeus, but Jesus summons him to come forward. There follows an exchange of words between Jesus and Bartimaeus, who now addresses Jesus as Rabboni, a word meaning "my master," found only here in this gospel. Jesus then heals Bartimaeus of his blindness, attributing the healing to Bartimaeus's faith, presumably his trust in God and in Jesus' power to heal. There is obviously a play on words here. The verb "save" means "heal," but it also has a more theological meaning: "to bring salvation to" or "to preserve from eternal death." The play on words is clearly intentional and sends a powerful message to the evangelist's readers or listeners: it is faith in God and in Jesus that brings salvation.

The pericope concludes with Bartimaeus joining the crowd headed on the road to Jerusalem for the Passover festival. The early Christians who heard or read of Bartimaeus's following Jesus "on the road" would likely have understood that they too were expected to follow Jesus on the road to suffering and perhaps even death.

Because of the identity of Jesus as the Son of David, this miracle story serves as a suitable prelude to Jesus' triumphal entry into Jerusalem.

CONCLUSIONS AFTER CHAPTER 10

Chapter 10 introduces a series of pericopes leading up to Jesus' triumphal entry into Jerusalem at the beginning of the next chapter: several sections of purported sayings or teachings of Jesus, and a single miracle story.

The first part of the chapter, verses 1–31, deals with a series of alleged sayings or teachings of Jesus on issues relating to the family:

1. Verses 2–12 concern teaching about marriage and divorce;
2. Verses 13–16 concern children;
3. Verses 17–22 and (3a) 23–27 concern matters of possessions and property; and
4. Verses 28–31 concern matters involving family, households, and farms.

These alleged sayings or teachings of Jesus are probably drawn by the evangelist from a single written source that dealt with these issues as they related to life in the church. It is difficult to discern whether any of this material reaches back to the historical Jesus. There was perhaps some recollection of Jesus' teaching at the time when this material was collected into the evangelist's written source, but very little or none of the material likely reaches back to Jesus in its current form.

Jesus' Third Prediction of His Suffering, Death, and Resurrection (10:32-34) is clearly the work of the church. This material is more detailed than the two earlier predictions in 8:31 and 9:31 and mirrors details of the Passion Narrative in chapters 14-16, an example of *vaticinium ex eventu*, prophecy *out of* or *after* the event.

The pericope in 10:35-41 tells a story of Jesus' disciples—James and John—who request from Jesus precedence on his right and on his left when Jesus enters into his glory or his glorious manifestation at the time of his Second Coming. Jesus asks James and John whether they are prepared to suffer in the way in which Jesus himself is about to suffer, to which they answer affirmatively. Yet Jesus does not and cannot extend precedence to them in the kingdom of God, as they request.

The material in 10:42-44 builds on the theme of precedence introduced by James and John. Jesus calls on his followers not to exercise authority over one another, but rather to serve one another and the Christian community. This teaching is followed by a single saying of Jesus (v. 10:45) that summarizes what has just been said and that likely served as an early Christian theme: "The Son of Man did not come to be served, but to serve, and to give his life as a ransom in behalf of many."

Chapter 10 closes with a miracle story: Jesus Heals the Blind Man Bartimaeus outside Jericho, the message of which is clear. Although Jesus' disciples have not always understood clearly who Jesus is, it is a blind man who actually "sees" and understands that Jesus is the Messiah, the Son of David. It is ultimately faith in God and in Jesus as Messiah that brings salvation. Interestingly, Jesus does not command Bartimaeus's silence after healing him of his blindness. The reason is clear: apparently the Messianic Secret is now over.

The stage is set for Jesus to enter Jerusalem and undergo the suffering and death that he predicted to his disciples on three occasions.

Chapter 11

Jesus' Triumphal Entry into Jerusalem and what follows in chapters 11–13 serve as a preamble to that portion of the gospel known as the Passion Narrative, which probably begins in 14:1. This preamble has a clever but artificial literary organization that is compressed into a period of three days (see 11:1; 11:12; 11:19–20; 14:1):

1. A series of events that precede Jesus' teaching (11:1–25)

    Day 1 (from the beginning of the day at sunset to the next sunset, 11:1–11)
    Jesus' Triumphal Entry into Jerusalem (11:1–11)

    Day 2 (from sunset to sunset, 11:12–19)
    The Cursing of the Fig Tree (11:12–14)
    The Cleansing of the Temple (11:15–19)

    Day 3 (from sunset to sunset, 11:20—13:37)
    The Lesson from the Withered Fig Tree (11:20–21)

2. Jesus' teaching in Jerusalem (11:22–13:44)

    Day 3 (continued)
    Sayings of Jesus on Faith and Prayer (11:22–25)
    The Question of Jesus' Authority (11:27–33)
    The Parable of the Evil Winegrowers (12:1–12)
    On Paying Taxes to Caesar (12:13–17)
    The Question about the Resurrection (12:18–27)
    The Greatest Commandment (12:28–34)
    The Question about David's Son (12:35–37)
    Criticism of the Scribes (12:38–40)

The Poor Widow's Contribution (12:41–44)

3. A compilation of Jesus' apocalyptic teaching (13:1–37)

Day 3 (continued)
Jesus Predicts the Destruction of the Temple (13:1–2)
Four Disciples Question Jesus Privately (13:3–4)
Jesus' Warning about Imposters (13:5–6)
Sayings of Jesus on Signs of the Beginning of the End (13:7–8)
Sayings of Jesus on Persecution (13:9–13)
The Abominable Desecration (13:14–20)
Warnings against False Messiahs and False Prophets (13:21–23)
A Prophecy of the Coming of the Son of Man (13:24–27)
The Lesson of the Parable of the Fig Tree (13:28–29)
Two Sayings about the Certainty of Imminent Consummation (13:30–31)
Saying on the Unknown Hour and Day (13:32)
An Exhortation to be Alert and the Parable of the Absent Householder (13:33–36)
The Application is to Everyone (13:37)

The three-day scheme is probably the evangelist's creation, given the imbalance of the events of the three days. Day 1 has only a single event, Day 2 has two events, and Day 3 has nine, plus the entire collection of Jesus' Apocalyptic sayings in chapter 13. Perhaps Jesus' Triumphal Entry into Jerusalem on Day 1 is so special that it must stand alone; the Cursing of the Fig Tree and the Cleansing of the Temple on Day 2 are viewed as a pair with the same basic message. Everything else on Day 3 is a collection of assorted miscellany. Interestingly, references to the Story of the Fig Tree frame a block of material immediately before the Cleansing of the Temple (11:15–19) and immediately after the A Prophecy of the Coming of the Son of Man (see 13:24–27 and 13:28–29). The significance of this, if any, is not clear.

JESUS' TRIUMPHAL ENTRY INTO JERUSALEM

11:1 And when they drew near to Jerusalem, to Bethphage and Bethany, to the Mount of Olives, he sent two of his disciples;

CHAPTER 11

2 and he said to them, "Go into the village ahead of you; and immediately as you enter into it, you will see a colt tied up, on which no person has yet sat. Untie it and bring it.

3 And if anyone says to you, 'Why are you doing this?' say, 'The Lord needs it, and he will immediately send it back here.'"

4 And they went and found a colt tied near a door outside on the street, and they untied it.

5 And some of those who were standing there said to them, "What are you doing untying the colt?"

6 But they said to them just as Jesus said. And they let them go.

7 And they brought the colt to Jesus, and they threw their outer garments upon it, and he sat on it.

8 And many spread their outer garments on the road, and others leaves they had cut from the fields.

9 And those who preceded and those who followed cried out: "Hosanna! Blessed is the one who comes in the name of the Lord!

10 Blessed is the coming kingdom of our father David! Hosanna in the highest heights!"

11 And he entered into Jerusalem and into the temple precinct. And when he had looked around at everything, as the hour was already late, he went out to Bethany with the Twelve.

The story of Jesus' Triumphal Entry into Jerusalem is prefaced with a story that has its roots in Zech 9:9:

> Rejoice greatly, O Daughter Zion!
>   Shout aloud, O daughter Jerusalem!
> Lo, your king comes to you;
>   triumphal and victorious is he,
> humble and riding on a donkey.
>   on a colt, the foal of a donkey.

In fulfillment of this prophecy the evangelist, or more likely his source, has Jesus send two of his disciples into the village (perhaps Bethphage) to secure the colt on which Jesus will ride into Jerusalem (v. 2). Now that blind Bartimaeus has "seen" and acknowledged Jesus as the Son of David (10:46–52), Jesus is ready to demonstrate publicly that he is, in fact, the people's messianic king. The fact that this colt has never before been ridden also illustrates its purity to carry the king.

The beginning of this pericope has Jesus at the Mount of Olives, recalling still another messianic text from Zech 14:4:

> On that day, his feet shall stand on the Mount of Olives, which stands before Jerusalem on the east . . . .

This additional allusion to a passage from Zechariah is not a coincidence. We are beginning to see what will increasingly become a story constructed out of passages from the Hebrew Bible with little regard to history or historic memory.

It seems clear that the passages in Zechariah are the basis for the story of Jesus' Triumphal Entry into Jerusalem as the king and not as simply one more pilgrim arriving in the city for the Passover festival. Jesus' entry is messianic; he arrives in Jerusalem as a king, who will "usher in the kingdom of our father David" (v. 10). The people recognize who Jesus is and throw their garments on the ground out of respect for the arriving king. Clearly, in its present form, the story is a legend, as it reflects a post-crucifixion and post-resurrection Christology. Furthermore, it is not unlikely that the story may be modeled after other stories of royal visits or triumphal entries following heroic victories in battle.

The shout "Hosanna" is reminiscent of Ps 118:25:

> "Save us (Hebrew or Aramaic *hosanna*), we beseech you, O Lord."

Interestingly, the evangelist does not translate this Hebrew or Aramaic word into Greek, perhaps because it was part of the liturgy in his church in the original language and, therefore, familiar to the evangelist's audience. The following phrase, "Blessed is the one who comes in the name of the Lord," quotes Ps 117:26a exactly.

The final cry of the crowd in verse 10, "Blessed is the coming kingdom of our father David, Hosanna in the highest heights (i.e., of heaven)," is not biblical. It is, however, clear that this verse claims that Jesus is both king and son of David, the very title by which blind Bartimaeus had just identified him in the previous pericope (10:46–47). Yet, Jesus will not be the political king, the Son of David whom some Jews expected. The Jesus of our gospel has already indicated he will be a suffering Messiah on the order of the suffering servant of Deutero-Isaiah. Moreover, the evangelist also seems to have in mind Jesus' future kingship on the order of what was predicted in Dan 7:13–14:

> As I watched in the night visions,
> I saw one like a human being coming with the clouds of heaven.
> And he came to the Ancient One and was presented before him.
> To him was given dominion and glory and kingship,
> that all peoples, nations, and languages should serve him.
> His dominion is an everlasting dominion that shall not pass away,
> and his kingship is one that shall never be destroyed.

The pericope ends with Jesus entering the temple precinct, where he looks around and observes what is going on (v. 11). It is late in the day, so he retreats with the Twelve to Bethany, where he can contemplate and plan what he will do when he returns to the temple on the following day.

THE CURSING OF THE FIG TREE

> 11:12 And on the following day, as they were going out from Bethany, he was hungry.
>
> 13 And seeing from afar a fig tree with leaves, he went to see whether perhaps he could find something on it. When he came upon it, he found nothing but leaves, for it was not the time for figs.
>
> 14 And answering he said to it, "May no one eat fruit from you ever again." And his disciples were listening.

The pericope of the cursing of the fig tree surely carries significant meaning that is hidden within the story. The story, otherwise, makes little or no sense. Jesus is hungry, but he looks for figs out of season. In response to finding no figs on the tree, Jesus curses the tree and commands that it never again produce fruit. The figs are obviously a metaphor, and the pericope an enacted parable.

Unlike some scholars, I do not think this is a miracle story in which Jesus' word simply results in the death of a fig tree. That is not the point of the story. The position of this pericope between Jesus' Triumphal Entry into Jerusalem and the Cleansing of the Temple likely provides a clue to its meaning. The pericope should be understood in its context. It is not entirely clear whether the fig tree represents Israel, which produces no fruit and is, therefore, condemned to fail, or the temple, whose fate is doomed because it does not produce the fruit for which it was intended. Yet the intention of the story is clear: there is no fruit on the tree, and the tree is condemned to wither to its roots (see 11:20). Israel and/or the temple are withered to their roots. This passage also recalls Hos 9:16-17:

> Ephraim is stricken.
>> their root is dried up,
>> they shall bear no fruit.
> Even though they give birth,
>> I will kill the cherished offspring of the womb.
> Because they have not listened to him,
>> my God will reject them,
>> they shall become wanderers among the nations.

See also Jer 8:13:
> When I wanted to gather them, says the LORD,
>> there are no grapes on the vine,
>> nor figs on the tree;
> even the leaves are withered,
>> and what I gave them has passed away from them.

The cursing of the fig tree is Jesus' message of eschatological judgment against Israel and/or the corrupt cult of the Jerusalem temple. In that regard this pericope anticipates the Cleansing of the Temple that immediately follows. See also the Lesson of the Withered Fig Tree below (11:20-21).

THE CLEANSING OF THE TEMPLE

11:15 And they went into Jerusalem. And he went into the temple precinct and began to drive out those who were selling and those who were buying in the temple precinct, and he overturned the tables of the money changers and the seats of those who were selling the doves.

16 And he would not let anyone carry a vessel through the temple precinct.

17 And he taught and said to them, "Has it not been written, 'My house shall be called a house of prayer for all the nations?' But you have made it a den of robbers."

18 And the chief priests and the scribes heard it and they were considering how they might destroy him; for they feared him, for the entire crowd was astonished at his teaching.

19 And when evening came, they went outside the city.

The Cleansing of the Temple is clearly one of the most important stories in this gospel and certainly one of the most important events in the life of Jesus. It is the event that probably led to Jesus' arrest, trials, and eventual execution. It seems almost certain that the gospel is reporting an actual event although the details are probably not entirely accurate. In its present form, the pericope is best classified as a legend, although it might also be considered an enacted parable.

The temple precinct in Jerusalem was a huge mounted area (approximately 1575 feet by 985 feet, or roughly thirty-five acres—about the size of six football fields) that could accommodate hundreds of thousands of pilgrims. Jesus' "cleansing" was probably localized in one small area and was likely a symbolic prophetic act designed to show God's disfavor with the bazaar-like atmosphere of the temple cult within the walls of the temple precinct. At the time of a festival, pilgrims entered the temple precinct to purchase oil, wine, food, and sacrificial animals that were sold by merchants. Money changers enabled the pilgrims to change their Greek or Roman money into Jewish or Tyrian coins (specifically the shekel currency of Tyre), so they could pay the half-shekel temple tax. At this time, Jews were not permitted to have their own currency, and foreign currency could not be used to pay the temple tax. This businesslike or even carnivallike atmosphere offended God in Jesus' mind. Jesus' angry action demonstrated symbolically God's disapproval that the "house of prayer for all peoples" (Isa 56:7c) had been converted into a den of robbers.

The implication of verse 16 may be that people were carrying ordinary containers through the temple precinct, using the temple precinct as a cut-through or shortcut to get from one area of Jerusalem to another.

The details of the story are not entirely clear. Jesus may have thought that such transactions should take place outside the temple precinct and not on the temple grounds in order to preserve the sacred character of the temple area. If Jesus took action for this reason, then the quote in verse 17 from Isaiah 56 may actually go back to Jesus. However, it is more likely that the quote from Isaiah is simply a part of the evangelist's story.

Verse 18 implies the chief priests and the scribes, both members of the Jewish court—the Sanhedrin—were fearful of taking action against Jesus because of his popularity with the crowd. That may actually be true.

Although some have suggested it is only Jesus who leaves the temple in verse 19 and that the verb should, therefore, be singular, it is likely that the opening words of verse 15a and the closing words of verse 19 are editorial additions of the evangelist. Inasmuch as the unspecified "they" arrived in verse 15, the same unspecified "they" have to leave in verse 19.

THE LESSON OF THE WITHERED FIG TREE AND ADDITIONAL SAYINGS OF JESUS ON FAITH AND PRAYER

11:20 And as they were passing by early in the morning, they saw the fig tree withered from its roots.

21 And Peter remembered and said to him, "Rabbi, look! The fig tree that you cursed has withered."

— — —

11:22 And Jesus answered and said to them, "Have trust in God.

— — —

11:23 Truly, I say to you, "Whoever says to this mountain, 'Be taken up and thrown into the sea,' and does not doubt in his heart but believes that what he says happens, it will be for him.

— — —

11:24 Therefore I tell you, all things you ask when you pray, believe that you received it (sic), and it will be yours.

— — —

11:25 "And when you stand praying, if you have anything against anyone, forgive, so that your Father in heaven may also forgive you your transgressions.

The evangelist picks up where the Cursing of the Fig Tree left off in 11:12–14 with events of the following day in 11:20–21: the fig tree is now dead. He then adds several unrelated Sayings on Faith or Trust (11:22–23) and Prayer (11:24–25). The evangelist did something similar earlier in the gospel by adding individual sayings onto pericopes in 2:21-22 (The New and the Old); 2:28 (On the Sabbath); 3:27–30 (On the Strong Man, On Blasphemy, and An Unclean Spirit); and 10:11–12 (On Adultery).

As Jesus and his disciples head back to Jerusalem from Bethany, Peter addresses Jesus as "rabbi" (meaning master or teacher) and indicates to Jesus that the fig tree he cursed the previous evening has now withered to its roots. Jesus changes the subject and begins instead to speak about faith (or trust) and prayer, implying that the appellation "rabbi" in this passage has the connotation of teacher.

As we have seen, the Story of the Fig Tree signifies that the old order, whether Israel as a whole, or the temple cult, or perhaps the leadership in Jerusalem, is rotting from its very roots and will soon die. However, although the old order is passing away, it is not yet time for the new age of God's rule to arrive. That will presumably happen only after Jesus' passion, death, and resurrection have come to pass. In fact, it appears that the coming of the new age depends on the faith, trust, prayer, and forgiveness of Jesus' followers—first his disciples, as in the story, and later by members of the church to which the evangelist addressed this message.

Jesus' command to have faith in God (v. 22) is perhaps better translated "have confident trust in God," or simply "have confidence in God." The related saying in verse 23 is, of course, metaphorical or allegorical. Jesus is saying that by having confidence or trust in God, people can accomplish almost anything, a reinforcement of what was said in 9:23, "If you are able, all things are possible to the one who believes," and 10:27, "All things are possible for God." The saying in verse 24 expresses the same confidence in the power of prayer—teaching applicable not only to Jesus' disciples, but to the evangelist's church, whose members are urged to pray with hope and steadfast conviction. The evangelist connects the power of prayer with trust in God.

The final saying in verse 25 mirrors some of the language of the Lord's Prayer in Matt 6:9 and 14. The phrase "your Father in heaven" and the word "trespasses" or "transgressions" link verse 25 to the version of the prayer found in the Gospel of Matthew but not in the Gospel of Luke. This similarity does not necessarily mean the evangelist already knew a version of the Lord's Prayer similar to what is found in Matt 6, but it does suggest an early connection between prayer and the forgiveness of others' transgressions or trespasses.

— — —

[11:26 But if you do not forgive, neither will your Father in heaven forgive your trespasses."]

Verse 26 is in brackets, because the manuscript tradition does not support its presence in the autograph of the gospel. It appears in some manuscripts of the earliest gospel, but probably by subsequent assimilation to the text of Matt 6:15.

THE QUESTION OF JESUS' AUTHORITY

11:27 And they went into Jerusalem again. And as he was walking in the temple precinct, the chief priests and the scribes and the elders came to him.

28 And they said to him, "By what authority are you doing these things? Or who gave you this authority to do these things?"

29 But Jesus said to them, "I will ask you one question; and answer me, and I will tell you by what authority I do these things:

30 Was the baptism of John from heaven or from humankind? Answer me."

31 And they were deliberating among themselves, saying, "If we say, 'From heaven,' he will say, 'Why then did you not believe him?'

32 But if we say, 'From humankind'"—they were afraid of the crowd, for they were all convinced that John was really a prophet.

33 And they answered and said to Jesus, "We do not know." And Jesus said to them, "Neither will I tell you by what authority I do these things."

This pronouncement story focuses on the question of the source of Jesus' authority. The implication of the pericope is clear: Jesus' authority comes from God. Those who question Jesus' authority represent the Jerusalem leadership, and the timing and setting of the story in the temple precinct reinforce the importance of the issue of authority. The appearance of the chief priests and the scribes recalls 11:18, in which it is reported that the chief priests and the scribes "were considering how they might destroy him"; and 8:31, in which Jesus first predicted that he would "be rejected by the elders and the chief priests and the scribes." There may even be a hint of the Messianic Secret in this pericope: Jesus is not yet ready to reveal to everyone the source of his authority.

It is not clear who "they" are in 11:27, although the third-person-impersonal plural of the verb is common in the gospel. If it refers to Jesus' disciples, they play no role elsewhere in this pericope. The question from the chief priests, the scribes, and the elders obviously refers to Jesus' prophetic cleansing of the temple. They would hardly have been concerned about Jesus' cursing of the fig tree.

The word "authority" (Greek *exousia*) implies, in this context, divine inspiration or prophetic authority from God. Does Jesus' authority in cleansing the temple come from God, or has he assumed for himself more authority than he actually has? The question that the Jewish leadership posed to Jesus was whether Jesus had legitimate authority to do what he did in the temple precincts.

As in 10:3, Jesus replies to the Jewish leadership's question with a question of his own about the source of John's baptism. The phrase "from heaven" in verse 31 is a common Jewish circumlocution of the time, meaning "from God." The pericope is particularly interesting because of the mention of John the Baptist. If Jesus was originally a follower of John and began his own ministry only after John's arrest, then the implication may be that

Jesus inherited from John the authority that God had originally bestowed on John.

CONCLUSIONS AFTER CHAPTER 11

Chapter 11 opens with Jesus' Triumphal Entry into Jerusalem (vv. 1–11), a major turning point in the gospel. The entry itself is prefaced with the story of Jesus' arrival at the Mount of Olives and the acquisition of a colt on which Jesus will ride into the city in fulfillment of prophecies in Zechariah. The fulfillment of these Old Testament proof texts indicates that Jesus is entering Jerusalem as Israel's messianic king, the Son of David. Additional Old Testament proof texts from Psalms and Daniel are woven into the outcries from the crowd who welcome Jesus as their king.

Jesus' second day in Jerusalem is marked by two events, two obviously interrelated stories that bear the same significance. The first story is the Cursing of the Fig Tree (vv. 12–14), an enacted parable into which the evangelist or his source has woven elements from Hosea and Jeremiah. By his word alone, Jesus expresses his anger that the fig tree has not produced the desired fruit. We will see later in verses 20–21 that Jesus' cursing of the tree has withered the tree to its roots; it is dead. The clue to the meaning of this story is in the next pericope, the Cleansing of the Temple (vv. 15–19), in which Jesus again shows his anger with wayward Israel, the perversion of the temple cult, and the misguided Jewish leadership through still another enacted parable as he drove out the vendors, overturned the tables of the money changers, and threw aside the chairs of those who were selling sacrificial animals. Whereas the Cursing of the Fig Tree is likely a metaphoric parable, the Cleansing of the Temple probably has roots in history and is likely the critical event—the enacted parable—that resulted in Jesus' arrest, crucifixion, and death.

It is now Jesus' third day in Jerusalem, and the remainder of chapter 11 and all of chapters 12 and 13 report events on this single day. The day begins with Jesus and the Twelve passing by the withered fig tree early in the morning (vv. 20–21). This is followed by a series of unrelated sayings of Jesus (vv. 22–25), presumably addressed to the Twelve, regarding trust or faith in God, the power of prayer, and the need to forgive other people's transgressions if one expects to be forgiven by God of one's own transgressions. It is likely that these sayings came from a teaching manual in the evangelist's church.

The final pericope in this chapter is a follow-up to Jesus' Cleansing of the Temple. The chief priests, the scribes, and the elders confront Jesus and ask him by what authority he engaged in such disruptive action on the previous day in the temple precincts (vv. 27–33). The story is crafted as a dialogue between the Jewish leaders and Jesus, in which Jesus refuses to state the obvious, which is clear to the evangelist's readers and listeners: Jesus' authority, like the authority of John the Baptist, obviously comes from God.

There is almost an arc of personality change from the earlier chapters, where Jesus is more humble and helpful to a more impatient and authoritative personality in this chapter. Is this development historical or is it a feature of the evangelist, who is preparing the reader or the listener for the final events in Jesus' life?

The only pericope in this chapter that likely reflects an historical event is the Cleansing of the Temple, although the details of the story are not entirely certain. It is also obvious that Jesus entered Jerusalem for the Passover festival. However, the account of Jesus' entry has been fashioned, either by the evangelist or more likely by the evangelist's source, in light of Old Testament passages that were appropriated to indicate that Jesus' entry was a triumphal arrival that reflected the people's acknowledgement and acclamation of Jesus' messiahship. The evangelist is likely responsible for including the story of the fig tree and the miscellaneous didactic alleged sayings of Jesus that probably served as teachings in the evangelist's church.

Chapter 12

THE PARABLE OF THE EVIL WINEGROWERS

12:1 And he began to speak to them in parables: "A man planted a vineyard and put a fence around it and dug a pit for the wine press and built a watchtower. And he rented it out to winegrowers and went on a journey.

2 And at the proper season, he sent a slave to the winegrowers, so that he might receive from the winegrowers some of the fruit of the vineyard.

3 And they seized him and beat him and sent him away empty-handed.

4 And again he sent to them another slave, and they beat him on the head, and treated him shamefully.

5 And he sent another, and they killed him; and many others as well, some they beat, others they killed.

6 He still had one other, a beloved son. Finally, he sent him to them, saying, 'They will respect my son.'

7 But those winegrowers said to one another, 'This is the heir. Come, let us kill him, and the inheritance will be ours.'

8 And they seized him and killed him and threw him outside the vineyard.

9 What then will the owner of the vineyard do? He will come and destroy the winegrowers and give the vineyard to others.

— — —

12:10 Have you not read this Scripture: 'A stone that the builders rejected has become the cornerstone.

11 This was the Lord's doing, and it is marvelous in our eyes?'"

12 And they wanted to arrest him, and yet they feared the crowd, for they knew he had spoken the parable against them. And so they left him and went away.

The parable of the Evil Winegrowers is much more than a parable. Parables generally make a single cogent point by telling a story, such as the common formula "The kingdom of God is like . . . ." This particular parable is more of an allegory—an allegoric parable or a parabolic allegory. Moreover, it is clear that this particular parable is a creation not of Jesus, but of the church.

The opening words of the parable are reminiscent of Isa 5:1–7, which the author of this parable clearly had in mind:

> 5:1 Let me sing for my beloved
>   my love-song concerning his vineyard.
> My beloved had a vineyard
>   on a very fertile hill.
> 2 He dug it and cleared it of stones,
>   and planted it with choice vines;
> he built a watchtower in the midst of it,
>   and hewed out a wine vat in it;
> he expected it to yield grapes
>   but it yielded wild grapes.
> 3 And now, inhabitants of Jerusalem
>   and people of Judah,
> judge between me
>   and my vineyard.
> 4 What more was there to do for my vineyard
>   that I have not done in it?

> When I expected it to yield grapes,
> > why did it yield wild grapes?
> 5 And now I will tell you
> > what I will do with my vineyard.
> I will remove its hedge,
> > and it shall be devoured;
> I will break down its wall,
> > and it shall be trampled down.
> 6 I will make it a waste;
> > it shall not be pruned or hoed,
> > and it shall be overgrown with briers and thorns;
> I will also command the clouds
> > that they rain no rain upon it.
> 7 For the vineyard of the LORD of hosts
> > is the house of Israel,
> And the people of Judah
> > are his pleasant planting;
> he expected justice,
> > but saw bloodshed;
> righteousness,
> > but heard a cry!

The parable is addressed to the chief priests, the scribes, and the elders of 11:27–28, who questioned the source of Jesus' authority. The symbolism of the elements in the allegory is clear:

- The vineyard is Israel, or perhaps more specifically Jerusalem and its temple cult;
- The owner of the vineyard is God;
- The winegrowers are the Jewish leaders and rulers;
- The various slaves are Israel's earlier prophets, who were rejected;
- The beloved son is Jesus;
- The punishment is the forthcoming destruction of Israel or Jerusalem;
- The new winegrowers are the Gentile church;
- The cornerstone is also Jesus, or more specifically the risen Lord.

The reference to the owner's "beloved son" is reminiscent of the baptism (1:11), when Jesus is referred to by the voice from heaven as "my Son, the Beloved" and of the transfiguration (9:7), when the voice from the cloud also calls Jesus "my Son, the Beloved."

Verse 9 also reflects the view of the church that in the last days Jesus will come again as God's agent to inaugurate the eschatological age of God's reign.

It is likely that the original form of the story is verses 1–9, and verses 10–12 are an addition, perhaps by the evangelist. The question posed in verses 10–11 is taken verbatim from Ps 118:22–23 and addresses the question posed previously in 11:28: Yes, Jesus' authority comes from God.

Inasmuch as Jesus not only refers to his own death but essentially claims in 12:6 to be the Son of God, a claim made by the church only after Jesus' death, this parable was obviously composed by the church. See Rom 1:3–4, where with reference to Jesus, Paul says:

> . . . the gospel concerning his Son, who was descended from David according to the flesh and *was declared to be Son of God with power according to the spirit of holiness by resurrection from the dead,* Jesus Christ our Lord . . . . (italics mine)

This adoptionist theology, the earliest such claim in the New Testament, makes it clear that Jesus' sonship was traced by the early church to Jesus' resurrection. The evangelist expresses a similar adoptionist theology in his account of Jesus' baptism, but thereafter in this gospel Jesus' sonship remains a secret by means of the evangelist's device of the Messianic Secret.

The claim that the risen Lord is the cornerstone is followed by Jesus' words in verse 11: "This was the Lord's doing, and it is marvelous in our eyes," a quote from Ps 117:23.

The pericope ends by stating that the Jewish authorities wanted to arrest Jesus, but were afraid to do so because of the crowd.

ON PAYING TAXES TO CAESAR

> 12:13 And they sent to him some of the Pharisees and the Herodians, so that they might trap him in what he might say.
>
> 14 And they came and said to him, "Teacher, we know that you are an honest man and that you show deference to no one; for you do not pay attention to outward appearance, but you truly teach

the way of God. Is it permitted to pay the poll tax to Caesar, or not?

15 Should we pay, or not?" But knowing their hypocrisy, he said to them, "Why are you testing me? Bring me a denarius so that I may see it."

16 So they brought one. And he said to them, "Whose image is this and whose inscription?" So they said to him, "Caesar's."

17 So Jesus said to them, "Render to Caesar what belongs to Caesar, and to God what belongs to God." And they were utterly amazed at him.

This pericope is a pronouncement story *par excellence*: a dialogue between Jesus and an opponent followed by an authoritative saying or pronouncement by Jesus. There is no christological element in this story, so the pronouncement may be a genuine saying of Jesus; however, the pronouncement story form is a fabricated literary device of the evangelist or his written source.

The indefinite "they" of verse 13 has no antecedent and is a common feature of this gospel. Grammatically, it could be "the chief priests and the scribes" of 11:27, but that reference is remote, and most of the pericopes in this gospel are free-standing units. The location of the events of this story is also unclear. The Herodians of verse 13 were people who were loyal to the rule of the Herodian family, specifically at this time Herod Antipas, who had recently killed John the Baptist.

The Pharisees and the Herodians approach Jesus in an effort to trick him. They begin by flattering him, probably to catch him off-guard. They address him respectfully as "Teacher" and then ask him whether it is lawful under the Jewish law to pay the poll tax to the Romans. This issue was controversial among Jews during the Roman occupation. The Roman emperor at this time was Caesar Tiberius (14–37 CE).

The reference to "the Way" in verse 14 may be an allusion to the name by which early followers of Jesus were known in Jerusalem after his death (see Acts 9:2; 18:25; 19:9, 23; 22:4; 24:14, 22). The word translated as "poll tax" is *kensos*, a Greek rendering of the Latin *census*, the tax paid to the Roman imperial treasurer. Jews resented paying the tax for two reasons: first, it represented Roman rule over them, and secondly, the coin bore the image and the name of the Roman emperor. Either a "yes" or a "no" to this question would pose a problem for Jesus, with either the Jews or the Romans.

Jesus' solution to the question is relatively simple: The people have a responsibility to serve God, but Caesar is obviously in charge of issues regarding the state, so the people are required to pay the tax. This position is consistent with what Paul wrote to the church at Rome (Rom 13:1, 6–7) in about 55–56 CE:

> Let every person be subject to the governing authorities, for there is no authority except from God, and those authorities that exist have been instituted by God . . . . For the same reason you also pay taxes, for the authorities are God's servants, busy with this very thing. Pay to all what is due them—taxes to whom taxes are due, revenue to whom revenue is due, respect to whom respect is due, honor to whom honor is due.

A version of this pericope was found in 1934 on a papyrus fragment known as Papyrus Egerton 2, generally dated about 150–200 CE. On the front side of this papyrus we find this text:

> Coming to him, they began to question him trying to put him to the test, saying: "Teacher, Jesus, we know that you have come from God, for the things you do give evidence surpassing all the prophets. Therefore, tell us: "Is it lawful to pay to kings things that pertain to their rule? Shall we pay them or not?" But Jesus, seeing their intention and being deeply moved, said to them, "Why do you call me teacher with your mouth, when you don't hear what I say? Well did Isaiah prophesy concerning you, saying: 'This people honor me with their lips, but their heart is far from me, showing reverence in vain for the precepts of men . . . '"(my translation).

The similarity to our pericope is striking, although it does not appear that the author of the text of Papyrus Egerton 2 was copying from the earliest gospel. The form of the story in Papyrus Egerton 2 is simpler and less developed than the text of our oldest gospel. Although the stories are similar, the version in the earliest gospel is more structured in the literary form of a pronouncement story. I would conclude that neither is dependent on the other, but that they are both probably drawn from early tradition, whether written or oral.

THE QUESTION OF THE RESURRECTION

12:18 And Sadducees, who say there is no resurrection, came to him; and they questioned him, saying:

19 "Teacher, Moses wrote to us that if a man's brother dies and leaves behind a wife and no child, his brother should take the wife and raise up children for his brother.

20 There were seven brothers. And the first took a wife; and when he died, he left no offspring.

21 And the second took her, and he died and left no offspring. And the third likewise.

22 And the seven left no offspring. Last of all, the woman also died.

23 In the resurrection, when they rise again, whose wife will she be? For the seven had her as wife."

24 Jesus said to them, "Are you not therefore mistaken, because you do not know the Scriptures nor the power of God?

25 For when they rise from the dead, they neither marry nor are given in marriage, but are like angels in heaven.

26 But concerning the dead, that they are raised, have you not read in the book of Moses, in the story about the bush, how God spoke to him, saying, 'I am the God of Abraham and the God of Isaac and the God of Jacob?'

27 He is not God of the dead, but of the living. You are very much mistaken."

This pericope is the third consecutive pronouncement story. There is a dialogue about marriage traditions in Judaism and resurrection, followed by a pronouncement of Jesus. It is quite possible this story reflects a teaching of the historical Jesus on the matter of resurrection in the age to come. It is interesting that the question in verse 23 is posed by the priestly party of

Sadducees, who did not believe in the resurrection of the dead. A hostile group is once again asking Jesus a question in order to trip him up.

The Sadducees politely address Jesus as "Teacher," just as the Pharisees and the Herodians did in the previous pericope. The reference to the law that Moses laid down is Deut 25:5–6:

> When brothers reside together, and one of them dies and has no son, the wife of the deceased shall not be married outside the family to a stranger. Her husband's brother shall go in to her, taking her in marriage, and performing the duty of a husband's brother to her, and the firstborn whom she bears shall succeed to the name of the deceased brother, so that his name may not be blotted out of Israel.

There are two differences between the passage in Deuteronomy and the gospel pericope. The gospel omits the limitations "when brothers reside together" and "has no son," although the latter may be implied, inasmuch as it was sons that were necessary for the continuation of the family. In fact, the main purpose of marriage was to produce male heirs to maintain family property within the family.

The intention of the Sadducees was to point out how ridiculous the idea of resurrection was, because it leads to the possibility that a woman could have seven husbands in the afterlife. The Sadducees' rejection of belief in the resurrection is the result of the fact that their only Scripture was the five books of Moses: Genesis, Exodus, Leviticus, Numbers, and Deuteronomy, whereas resurrection creeps into Judaism, probably from Persian influence, only after the Babylonian Exile of 587/586–538 BCE in such passages as Job 19:25–27; Ps 73:24–25; Isa 26:19; Ezek 37:1–14; and Dan 12:2. Although some of these references are preexilic, later generations read meaning into these passages that was not there in their original context. Previously Jews believed the dead went to Sheol, a tunnel under the earth through which the sun passed at night to rise the next morning in the east. All the dead went to Sheol, where they had an inactive shadowy existence without God. Sheol was neither a place of reward nor a place of punishment.

For the benefit of the Sadducees, Jesus cites the story of the burning bush in Exod 3:6, part of the Sadducees' Scripture. In fact, both parties cite the Pentateuch in making their arguments. The mistake of the Sadducees is that they understood the resurrection incorrectly as if it were simply an extension of earthy existence. In the resurrection, Jesus points out, matters like marriage and offspring are irrelevant.

There is some question in this pericope whether the actual pronouncement was originally in verse 25, and whether verses 26–27 were added by the evangelist. Alternatively, this might be a twofold pronouncement in verses 24 and 27.

THE GREATEST COMMANDMENT

12:28 And one of the scribes was approaching and heard them deliberating, and, perceiving that he had answered them well, asked him, "Which is the first commandment of all?"

29 Jesus answered him, "First is: 'Hear, Israel, the Lord our God, the Lord is one.

30 And you shall love Lord your God with all your heart, and with all your being, and with all your mind, and with all your strength.'

31 The second is this: 'You shall love your neighbor as yourself.' There is no other commandment greater than these."

32 And the scribe said to him, "Well said, Teacher. You have spoken in accordance with truth, 'He is one, and there is no other except him'

33 and 'to love him with all the heart, and with all the understanding, and with all the strength,' and 'to love one's neighbor as oneself' is much more than all the whole burnt offerings and sacrifices."

34 And when Jesus saw that he answered wisely, he said to him, "You are not far from the kingdom of God." And after that no one dared to ask him any question.

This is the fourth pronouncement story in this sequence. It is connected to the preceding pericope by the evangelist's editorial introduction: one of the scribes overheard Jesus and the Sadducees discussing the issue of the resurrection. The scribe was impressed by Jesus' answer to the Sadducees and, therefore, had a question he wanted to ask Jesus, "What is the greatest, the most important, commandment of all?"

Love for God is rarely mentioned in the New Testament—only here in the Synoptic Gospels and a few times in Paul's letters. The emphasis in Judaism and early Christianity is usually on God's love for his chosen people, which serves as an example from which human love is derived.

The scribe asks Jesus which commandment is most important? Jesus' answer is to quote the *shema'* (Deut 6:4), the prayer that pious Jews are enjoined to recite twice a day:

> Hear, Israel: "The LORD is our God, the LORD alone," or
>
> Hear, Israel: "The LORD our God, the LORD is one," or
>
> Hear, Israel: "The LORD our God is one Lord," or
>
> Hear, Israel: "The LORD is our God, the LORD is one."

[I might note, as an aside, that in my opinion the *shema'* made more sense when the divine name was still spoken and not the later euphemism "The Lord," after it was forbidden to speak the divine name—thus: Hear, Israel: "Yahweh is God; Yahweh is one." Interestingly, in the Greek Septuagint text of verse 30, there is no article "the" before the word "LORD."]

In his reply to Jesus, the scribe completes the language of the *shema'* by adding the words of Deut 6:5 with some deviation from what Jesus said in verse 30 but in agreement with the text of the Septuagint, the Greek translation of the Hebrew Bible.

Jesus in v. 30	Scribe in v. 33, and Septuagint
kardia, heart	*kardia*, heart
psyche, being	*synesis*, understanding
dianoia, mind	
ischys, strength	*ischys*, strength

The scribe substitutes *synesis* (understanding) for *psyche* (being or soul or life) and omits *dianoia* (mind) to bring Jesus' statement into conformity with the Greek translation of the original Hebrew. Early scribes of the New Testament perceived this inconsistency, and many manuscripts reflect changes to correct this difficulty. The intention of this elaboration is to describe unconditional love with every conceivable human emotion.

The scribe asked Jesus for the single greatest commandment; Jesus gives two. The second commandment (12:31) quotes Lev 19:18b: "You shall love your neighbor as yourself." In its original context in Leviticus, this commandment applied only to fellow Israelites, as did all of the original Ten Commandments. They were an in-group ethic. In the context of our gospel, the commandment probably applies only to other Christians or to other Christian communities. It likely did not have a universal meaning at this time or in this context. Loving one's neighbor probably meant showing your neighbor benevolence, compassion, support, etc.

This is not the first time these two commandments were joined together, but in the context of Jesus' teaching it is almost as if they are one commandment, an indivisible and inseparable whole. To love God is to love one's neighbor, and to love one's neighbor is to love God. This single command reflects the focus of the original Ten Commandments: the first four concern one's relationship with God, the remaining six concern one's relationship with one's fellow Israelites.

It is the scribe, not Jesus, who says that following Jesus' twofold commandment is better than all burnt offerings and sacrifices, an observation that is reminiscent of Hos 6:6:

> For I desire steadfast love and not sacrifice,
> the knowledge of God rather than burnt offerings.

It is tempting to see this observation as an additional slap at the temple cult in Jerusalem, especially if the evangelist's audience was Diaspora Jewish Christians and Gentile Christians. It is not clear whether this pericope faithfully reports a specific moment in Jesus' ministry, but the combination of the twofold love commandment is clearly consistent with Jesus' teaching.

The fact that Jesus tells the scribe "You are not far from the kingdom of God" is interesting because it is quite different from the eschatological conception of the kingdom of God that likely reflects the teaching of the historical Jesus and that dominates this gospel. It appears Jesus' comment to the scribe suggests that the kingdom is presently approachable and almost within reach, perhaps already within the life and the ministry of Jesus.

The evangelist's hand is evident in the final sentence: "And after that no one dared to ask him any question."

THE QUESTION ABOUT DAVID'S SON

12:35 And answering, Jesus said, as he was teaching in the temple precinct, "How can the scribes say that the Messiah is a Son of David?
36 David himself said in the Holy Spirit:
> 'Lord said to my Lord,
>> "Sit at my right hand,
> until I put your enemies

under your feet.'"

37 David himself calls him 'Lord'; and how can he then be his son?" And the large crowd listened to him gladly.

In this pericope it is Jesus who asks the question of his unnamed listeners while he is teaching in the temple precinct. The last mention of Jesus' location is in 11:27, where he is walking in the temple precinct. There is no mention of spatial location in the intervening four pericopes, so the evangelist apparently wants to remind the reader of Jesus' location. This pericope is linked to the previous pericope in verses 28–34 and to the following pericope in verses 38–40 by their common references to "scribes."

The participle "answering" in the opening words of verse 35 is redundant, but not untypical of the evangelist's literary style. Jesus' question regarding the teachers and interpreters of the Jewish law ("How can the scribes say that the Messiah is a Son of David?") seems to imply that Jesus disagrees with the scribal teaching.

The evangelist and his audience assume that David is the author of the quoted psalm (Ps 110), which in its original context was probably an enthronement hymn, composed for the installation of a king of Judah in Jerusalem long after David's time.

It is not clear from the context to whom Jesus is posing this question in the temple precinct. It does, however, appear from Jesus' question that the scribes believed the Messiah would be a political Messiah, a Son of David, who would restore the Davidic monarchy in Jerusalem. What is not clear is whether, even in the story, Jesus subscribed to this belief either by genealogical descent or simply by messianic claim. Jesus' genealogical descent from David is claimed in the gospels of Matthew (Matt 1:1–17) and Luke (Luke 3:23–38) as well as in Rom 1:3 and 2 Tim 2:8. The restoration of the Davidic line of kings in Israel was assumed in many passages in the Old Testament (Ps 89:20–37; Isa 9:7, 11:1–9; Jer 33:6–7, 14–18; Ezek 34:23–24; 37:24; see also Ps Sol 17:4–45 and John 7:42).

The early church apparently interpreted the passage in Ps 110 as a reference to Jesus that may have been circulated in the early church in a collection of *testimonia* or Old Testament proof texts. It is cited by Jesus himself, but it is not clear in this pericope whether Jesus considered descent from David as proof that he was the royal Messiah. It is uncertain whether in this pericope Jesus was looking for popular support for his messianic claim either as a Son of David or, more likely, as a very different kind of Messiah.

The three questions posed by others to Jesus in the three previous pericopes and the question posed by Jesus in this pericope may mimic the questions asked at the traditional Passover meal. It is irrelevant whether the Last

Supper was actually a Passover meal, but it was certainly so interpreted by the church. Now, and in a new context, the celebration of the events leading up to Easter appears to follow the model of the Passover meal in Judaism. However, for Christians, the salvific event is not the Exodus from Egypt, as in Judaism, but the new deliverance that has come as a result of Jesus' passion, death, and resurrection. The Lord's Supper is the new Passover that probably had its origin in Jewish Christianity, likely in the Jerusalem Church.

In the eyes of the early Christian community, Jesus is apparently making claims to Davidic descent and, therefore, to messiahship. Once again, we are witnessing in this gospel the gradual but guarded unfolding of the Messianic Secret.

This pericope is a product of the church with an introduction probably provided by the evangelist. It is unlikely to have had its origin in the life of the historical Jesus. The passage is not easily categorized by literary form. It may simply be a saying for which the evangelist provided a setting.

CRITICISM OF THE SCRIBES

> 12:38 And he said in his teaching, "Watch out for the scribes, who like to walk around in long robes and be greeted with respect in the marketplaces
>
> 39 and have seats of honor in the synagogues and the places of honor at dinners.
>
> — — —
>
> 40 These men devour the houses of widows and for the sake of appearance say long prayers. These men will receive a greater condemnation."

This pericope is again a saying or collection of sayings condemning the scribes for their ostentation, their sense of authority and self-importance, and their desire for public deference, adulation, and privilege. These sayings underscore a serious clash between Jesus and the scribes, although it is not entirely clear whether the break actually took place toward the end of Jesus' ministry or in the church only after Jesus' death.

It is also not clear whether verse 37b was meant to conclude the previous pericope or to introduce this pericope. In either case, it provides a transition between the two stories. Verse 40 may be a separate saying, linked to verses 38–39 because of the similarity of their subject matter: the hypocrisy of the scribes.

THE POOR WIDOW'S CONTRIBUTION

> 12:41 And he sat down opposite the temple treasury and watched the crowd put money into the temple treasury. And many rich people were putting in large sums.
>
> 42 And a poor widow came and put in two *lepta* (small Greek copper coins), which makes a *quadran* (the smallest Roman coin).
>
> 43 And he called his disciples to him and said to them, "Truly, I say to you, this poor widow put in more than all those who were contributing to the temple treasury;
>
> 44 for they all contributed out of their abundance, but she out of her poverty put in everything she had, all she had to live on."

This pericope sounds as if it was originally a parable, although it is reported here as an actual event in the temple precinct. Some regard it as a pronouncement story, because it ends with a definitive statement by Jesus about contributing to the upkeep of the temple. The widow serves as the link to the previous pericope.

There is, however, a change in location, as Jesus now sits down in front of the temple treasury where he observes the contributions people are making. Jesus sees that rich people are putting in large sums of money but that they do so out of their abundant wealth. A poor widow, on the other hand, contributes two small coins, two Greek *lepta*, the smallest coin in circulation, which the evangelist converts into Roman coinage as one Roman *quadran*. Mention of the *lepta* may make it more likely that our earliest gospel was written not in Rome but rather in one of the eastern provinces like Syria, where the *lepta* was better known.

Jesus summons his disciples in verse 43 to make the point to them that the example of the widow may illustrate the cost of discipleship. The introduction of the teaching with "truly, I say to you" illustrates the importance that the evangelist attaches to this lesson. The evangelist frequently uses this introductory phrase to emphasize the importance of an element of Jesus' teaching (see e.g., 3:28; 8:12; 9:1, 41; 10:15; 10:29; 11:23; 13:30; 14:9, 18, 25, 30).

CONCLUSIONS AFTER CHAPTER 12

It is evident that the evangelist used the occasion of Jesus' visit to Jerusalem to include several pericopes dealing with elements of Jesus' teaching that appeared relevant at the close of Jesus' ministry. These units of tradition definitively answer the question of Jesus' authority, an issue posed in the final pericope of chapter 11.

Chapter 12 begins by saying that Jesus began to speak to an indefinite "them" in parables, yet there is only one parable in what follows: the Parable of the Evil Winegrowers (12:1–9). Moreover, this pericope is actually more of an allegory than a parable—with additional sayings material added, probably by the evangelist (12:10–12), presumably because these sayings seemed relevant to the evangelist in this context. This pericope is highly structured and likely a product of the church, as it is specific about Jesus as Son of God, a belief that apparently arose only after Jesus' death. We also see the important role of the Old Testament in the construction of the parable and in the saying(s) in verses 10–11.

There then follows a series of pronouncement stories, likely drawn by the evangelist from a single source: On Paying Taxes to Caesar (12:13–17); the Question of the Resurrection (12:18–27); and the Greatest Commandment (12:28–34). In the first of the pronouncement stories, Jesus is confronted by the Pharisees and the Herodians; in the second by the Sadducees; and in the third by the scribes—a full complement of the Jerusalem Jewish leadership.

In the first and second of the pronouncement stories, Jesus is graciously addressed by his adversaries as "Teacher," although it is clear that the adversaries are trying to entrap him. The third of the pronouncement stories is more cordial and deals with the question of the Greatest Commandment.

On Paying Taxes to Caesar (12:13–17) shows the Pharisees and the Herodians trying to create trouble for Jesus by asking him whether the Jewish law allows Jews to pay taxes to the Romans. Jesus understands their trickery and answers with the pronouncement "Return to Caesar what belongs to Caesar and to God what belongs to God."

The Question of the Resurrection (12:18–27) is built around Old Testament passages in Deut 25 and Exod 3. The Sadducees attempt to demonstrate that belief in the resurrection of the dead leads to serious difficulties, but Jesus refutes their claim by stating that their understanding of the resurrection is a misconception. The resurrection of the dead is not simply a continuation of this life: the God of Israel "is not God of the dead, but of the living."

The Greatest Commandment (12:29–34) is a more friendly exchange between Jesus and the scribes in which they basically agree that loving God and loving one's neighbor constitute the greatest commandment(s) in Judaism. The pericope ends with Jesus saying to the scribe, "You are not far from the kingdom of God."

Two more pericopes follow in which scribes seem to be the link to the previous pericope: the Question about David's Son (12:35–37) and Criticism of the Scribes (12:38–40). The former is a saying of Jesus, based on Ps 110:1; the latter is also a saying or a collection of sayings of Jesus critical of the haughty pretension of the scribes.

Chapter 12 ends with the Poor Widow's Contribution (12:41–44), a pronouncement story linked to the previous pericope by reference to widows in both.

It appears key words may link much of the material in chapter 12. If so, these key words may have served as the mnemonic devices necessary to remember these pericopes in order. If so, this material may reach back to a period of oral tradition before these stories were written down in what may have served as the evangelist's source for most of the material in this chapter.

In a single chapter, devoted to Jesus' teaching in the final days of his life, the evangelist reports that Jesus successfully met the challenges of the Jewish leaders in Jerusalem: Pharisees and Herodians, Sadducees, and scribes. It is also clear in the final pericope in this chapter that the cost of discipleship is very difficult: the widow with her two *lepta* is more generous than the wealthiest donors to the temple treasury. This story reminds us of the pronouncement story about the Rich Man (10:17–22). Discipleship requires unselfish beneficent action, not merely belief.

Chapter 13

THE APOCALYPTIC DISCOURSE

AN "APOCALYPSE" OR "REVELATION" is a literary form that describes visions or auditions about the end of history as we know it and the imminent future age of God's rule. Some scholars maintain that in anticipation of the Roman siege of Jerusalem in 70 CE the evangelist or someone before him built the apocalyptic discourse from an even earlier apocalypse composed by a Jewish or a Jewish-Christian "visionary."

The original apocalypse may have been written several years before the siege of Jerusalem to provide consolation, reassurance, and promise at a time when the political situation in Jerusalem was deteriorating. To this earlier apocalypse, the evangelist or someone before him may have added, from another written source, eschatological sayings attributed to Jesus. Although the evangelist likely used one or more written sources in composing the apocalyptic discourse, it is especially challenging, if not impossible, to divide this material into its component parts.

In its present form, the apocalyptic discourse apparently reflects the beliefs and hopes of the church to which the evangelist was writing, probably just a few years before the siege of Jerusalem at a time when the Jerusalem temple was likely still standing. Although in its present form chapter 13 is a composite unit, it makes sense to discuss the individual elements within the discourse. Hence, the divisions below reflect what are likely some of the component units, which are given individual headings and comments. These divisions are effectively noted by the evangelist, who begins every unit with a connective word, usually "and" (Greek *kai*) or "but" (Greek *de*).

JESUS PREDICTS THE DESTRUCTION OF THE TEMPLE

> 13:1 And as he went out of the temple precinct, one of his disciples said to him, "Teacher, look! What great stones and what great buildings!"
>
> 2 And Jesus said to him, "Do you see these great buildings? Not one stone will be left upon another stone that will not be thrown down."

Verse 1a serves as the evangelist's introduction to the apocalyptic discourse and reflects typical language of the anonymous author. Jesus is about to leave the temple precinct when one of his disciples comments on the magnificence of the buildings. This unit is a concise pronouncement story. Following a brief narrative, Jesus replies with the pronouncement: "Not one stone will be left upon another stone that will not be thrown down." The temple will be totally destroyed. Some scholars believe that this prediction of Jesus was written at a time when the Jerusalem temple was no longer standing, hence a date after 70 CE for the gospel, but this is not entirely clear.

FOUR DISCIPLES QUESTION JESUS PRIVATELY

> 13:3 And as he sat on the Mount of Olives opposite the temple mount, Peter and James and John and Andrew asked him privately,
>
> 4 "Tell us, when will these things be? And what will be the sign when all these things are about to be fully realized?"

Jesus heads east away from the temple precinct across the Kidron Valley and up the hill to the Mount of Olives, overlooking the temple mount. Peter, James, John, and Andrew (the first four disciples whom Jesus called in 1:16–20) then question Jesus privately about when the temple will be destroyed and what sign will warn that the destruction is near. This transition is probably a construction of the evangelist and serves to introduce Jesus' warning (v. 5) and the remainder of the apocalypse or revelation (vv. 6–37). Jesus speaks privately to the four disciples in the remaining verses of this chapter.

JESUS' WARNING ABOUT IMPOSTERS

> 13:5 But Jesus began to say to them: "Watch out that no one leads you astray.
>
> 6 Many will come in my name, saying, 'I am he,' and will lead many astray.

It is not entirely clear what is meant by Jesus' warning against deceivers or imposters who will come saying "I am he" (vv. 5–6)—perhaps early Christians, who claimed to be prophets speaking in Jesus' name but who were leading members of the church astray. It appears these imposters are making claims about themselves ("I am he," v. 6). Were they claiming at the time the gospel was written that they were the risen Christ now returning as the Son of Man, who would usher in the period of God's rule? Or was the evangelist referring to one or more of the messianic pretenders who appeared at the time of the Jewish revolt? The evangelist may be saying none of these deceivers is Messiah, because Jesus has already appeared as Messiah. It is likely that whoever these deceivers were, they were apparently predicting the imminence of the end time. And whatever verses 5–6 may mean, they are not an answer to the disciples' question in verse 4. This unit is likely a composition of the evangelist.

SAYINGS OF JESUS ON SIGNS OF THE BEGINNING OF THE END

> 13:7 But when you hear of wars and reports of wars, do not be disturbed; for such things must happen, but it is not yet the end.
>
> 8 For nation will rise up against nation, and kingdom against kingdom. There will be earthquakes in various places; there will be famines. These are the beginning of birth-pains.

In this unit Jesus begins to answer the question posed by the four disciples in verse 4. The events predicted in verses 7–8 (wars, reports of wars, nation rising against nation and kingdom against kingdom, earthquakes, and famines) were common apocalyptic expectations of what would precede the end time.

See such Old Testament passages as:

CHAPTER 13

Isa 13:13 ("I will make the heavens tremble; and the earth will be shaken out of its place"); Isa 14:30 ("but I will make your root die of famine"); Isa 19:2 ("I will stir up Egyptians against Egyptians, and they will fight one against the other, neighbor against neighbor, city against city, kingdom against kingdom");

Ezek 5:12 ("one-third of you shall die of pestilence or be consumed by famine among you; one-third shall fall by the sword around you);

Hag 2:6 ("in a little while, I will shake the heavens and the earth and the sea and the dry land");

Zech 14:4 ("and the Mount of Olives shall be split in two from east to west by a very wide valley").

See also examples in the Pseudepigrapha:

Sib Or 3.635–36 ("king captures king and takes his land, and nations ravage nations and potentates people");

4 Ezra 13.31 ("and they shall plan to war one against another, city against city, place against place, people against people, and kingdom against kingdom");

1 En 99.4 ("in those days the nations shall be stirred up, and the families of the nations shall arise on the day of destruction");

2 Bar 27.6–7 ("And in the fifth part famine and withholding of rain. And in the sixth part earthquakes and terrors"); 2 Bar 70.3 ("and they shall hate one another, and provoke one another to fight, and the mean shall rule over the honorable, and those of low degree shall be extolled above the famous"); 2 Bar 70:8 ("whoever gets safe out of the war shall die in the earthquake, and whoever gets safe out of the earthquake shall be burned by fire, and whoever gets safe out of the fire shall be destroyed by famine").

See also in the New Testament:

Rev 6:8 ("to kill with sword, famine, and pestilence"); Rev 11:13 ("there was a great earthquake"); Rev 16:18 ("and there came flashes of lightning, rumblings, peals of thunder, and a violent earthquake").

Jesus clarifies what will happen in the end time based on Jewish Scriptures and on his vision as a prophet. He encourages the people not to be afraid when these events begin to occur, because everything that happens is part of God's plan. This unit ends with Jesus telling the people "these" disasters that will unfold are just the beginning of the birth pains that will usher in the age of God's rule.

SAYINGS OF JESUS ON PERSECUTION

> 13:9 But watch out for yourselves; they will hand you over to councils, and you will be beaten in synagogues, and you will stand before rulers and kings, because of me, in order to give testimony to them.
>
> 10 And the good news must first be proclaimed to all the nations.
>
> 11 And when they arrest you and deliver you up, do not worry beforehand what you will say. But say whatever is given you in that hour; for you are not the ones speaking, but the Holy Spirit.
>
> 12 And a brother will deliver a brother to death, and a father a child; and children will rise up against parents and put them to death.
>
> 13 And you will be hated by all on account of my name. But whoever endures to the end will be saved.

This collection of sayings begins by identifying places in which followers of Jesus will be persecuted—in courts, in synagogues, and before rulers and kings (v. 9). They are exhorted not to worry in these situations, because the Holy Spirit will guide them in what to say (v. 11). The unit adds that there will be divisions within families and that Jesus' followers will be hated "on account of his name" (v. 13), presumably meaning because they are Christians. These too may be part of the birth-pains mentioned in verse 8 above. The followers of Jesus (Christians) are, however, urged to be steadfast to the end.

It is possible that verse 9 is a reference to the kinds of persecutions Christian missionaries were suffering when they went out to Jews and Gentiles to preach the good news. This interpretation is supported by what is obviously an intrusive insertion into the text in verse 10 ("And the good news must first be proclaimed to all the nations"), a phrase that interrupts the flow of this collection of sayings and that is, in this location, an inappropriate addition, probably by the evangelist. In fact, verses 9 and 11–13, if read in sequence without the intervening verse 10, have a poetic quality, perhaps reflecting their Aramaic past.

The reference to the Holy Spirit as the source of inspiration in verse 11 is a further indication this particular collection of sayings comes not from the mouth of Jesus but from the period of the early church, when such inspiration was commonplace. Likewise the fact that the followers of Jesus will be hated "because of my name" (v. 13) reflects the hand of the church or the evangelist.

Whatever else, the evangelist is clearly connecting the preaching of the good news to both Jews and Gentiles with the suffering and persecution of Christians, perhaps members of the evangelist's own church. And everything that is unfolding is, in the mind of the evangelist, evidence of the last days. Like Jesus in his final days, so too Jesus' followers will be "handed over" (vv. 9, 11, 12). This unit comes clearly from the early church and is not an authentic teaching of the historical Jesus.

THE ABOMINABLE DESECRATION

13:14 But when you see the 'Abominable Desecration' [or the 'Abomination of Desolation,' or the 'Desolating Sacrilege'] standing where he should not—let the reader understand—then let those who are in Judea flee to the mountains.

15 Let him who is on the roof not come down into the house nor enter to take something out of his house.

16 And let him who is in the field not go back to get his clothing.

17 But woe to women who are pregnant and to those who are nursing babies in those days!

18 But pray that it doesn't happen in winter.

19 For in those days there will be tribulation, such as has not been since the beginning of the creation which God created until now, nor will ever be.

20 And if the Lord did not shorten those days, nobody would be saved; but on account of the elect, whom he had chosen, he shortened the days.

There is an interesting contrast between the opening words of verse 7 ("but when you hear . . . "), "do not be disturbed," and the opening words of verse 14 ("but when you see . . . "), it is clear that it is now time to be terrified. We are at a new point in the unfolding of the eschatological drama, what the evangelist calls "tribulation" (v. 19).

Verse 14 is clearly a reference to Dan 11:31 and 12:11:

> 11:31 Forces sent by him will occupy and profane the temple and fortress. They shall abolish the regular burnt offering and set up *the abomination that makes desolate*.

> 12:11 From the time that the regular burnt offering is taken away and *the abomination that desolates* is set up, there shall be one thousand two hundred ninety days (italics mine).

The original context in Daniel refers to Antiochus IV Epiphanes, the Seleucid ruler from Syria, who began a persecution of the Jews in 168/167 BCE with a desecration of the Jerusalem temple. More specifically, Antiochus interrupted the offerings in the temple and erected on the altar of burnt offering a pagan altar, referred to as "the transgression that makes desolate," and slaughtered pigs on it (see also Dan 8:13–14; 9:27; and 1 Macc 1:54 ["they erected a desolating sacrilege on the altar of burnt offering"] and Josephus, *Antiquities of the Jews* 12.5.4 ["The king also built a pagan altar upon the temple altar and slaughtered swine thereon"]).

The reference to the Abominable Desecration in 13:14 may be to the Roman Emperor Caligula's attempt to have his statue placed inside the Jerusalem temple in 40 CE. The phrase "let the readers understand,"—almost an aside—is difficult to understand. If the reference is to Caligula, then this unit may be part of an early source used by the evangelist. If so, then this (Jewish?) source presumably chose intentionally not to identify Caligula by name for fear of repercussions from the Roman authorities.

What follows in verses 15–20 are stereotypical examples of crises the people might encounter in warfare with the Romans, whether in the context of the events of 40 CE or, in the case of the earliest gospel, at the beginning of the Jewish war in 66 CE. Just about everyone is encouraged to flee from Judea into the mountains. However, the degree of the distress sounds like much more than warfare with the Romans. Certainly verses 19–20 move beyond human warfare to the events that will accompany the end time.

Yet, God has chosen to shorten the time of tribulation in his mercy for his elect, his chosen ones—in the context of the gospel probably not the chosen people Israel, but rather the Christian community.

WARNINGS AGAINST FALSE MESSIAHS AND FALSE PROPHETS

> 13:21 And at that time if anyone says to you, 'Look, here is the Messiah!' 'Look, he is there!' do not believe it.

> 22 For false messiahs and false prophets will rise up and they will do signs and wonders to deceive, if possible, the elect.

> 23 But take heed; watch out; I have told you all things beforehand.

It appears this unit was written at a time when false messiahs and false prophets were making claims, suggesting a time at the beginning of the First Jewish War against Rome, beginning in 66 CE. This unit could be a Jewish apocalyptic claim, in which case the elect in verse 22 might originally have been the Jews, unlike the passage above, where it is more likely Christians (see v. 20).

Verse 21 may be built on Deut 13:1–3:

> If prophets or those who divine by dreams appear among you and promise you omens or portents, and the omens or portents declared by them take place, and they say, "Let us follow other gods" (whom you have not known) "and let us serve them," you must not heed the words of those prophets or those who divine by dreams . . . ."

It is possible that verses 21–23, together with verses 5–8, were part of a single unit, an older Jewish or Jewish-Christian apocalypse here reported as sayings of Jesus. Some consider verses 21–23 a doublet with verses 5–6, but in verses 5–6 the reference is clearly to Christians or pseudo-Christians, whereas that may not be the case in verses 21–23.

A PROPHECY OF THE COMING OF THE SON OF MAN

> 13:24 "But in those days, after that tribulation,

the sun will be darkened,

and the moon will not give its light;

25 and the stars will fall from the heaven,

and the powers in the heavens will be shaken.

26 And then the Son of Man will be seen coming in clouds with great power and glory.

27 And then he will send the angels, and gather together the elect from the four winds, from the farthest part of earth to the farthest part of heaven.

Verses 24–25 appear to be an allusion to Isa 13:10:

For the stars of the heavens and their constellations
> will not give their light;
the sun will be dark at its rising,
> and the moon will not shed its light.

Many of these words are rare in this gospel: e.g., "sun" (Greek *helios*) here and in 1:32; "will be darkened" (Greek *skotisthesetai*); "moon" (Greek *selene*); "light" (Greek *pheugos*); "stars" (Greek *asteres*); "will be shaken" (Greek *salegthesontai*), suggesting that these are likely words from a written source and not from the evangelist.

The phrase "And then they will see the Son of Man coming in clouds with great power and glory" in verse 26 is obviously an allusion to and an updated interpretation of Dan 13:7 ("I saw one like a Son of Man coming with the clouds of heaven") symbolizing the ushering in of a new, everlasting kingdom. See also 14:62 below. Verses 25–26 may be from an earlier source, and they may reflect an authentic teaching of Jesus because they mirror Jesus' sayings in 8:34–9:1, most especially 8:38 and 9:1 (see the discussion above in chapter 8):

8:38 Those who are ashamed of me and of my words
> in this adulterous and sinful generation,
of them the Son of Man will also be ashamed
> when he comes in the glory of the Father with the holy angels.

9:1 ... Truly I tell you, there are some standing here who will not taste death
> until they see that the kingdom of God has come with power.

These sayings all meet the criterion of dissimilarity or embarrassment, because Jesus is referring to someone other than himself as the eschatological Son of Man, who will be coming soon. In these verses, Jesus is making no claim about himself.

THE LESSON OF THE PARABLE OF THE FIG TREE IN SUMMER

> 13:28 "But learn from the similarity of the fig tree: When its branch has already become tender and has put forth its leaves, you know that the summer is near.
>
> 29 So you too, when you see these things happening, know that he is near—at the door!

Verse 28 marks the beginning of a series of loosely related sayings and parables around the general theme of vigilance in preparation for the imminent ominous events of the end time.

Verse 28 actually says "But learn from the parable (Greek *parabole*) of the fig tree." But there is no parable in these verses, and the reference is certainly not to the pericope of the withered fig tree in 12:12–14 and 12:20–24, which is also not a true parable. The meaning of the Greek word *parabole* in this context appears to be "similarity," "likeness," "comparison," "resemblance," "lesson," "example," "analogy," or "illustration," admittedly not the usual meaning of the word *parabole* in the gospels of the New Testament. Although somewhat different, almost any of these English words appear to illustrate the author's intent.

The final words of verse 29 are also ambiguous: they can mean "know that it is near" or "know that he is near." Both translations work in this pericope, although they are quite different in meaning. Is it "the end" that is near," or "the Son of Man" who is near? Perhaps the ambiguity of the original Greek is intentional, but there is no way to capture this subtlety in English, where we have to commit to one or the other: "it" or he."

The "things happening" in verse 29 are twofold: either the tender branch of the fig tree and the putting forth of its leaves, or everything described in verses 5b–27. The latter probably makes more sense.

TWO SAYINGS ABOUT THE CERTAINTY OF IMMINENT CONSUMMATION

> 13:30 Truly, I say to you, this generation will not pass away until all these things happen.
>
> 31 The heaven and the earth will pass away, but my words will surely not pass away.

According to Jesus, the arrival of the Son of Man is near. These may be actual sayings of the historical Jesus, as they conform to sayings of Jesus in 8:38–9:1 and 13:26–27 and also 14:62 (see below). If it is the evangelist or the church speaking, then the reference may be to Jesus' return as the Son of Man. Both possibilities actually work. The important difference is who will be coming within this generation: the Son of Man or Jesus as the Son of Man.

Earlier in this chapter the exhortations of Jesus were based on passages from Hebrew Scripture. Then the lesson of the fig tree was based on an example from nature. Now, in the remainder of this chapter, it is merely the authoritative words of Jesus that issue the warning. Everything that Jesus has predicted is going to happen while this generation is still alive, presumably within the next thirty or forty years.

"All these things" (v. 30) is everything described in verses 5–27, including the messianic and prophetic predictions, the wars and reports of wars, the persecutions, family betrayals, the heavenly signs, the coming of the Son of Man (or the Second Coming of Christ), and the gathering of the elect. Verse 31 may mark the end of the original apocalyptic discourse to which related material in verses 32–37 may have been added by the evangelist. These final verses (32–37) are more catechetical and practical.

SAYING ON THE UNKNOWN HOUR AND DAY

> 13:32 "But concerning that day or the hour no one knows, not the angels in heaven, nor the Son, but only the Father.

No one except God knows when the Day of the Lord will arrive, but it will be sometime soon. Once again this is not an authentic saying of Jesus. The reference to the Son precludes that possibility, unless, of course, it was originally a reference to the Son of Man. The imminent arrival of God's rule is certain, but the timing of the end is entirely in the hands of God. The arrival of the Son of Man will presumably follow the events described in verses 5b–27, and before this generation passes away.

The warning in verse 32 may be an effort to discourage people from calculating the time when the end will come. Or it may be an effort to explain why Jesus did not make a more specific prediction about when the Son of Man would come, or when he would return as the Son of Man. Clearly this verse indicates the Son's subordination to the Father. If it is a reference to the Son of Man, that would make sense. If it is a reference to Jesus, then it obviously reflects an early stage in the development of the church's Christology, when Christ was considered subordinate to God.

AN EXHORTATION TO BE ALERT AND THE PARABLE OF THE ABSENT HOUSEHOLDER

> 13:33 Take heed, stay awake; for you do not know when the time is.

— — —

> 13:34 [It is] like a man going away to a distant country, who has left his household and given authority to his slaves, to each his specific task, and he has commanded the doorkeeper to keep awake.

> 35 Keep awake, therefore, for you do not know when the lord of the house is coming—in the evening, or at midnight, or at the crowing of the rooster, or in the early morning—

> 36 lest, he come unexpectedly and find you sleeping.

The saying in verse 33 provides still one more exhortation to be alert. Yet this exhortation likely serves as an introduction to the parable in verses 34–36.

The parable itself begins abruptly (v. 34): "Like a man going . . . ." I've added the words "It is" to make better sense in English.

The reference to the coming of "the lord (Greek *kyrios*) of the house" in verse 35 may be an allusion to the second coming of Christ, a message that would suit the theme of the gospel at the time of its writing. In that case, the man away on the journey is the risen Jesus, and the household is the Christian community, perhaps even the members of the evangelist's church. The members of the household, the church, have been exhorted to do the work to which they have been assigned and to do it faithfully, because they do not know when Jesus will come again.

THE APPLICATION IS TO EVERYONE

> 13:37 But what I say to you, I say to all: keep awake!"

This saying, this exhortation, is intended for everyone, not just the slaves in the master's household, or the four disciples to whom Jesus was speaking, but to all followers of Jesus in the community to which the evangelist was writing: "Keep awake." You have no idea when the second coming of Jesus and the time of God's rule will arrive.

CONCLUSIONS AFTER CHAPTER 13

Chapter 13 is an apocalyptic discourse similar to apocalypses in Dan 7–13, 2 Esdras, the Revelation of John, and the *War of the Sons of Light against the Sons of Darkness* from the Dead Sea Scrolls. Whatever else, the evangelist was apparently providing his audience with an interpretation of events that were likely unfolding during the early stages of the First Jewish War with Rome, which began in 66 CE, about 35 years after Jesus' death. The author was probably aware that there were several individuals who were making claims at this time about what was unfolding, and some were making claims in the name of Jesus. The evangelist felt compelled to dismiss these false messiahs and false prophets, especially those who were apparently Christian prophets or visionaries, who claimed that they were speaking in the name of Jesus.

The apocalyptic discourse is represented as a teaching of Jesus to his first four disciples: Peter, James, John, and Andrew. That is to say, it is an esoteric teaching intended for very few within the inner circle. Is this chapter another element of the Messianic Secret, which is being revealed only gradually, presumably because this material was not actually a part of the teaching of the historical Jesus?

Put differently, there is a question whether any of the material in chapter 13 originated with the historical Jesus, or whether it is all simply teaching of the church. We identified some sayings of Jesus in this discourse that may be authentic: verses 26–27, 30–31, and perhaps verse 32, depending on how we understand this verse. In these three passages, it appears Jesus is speaking of someone other than himself, when he speaks of the imminent coming of the Son of Man. We have already seen similar sayings in 8:38 and 9:1. When we put these sayings together, they support a picture of Jesus as an eschatological prophet, who is announcing the imminent arrival of the period of God's reign and of the arrival of the Son of Man, who will usher in the age of God's rule.

Following Jesus' death, some Christians came to believe it was Jesus who would return as the Son of Man in his Second Coming. That belief certainly affected the way in which Jesus' teaching unfolded in the early church. If Jesus did not claim to be Messiah or Son of Man, and if he was *made* Lord and Messiah (Christ) and Son of God only *after* his death by virtue of his resurrection from the dead and exaltation into heaven (Acts 2:36; Rom 1:4), then why did Jesus and his disciples not know this? The Messianic Secret, perhaps a literary feature or creation of the evangelist, offers an explanation. The evangelist and his audience are, of course, convinced Jesus knew he was Messiah and Son of God, but he kept it a secret and periodically ordered silence to those who recognized him. Jesus gradually revealed the secret to his inner circle, his disciples, but they never really understood what Jesus was saying until after his death and exaltation (or resurrection).

If the apocalyptic discourse assumed its final form with the writing of this gospel in about 67 CE, then the evangelist is representing Jesus as Messiah or Messiah designate to his audience, beginning with Jesus' adoption at the time of his baptism by John the Baptist. But Jesus is also for the evangelist and his audience the one who will return as the future Son of Man to usher in the age to come.

The text of the gospel is full of inconsistencies, because the evangelist was apparently juggling different material from his multiple sources in order to paint a coherent picture. He was not entirely successful, and the contradictions within the gospel sometimes provide us with clues that we then have to resolve in order to paint a coherent picture and provide a reasonable, historical reconstruction of what happened, when, where, and why.

If the evangelist was writing in about 67 CE and using a variety of sources, he was attempting to create an account of the good news by using building blocks that were available to him in his written, and perhaps sometimes oral, sources. In this chapter, he was trying to interpret for his audience what was unfolding especially in the chaos in Jerusalem in the late 60s. The evangelist saw in these events the birth pains of the age to come, the end of history, and the inauguration of the period of God's rule. In his mind, the events that were unfolding were signs the end was near and that Jesus would return within the present generation to inaugurate the period of God's rule.

The evangelist's readers, or more accurately his listeners, inasmuch as the gospel was probably read to the Christian community, were urged to be ready and not be caught sleeping when Jesus returns and the end comes.

Chapter 14

THE PASSION NARRATIVE

CHAPTER 14 IS GENERALLY considered the beginning of the Passion Narrative. A written source of this final section of the gospel, perhaps the oldest material written in the form of a continuous story within the Christian community, was apparently known to the evangelist. This story was trying to make sense of the unforeseen events surrounding Jesus' crucifixion and death, an unanticipated challenge that Jesus' followers had to explain and justify.

The evangelist did not simply reproduce this early written source. As he typically did with all of the sources at his disposal, the evangelist adapted the earlier written Passion Narrative to serve this own purpose. He likely made additions to, and perhaps even subtracted from, his written source. The primary purpose of the original Passion Narrative was to address the perplexing unexpected problem of the crucified Messiah by referring to prophecies or proof texts in the Jewish Scriptures.

Most of the material in the Passion Narrative does not conform to the literary forms identified in the main body of this gospel: pronouncement stories, miracle stories, parables, sayings, and legends, although I classify most of the stories in chapters 14–16 as legends. There was, however, in the Jewish Scriptures a story of the death of a prophet that may have served as the prototype of the Passion Narrative—namely the account of the death of the prophet Zechariah in 2 Chr 24:20–22:

> 20 Then the spirit of God took possession of Zechariah son of the priest Jehoiada; he stood above the people and said to them, "Thus says God: Why do you transgress the commandments of the LORD, so that you cannot prosper? Because you have forsaken the LORD, he has also forsaken you." 21 But they conspired against him, and by the command of the king they stoned him to death in the court of the house of the LORD. 22 King

Joash did not remember the kindness that Jehoiada, Zechariah's father, had shown him, but killed his son. As he was dying he said, "May the LORD see and avenge."

Moreover, Greek and Latin biographies of the period and the Jewish apocryphal book 2 Maccabees also showed an interest in the deaths of people of renown, so such stories were not uncommon at the time of the writing of the earliest gospel or its presumed source of the material in these three chapters.

The original Passion Narrative may have evolved as an apologetic element in the liturgy of the early Christian community, when Jesus' followers developed and rehearsed annually a ritual or liturgy of ceremonial events during the week leading up to the church's celebration of Jesus' death and his resurrection at Easter. Not everyone agrees how this may have unfolded, but it is my purpose here to generate discussion, not to impose a particular solution to this important question.

Anticipating what follows, chapter 14 verses 1–52 purport to cover events leading up to the arrest of Jesus; verses 53–65 cover Jesus' trial before the high priest and the council; and verses 66–72 cover Peter's Denial of Jesus.

THE PLOT OF THE PRIESTS AND THE SCRIBES TO KILL JESUS

> 14:1 But after two days it was the Passover and the Feast of Unleavened Bread. And the chief priests and the scribes were looking for a way to arrest him by deceit and kill him.
>
> 2 For they said, "Not during the festival, lest there be an uproar of the people."

These two verses introduce the Passion Narrative. Verse 1 sets the date at two days before the Passover and the Feast of Unleavened Bread. There is, however, disagreement whether the dating is based on historical memory or whether it is simply part of a scheme on the part of the evangelist to set events into a liturgical calendar with everything from 11:1 onwards occurring within a single week. I favor the latter opinion, as I have seen little evidence in this gospel that historical accuracy was a concern of the evangelist. He is a storyteller, not a historian.

Jewish practice at the time was that Passover began in the late afternoon of Nisan 14, when lambs were slaughtered and offered in the Jerusalem temple. There followed a celebratory Passover meal between sunset and midnight, meaning Nisan 15, inasmuch as the Jewish calendar began the new day at sunset. The Feast of Unleavened Bread was celebrated for a week beginning on Nisan 14.

Verse 1 implies the chief priests and scribes had been conspiring for some time about how to arrest Jesus "with subtlety" or "with guile" or "with cunning" and then kill him (see 11:18, which expresses a similar sentiment). It is not clear in verse 2 whether the evangelist thought the priests and the scribes wanted to arrest Jesus before or after the festival. Of course, it is important to understand we are reading a story, not a reliable historical account of an actual meeting at which the chief priests and scribes discussed their plans to arrest Jesus. This unit is likely a construction of the evangelist.

THE ANOINTING OF JESUS AT BETHANY

14:3 And when he was in Bethany in the house of Simon the leper, as he was reclining at the table, a woman came in with an alabaster jar of genuine expensive spikenard oil. She then broke open the alabaster jar and poured the oil on his head.

4 But there were some who were indignant and said to one another, "Why was the oil wasted in this way?

5 For this oil could have been sold for more than three hundred *denarii* and the money given to the poor." And they scolded her.

6 But Jesus said, "Leave her alone. Why do you cause her trouble? She has performed a good deed for me.

7 For you will always have the poor with you, and whenever you want you can show kindness to them; but you will not always have me.

8 She did what she could. She has anointed my body for burial beforehand.

> 9 Truly, I say to you, wherever the good news is proclaimed in the whole world, what she has done will also be told in remembrance of her."

It is difficult to categorize this pericope, this apparent insert of the evangelist into the Passion Narrative. Technically, it is probably a pronouncement story, although it does have legendary elements. Verse 7ab (but not 7c) may be the original pronouncement, and verses 7c–9 later additions of the evangelist.

The opening words of the pericope are curious, because they contain two dependent clauses about Jesus ("when he was in Bethany in the house of Simon the leper" and "as he sat at the table") before the main clause, which has a totally different subject ("a woman came to him"). The structure of the sentence is awkward in both the original Greek and in English. The first dependent clause may be an addition of the evangelist, but it is not possible to know with certainty. The reference to "Simon the leper" is also interesting. He is otherwise unknown in this gospel. Perhaps he was known to the evangelist or to members of his church—once again, pure speculation.

The most important part of the story in its present form is the series of sayings attributed to Jesus. Verse 6 is part of the setting for Jesus' pronouncement in 7ab. Verses 7c, 8, and 9 are likely additions of the evangelist (v. 7c anticipates Jesus' death; v. 8 indicates Jesus' body has been prepared beforehand for burial; and v. 9 says the good news, or the gospel, will be proclaimed throughout the entire world, clearly a reflection of the life situation of the missionary Gentile church, or of the evangelist—not of the historical Jesus).

The unknown woman, who arrives mysteriously, brought an alabaster jar of expensive aromatic oil to anoint Jesus, perhaps for the festival. There is nothing to indicate otherwise until Jesus himself indicates he is being anointed beforehand for his burial. This detail is particularly significant in light of the fact that Jesus was not so anointed following his death according to the evangelist (see 16:1). If Jesus was, in fact, not anointed for burial, perhaps this story was created by the church or the evangelist to ensure that Jesus was properly anointed for burial by the mysterious woman at Bethany.

I would propose that this pronouncement story was known in a more primitive form to the evangelist, who then added it to the Passion Narrative at this critical moment to assure his audience that Jesus was, in fact, properly anointed for burial.

Moreover the proclamation of the news about this woman to the entire world is characteristic of the missionary message of the Gentile-Christian church and not Jesus, who apparently expected the imminent coming of the kingdom of God.

The location of this story immediately before Judas' betrayal is probably intentional, as it illustrates the contrast between the nameless woman's total devotion to Jesus and the outright treachery of a member of Jesus' inner circle of disciples.

JUDAS AGREES TO BETRAY JESUS

> 14:10 And Judas Iscariot, who was one of the twelve, went to the chief priests in order to hand him over to them.
>
> 11 But when they heard it, they were glad and promised to give him money. And he began to look for an opportunity how to hand him over.

The action of Judas Iscariot, one of the Twelve, is represented by the evangelist as pure betrayal.

Verses 10–11 may have directly followed verses 1–2 in the evangelist's source, suggesting the story of the woman with the oil was inserted by the evangelist between these two units. The name Judas Iscariot appears earlier in the list of apostles in 3:13–19, where he is identified as the future betrayer. He is also mentioned in 14:43 in the context of Jesus' arrest. Interestingly, no reason is given for Judas's betrayal. The money is a reward after the fact, not the reason for Judas's treachery.

The historical value of this account seems quite certain. The church would not have ascribed the betrayal to one of Jesus' disciples if this were not the case. However, no motive is given for the betrayal. Judas's motive is pure speculation and has been so for almost 2,000 years, but it may be that he was simply disillusioned with the way in which events were unfolding in Jerusalem. No one seems to have expected this downturn in Jesus' ministry, probably not even Jesus himself.

The passage in Isa 53:6 is part of the Jewish Scriptures that may have informed much of what unfolds in Jesus' final days in Jerusalem and probably implies that Jesus' death was part of God's purpose ("and the LORD has laid on him the iniquity of us all"). The simple reason given for Judas's betrayal is "in order to turn Jesus over to the chief priests." Nothing less and nothing more.

THE PREPARATIONS FOR THE PASSOVER MEAL

14:12 And on the first day of the Unleavened Bread, when they sacrificed the Passover lamb, his disciples said to him, "Where do you want us to go and prepare in order that you may eat the Passover meal?"

13 And he sent out two of his disciples and said to them, "Go into the city, and a man carrying a jar of water will come to you; follow him.

14 And wherever he enters, say to the master of the house, 'The Teacher says, "Where is my guest room, where I may eat the Passover meal with my disciples?"'

15 And he will show you a large upstairs room, furnished and ready; and prepare for us there."

16 And the disciples went out and went into the city and found everything just as he had told them; and they prepared for the Passover meal.

The introductory words of verse 12 imply that the Lord's Supper (vv. 22–25) occurred within the Passover meal on Nisan 15, after sunset on Nisan 14, the day when the Passover lambs were sacrificed in the late afternoon. Verse 17 ("and when evening had come") marks the transition from Nisan 14 to Nisan 15.

The words of this pericope bear a striking resemblance to the description of the events preceding the triumphal entry into Jerusalem (11:1–6):

11:1–6	14:13–16
11:1 and . . . he sent two of his disciples	14:13 and he sent two of his disciples
2 and he said to them, "Go into the village, . . . and . . . you will see . . .	and said to them, "Go into the city, and . . . will come to you
3 say . . . the Lord	14 say . . . the Teacher
4 and they went and found . . .	16 and the disciples went . . . and found
6 just as Jesus said. And	just as he had told them . . . ; and

The similarities almost suggest a doublet. Alternatively we may be dealing with the literary style of the evangelist, who may have composed both stories, which, consequently, may have little historical value. This pericope has other problems as well, not least of which is the contradiction between verses 13 and 16: Jesus sent two of his disciples ahead (v. 13) to prepare for the Passover meal (v. 16); and he then arrives (see v. 17 below) with all Twelve. Also, how does Jesus know about the man with the jar of water or about the house with a large upper room? It appears that both narratives were composed by the evangelist, based perhaps on existing oral tradition.

This pericope is often considered a legend by those who do not assign any historical value to it. It may be a construction of the evangelist. Minimally, it has legendary elements. A factor to consider in this regard is whether verses 13–15 imply Jesus' foreknowledge, or whether an arrangement was made previously with the owner of the house.

THE PROPHECY OF THE BETRAYAL

14:17 And when evening came, he came with the Twelve.

18 And as they reclined in their places and were eating, Jesus said, "Truly, I say to you that one of you who is (sic) eating with me will hand me over."

19 They began to be distressed and to say to him one by one, "Is it I?"

20 But he said to them, "It is one of the Twelve, who is dipping with me in the bowl.

21 For, on the one hand, the Son of Man goes just as it is written concerning him; on the other hand, woe to that man by whom the Son of Man is betrayed! It would be better for him if that man had not been born."

The Prophecy of the Betrayal is an example of a *vaticinium ex eventu*, a prophecy *out of* or *after* the event. It is inconsistent with the preceding story, as Jesus arrives with all Twelve disciples, even though two had been sent ahead (14:13–16) and were presumably already at the house.

The story is probably a construction of the evangelist, who could not imagine that Jesus did not know in advance that Judas would betray him shortly after the meal. The final verse (v. 21) makes sense only to an audience that already equated the Son of Man with the Suffering Servant of Deutero-Isaiah and Dan 7:21. The explanation for Jesus' suffering and death is stated in verse 21: these events occurred in fulfillment of Scripture (i.e., "as it is written"), although the specific Scripture is not identified.

THE INSTITUTION OF THE LORD'S SUPPER

> 14:22 And while they were eating, he took bread, gave thanks and praise, broke it, and gave it to them and said, "Take; this is my body."
>
> 23 And he took a cup, and when he had given thanks he gave it to them, and they all drank from it.
>
> 24 And he said to them, "This is my blood of the covenant, which is poured out for many.
>
> 25 Truly, I say to you, I will surely not drink of the fruit of the vine again until that day when I drink it new in the kingdom of God."

These verses allege to report what is surely a centerpiece in the history of Christianity: the institution of the eucharist. They may be the most scrutinized verses in the two-thousand-year history of Christianity. Yet, there is considerable debate whether this story reflects an historical event in the final days of Jesus' life or is simply an aetiological legend, a story that professes to explain the origin of and the justification for the Christian fellowship meal.

Table fellowship is important in Judaism. Earlier in this gospel, the evangelist tells a story of Jesus eating with tax collectors and sinners (2:16), perhaps an early indication on the part of the evangelist that the eschatological age of forgiveness and deliverance was already arriving during the life and ministry of Jesus. The common meal served as an indication of inclusiveness, friendship, oneness, and peace in Judaism and subsequently in early Christianity.

The earliest account of the Lord's Supper comes not in the earliest gospel, but more than a decade earlier from Paul in 1 Cor 11:23–26:

CHAPTER 14

> 23 For I received from the Lord what I also handed on to you, that the Lord Jesus on the night when he was betrayed took a loaf of bread, 24 and when he had given thanks, he broke it and said, "This is my body that is for you. Do this in remembrance of me." 25 In the same way he took the cup also, after supper, saying, "This cup is the new covenant in my blood. Do this as often as you drink it, in remembrance of me." 26 For as often as you eat this bread and drink the cup, you proclaim the Lord's death until he comes.

Writing to the church at Corinth in ca 54, Paul implies he "received from the Lord" the tradition about the Lord's Supper, which he in turn previously passed on to the Corinthians, presumably during his visit to Corinth in ca 51–52, some twenty years after Jesus' death. The source of the tradition that Paul received is unclear, but he obviously implies its antiquity, genuineness, and reliability.

The blessing of the bread in verse 22 is not so much a blessing as it is an expression of thanksgiving to God for his blessings. The form for this in Judaism was and still is: "Blessed are you, O Lord, our God, King of the universe, who brings bread from the earth."

The pattern of the words "took," "gave thanks," "broke," and "gave" in verse 22 is reminiscent of the miracle stories of the Feeding of the Five Thousand Men (6:30–44) and the Feeding of the Four Thousand (8:1–9) earlier in this gospel. These stories both have obvious eucharistic overtones (6:41 and 8:6).

Our gospel and Paul both agree and disagree in important ways:

1. In both, the Lord's Supper occurred on the night when Jesus was betrayed (14:17–21 and 1 Cor 11:23).

2. In both, Jesus says regarding the bread, "this is my body," although the word order in the original Greek text is slightly different in the two accounts, and Paul has, additionally, "that is for you" (1 Cor 11:24).

3. With respect to the cup, the evangelist says "this is my blood of the covenant, which is poured out for many," whereas Paul says, "this cup is the new covenant in my blood" and adds "do this as often as you drink it in remembrance of me" (1 Cor 11:25).

4. The evangelist ends with the words "Truly I tell you, I will by no means drink of the fruit of the vine until that day when I drink it new in the kingdom of God," whereas Paul ends with the words "For as often as you eat this bread and drink the cup, you proclaim the Lord's death until he comes" (1 Cor 11:26).

The agreement is striking, but so too is the disagreement. Both accounts probably reach back to an early eucharistic tradition in the church, but not necessarily to the time of Jesus.

There is, moreover, an interesting and important grammatical issue in verse 22. The word for "bread" in Greek is *artos* and is masculine in gender, whereas the form used for the word "this" (Greek *touto*) is neuter in gender, so the original Greek does *not* mean that the "bread" *is* the "body" (Greek neuter *soma*). The meaning of the phrase "this is my body" is unclear and is probably not a simple equation "bread = body."

If the story of the institution of the Lord's Supper is of Palestinian and, therefore, of Aramaic origin, it should be noted that there would be no word for "is" in the Aramaic original of verses 22 and 24. In any case, the apostles and, thereafter, Christians were surely not eating the body and drinking the blood of Jesus. Such a thought would be anathema to any Jew. It is perhaps best to understand the word "is" or the missing Aramaic copular verb to mean something like "represents" or "means" or "signifies." Imperfect translations to be sure, but words that indicate the significance of the eucharistic meal to the church, which through the meal participated vicariously in Jesus' sacrificial death. The imagery of participating in Jesus' death mirrors the meaning of the Passover meal in which Jews participate vicariously in the Exodus from Egypt. The fact that the bread symbolizes Jesus' body, which in the eyes of the church has been sacrificed for them, points, moreover, to the likelihood that this language comes from the church and not from the historical Jesus.

There are other elements in the text that betray the likelihood that, at least in its present form, the words of institution are not authentic to Jesus. The reference to the "blood of the covenant" and the words "which is poured out for many" (verse 24) suggest the hand of the church. It was the church that was the new covenant in his blood (see e.g., Heb 8:6–12 in fulfillment of Jer 31:31–34). Moreover, the reference to the redemptive quality of Jesus' blood reflects a teaching of the church, not of the historical Jesus. Furthermore, verse 25 is not only eschatological, but it is also christological in speaking of Jesus in his future glory with God.

There is no suggestion in the text that Jesus is in an any way actually present in the eucharistic elements of bread and wine, an issue that has mistakenly preoccupied the church for centuries. Thomas Aquinas's transubstantiation (the conversion of the "substance" of the eucharstic elements of bread and wine into the body and blood of Christ with only the "appearance" of bread and wine remaining) and Martin Luther's consubstantiation (the bread and wine remain bread and wine, but "in," "with", and "under," they are spiritually the flesh and blood of Jesus) are theological readings into the text of meanings that were certainly not intended by or even comprehensible to the authors of any of the gospels. The words "this is my body," etc. are figurative and symbolic.

The saying in verse 25 is only loosely connected to the story of the institution of the eucharist. It is not clear whether it was drawn from an earlier source or was a creation of the evangelist, but it is clearly an addition to verses 22–24. Verse 25 does, however, reflect Semitic and Jewish origin, inasmuch as the idea of the messianic banquet in the kingdom of God is found in ancient Jewish writings (Isa 25:6; 1 En 62:14; 2 Bar 29:5–8). So too the use of *amen* ("truly") at the beginning of verse 25 suggests a Palestinian tradition and, therefore, the probable antiquity of this verse.

The story of the Last Supper is likely derived from an early Christian liturgy of Palestinian origin and not from memory of an actual event on the eve of Jesus' arrest and trial. As such, these verses served the evangelist as a way of interpreting the meaning of Jesus' death within the context of Jesus' ministry before the events actually unfolded. Most importantly, these verses served the church as an interpretation of its liturgical meal in light of Jesus' suffering and death.

PETER'S DENIAL FORETOLD

14:26 And after they had sung a hymn, they went out to the Mount of Olives.

27 And Jesus said to them, "You will all fall away, for it is written:

'I will strike down the shepherd,

and the sheep will be scattered.'

28 "But after I am raised, I will go ahead of you to Galilee."

29 But Peter said to him, "Even if they all fall away, yet I will not."

30 And Jesus said to him, "Truly, I say to you that today, even this night, before a rooster crows twice, you will deny me three times."

31 But he said more vehemently, "Even if I have to die with you, I will definitely not deny you!" And they all spoke similarly.

This unit is primarily a collection of sayings of Jesus and Peter with a quotation in verse 27 from Zech 13:7b. Verse 28 is possibly an interruption in what otherwise appears to be a dialogue between Jesus and Peter, followed by the agreement of all of Jesus' disciples.

This pericope purports to report a conversation following the Lord's Supper, when Jesus and his disciples were walking to the Mount of Olives. Both the original Hebrew and the Septuagint Greek translation of Zechariah have the imperative form of the verb "strike down" or "smite" (i.e., smite or strike down the shepherd). The change to the future tense is obviously due to subsequent Christian retrospection in either the evangelist's written source or in a collection of *testimonia* (early Christian proof texts). There is no reason to assume Jesus actually anticipated his disciples' abandonment.

The saying from Zechariah reflects the hand of the church and may be a simple reflection backward in time to explain the passion of Jesus and the defection of his disciples. It is evident that in this quotation from Zechariah the evangelist understood Jesus' death as the will of God: "I [God] will strike down the shepherd [Jesus], and the sheep (the disciples) will be scattered." The message is clear for those followers of Jesus who could not make sense of Jesus' humiliating death: Jesus was a willing subject in God's plan, as predicted in the Jewish Scriptures.

Verse 28, the perceived intrusion into the text, is the evangelist's fourth reference to Jesus' resurrection (see 8:31; 9:9; and 10:34 above; a fifth reference to the resurrection follows in 16:6–7). Verse 28 may have been introduced into the story by the evangelist in anticipation of 16:7 ("But go, tell his disciples and Peter that he is going ahead of you to Galilee; there you will see him, just as he told you"). There is some disagreement regarding the meaning of Jesus' words in verse 28. Is he referring to resurrection appearances in Galilee, or to what Christians came to believe would be Jesus' second coming as the Son of Man? I am inclined to agree with the former position. It is likely that some or all of Jesus' disciples returned to Galilee after his crucifixion and death and that it was there in Galilee that Peter and then others had experiences (perhaps dreams) that Jesus had been raised from the dead and was in some way still with them. Perhaps the evangelist had no record—written or oral—about such experiences or visions, so the evangelist's story ends with the resurrection in 16:8, but with no report of resurrection appearances. The references in verses 14:28 and 16:6–7 about Jesus going to Galilee ahead of his disciples may simply allude to unspecified resurrection appearances in Galilee, details of which were unfamiliar to the evangelist and his audience.

This pericope may be a construction of the evangelist or his written source, composed to anticipate events that were to follow in the Passion Narrative: the shepherd who will be struck down, the denial of Peter and the other disciples, Jesus' death and vindication through his resurrection and appearances in Galilee.

Likewise in this pericope, there is focus on Jesus' disciples, who will deny Jesus and be scattered. Most especially, in this regard, there is Peter, who professes his willingness to die rather than fall away from Jesus. Clearly, Peter does not understand the situation that is about to unfold and how difficult the test will be. Earlier in this gospel, Jesus' disciples James and John affirmed that they could endure anything that Jesus had to suffer (10:38–39a). They too were wrong.

It appears the evangelist's theme of the Messianic Secret and the disciples' ongoing misunderstanding of Jesus' messiahship is about to be tested.

JESUS AND THE DISCIPLES IN GETHSEMANE

14:32 And they went to a place called Gethsemane. And he said to his disciples, "Sit here while I pray."

33 And he took Peter and James and John with him, and he began to be distressed and to be apprehensive.

34 And he said to them, "My soul is exceedingly sorrowful, even to the point of death. Stay here and keep awake."

35 And he went a little farther and fell on the ground and prayed that, if it was possible, the hour might pass away from him.

36 And he said, "Abba, Father! All things are possible for you. Take this cup away from me. But not what I want, but what you want."

37 And he went and found them sleeping, and he said to Peter, "Simon, are you asleep? Were you unable to stay awake for one hour?

38 Stay awake and pray that you will not be tested. On the one hand, the spirit is willing; on the other hand, the flesh is weak."

39 And again he went away and prayed, speaking the same words.

40 And he returned again and found them sleeping, for their eyes were becoming very heavy; and they did not know how to answer him.

41 And he went the third time and said to them, "Are you still asleep and resting? It is enough! The hour has come; behold, the Son of Man is being betrayed into the hands of the sinners.

42 Get up, let us go. Behold, my betrayer has drawn near."

The pericope of Jesus and the Disciples in Gethsemane is possibly based on an early written source and may have some claim to historicity. However, in its present form it should be classified as a legend. Jesus shows real emotion for the first time anywhere in this gospel. He reflects a degree of humanity quite different from that of the miracle worker of previous chapters. Admitting the likelihood that this story may be quite old does not, however, mean that it is accurate in its detail. The most likely witnesses to the "events" in this story are, after all, described as being asleep most of the time.

Gethsemane, which means "oil press" in Hebrew and Aramaic, was likely an olive farm east of the Kidron Valley on the slope of the Mount of Olives, where olives were grown and then pressed into oil. The evangelist maintains that it was here that Jesus showed significant passion about what was unfolding and asked his disciples to stay awake and keep watch, while he prayed.

The narrative unfolds in eight steps:

1. Jesus arrived at Gethsemane with his disciples and asked them to sit down while he went to pray (v. 32). Verse 32 appears to be redactional work typical of the evangelist.

2. Jesus took Peter, James, and John to another area, where he displayed emotional distress and agitation with what was unfolding (vv. 33–34). The decision to take Peter, James, and John with him may also be an addition by the evangelist (see 5:37; 9:2; 13:3) to a written source to which he had access.

3. Jesus left Peter, James, and John and went to another place to pray alone. There, Jesus fell on the ground and asked God to deliver him

from what was about to unfold. His words of distress in verse 34a are reminiscent of Pss 42:6, 11a and 43:5, suggesting the clear hand of the church in the composition of this story. There Jesus prayed alone for deliverance but then corrected himself by saying to God, "Not what I want, but what you want" (vv. 35–36).

4. Jesus went back to Peter, James, and John, found them asleep, and addressed Peter alone, asking him why he did not stay awake and keep watch for the hour that Jesus was away praying alone (v. 37). Jesus even implies that Peter and the other disciples are being tested (v. 37). He urges them to stay awake and not fail the test (v. 38).

5. Jesus then went away again and prayed alone just as he had before (v. 39).

6. Jesus came back to Peter, James, and John and again found them asleep (v. 40).

7. Jesus apparently then went away once again to pray (implied but not mentioned specifically in the text).

8. Jesus returned for a third time and found Peter, James, and John asleep once again. Jesus basically tells them that enough is enough and that the Son of Man is about to be betrayed into the hands of sinners (v. 41). In fact, the betrayer is approaching: "Get up, and let's go" (v. 42).

The use of "Abba," Aramaic for "Father," followed by the Greek word *pater* (Father) in verse 36 may suggest use by a bilingual community that spoke the Aramaic and Greek words in tandem, possibly in liturgy—perhaps one more bit of evidence to suggest Antioch of Syria as the gospel's place of composition.

"The hour has come" in verse 41 is probably eschatological in its meaning and not simply the time for Jesus' betrayal, capture, and arrest. Jesus is about to be delivered into the hands of sinful men. But strengthened by prayer, he is now ready to accept God's plan of suffering and death. "Behold, the Son of Man is being betrayed into the hands of the sinners." The obvious reference in verse 41b to the *suffering* Son of Man clearly reflects the post-resurrection belief of the church and not the teaching of the historical Jesus.

The story in Gethsemane represents in this gospel Jesus' total submission to God's will in the form of his sacrificial love for humankind. Although most of the details in this pericope are probably not historical, there may be historic memory that it was in Gethsemane that Jesus was betrayed and arrested.

THE BETRAYAL AND ARREST OF JESUS

14:43 And immediately, while he was still speaking, Judas, one of the Twelve, arrived, and with him a crowd with swords and clubs, from the chief priests and the scribes and the elders.

44 But the one betraying him had given them a signal, saying, "Whomever I kiss, he is the one; seize him and get him away securely."

45 And as soon as he had come, he immediately went to him and said, "Rabbi!" and he kissed him enthusiastically.

46 But they laid their hands on him and seized him.

— — —

14:47 But one of those who stood by drew his sword and struck the slave of the high priest, and cut off his ear.

— — —

14:48 And Jesus answered and said to them, "Have you come out, as against a robber, with swords and clubs to arrest me?

49 Daily I was with you in the temple precinct teaching, and you did not seize me. But in order that the Scriptures may be fulfilled."

50 And they all left him and fled.

The hand of the evangelist is evident in the opening words: "And immediately" (Greek *kai euthus*) and the participial clause "while he was still speaking," which connects this pericope to the preceding Gethsemane story. The Greek in verse 43 is awkward, and I have tried to preserve that awkwardness in my translation.

The arrival of Judas is curious, because there is no indication that Judas was not already with Jesus in Gethsemane. It appears from the text that

Judas arrived from the chief priests, the scribes, and the elders, along with a crowd gathered by the Jewish authorities. It is not at all clear from the text that any Jewish authorities were present for Jesus' arrest. The ambiguous "them" and "they" in verses 44, 46, and 48 and "one of those who stood by" in verse 47 provide no clue as to who was actually involved in these events. They reflect a common literary device of the anonymous author.

Verse 47 implies it was one of the bystanders, not one of Jesus' disciples, who cut off the ear of the high priest's slave. Jesus seems to ignore this event, and we find him instead saying in verses 48–49 not that he objects to his arrest but that he objects to the force involved in his arrest—as if he were merely a common criminal. Jesus asks, "Why didn't you just arrest me in the temple precinct, when I was there every day teaching?" Even more curious is Jesus' introduction in verse 49b of "But in order that the Scriptures may be fulfilled," when it is not at all clear what Scriptures the church or the evangelist had in mind. This ambiguity is reminiscent of what Paul wrote to the church at Corinth in 1 Cor 15:3–4:

> For I handed on to you as of first importance what I in turn had received: that Christ died for our sins *in accordance with the Scriptures*, and that he was buried, and that he was raised on the third day *in accordance with the Scriptures*.

It may be that verse 49b comes from an early period in the church when there was an allusion to generic Scriptures, before the church undertook the laborious task of identifying specific scriptural passages of the sort that we find in the Gospel of Matthew and in the Acts of the Apostles, both of which are later writings. It is not clear that the evangelist had particular Scriptures in mind (such as Isa 53:12, which is cited in Luke 22:37, but in a totally different context). Both verse 49b and Paul's comment in 1 Cor 15 imply that events in Jesus' life occurred in accordance with the generic *Scriptures* (plural), confirming that God was active in these events in Jesus' life. It was all part of a divine plan. It was probably a later generation that actually undertook the identification of specific relevant scriptural proof texts to argue the case more convincingly.

The fact that Jesus says in verse 49a that he was with them daily teaching in the temple precinct seems to imply the authorities had plenty of time to arrest him if the disruptive cleansing of the temple (11:15–19) was the primary reason for Jesus' arrest. In fact, the reason for Jesus' arrest is not entirely clear, except that he apparently posed some sort of threat to the Jewish authorities in Jerusalem.

Some have argued that the original pericope ended with verse 46 and that verses 47–50 are only loosely connected to the pericope. It is not always easy to separate the evangelist's source(s) from the evangelist's editorial material.

The meaning of the "all" who fled in verse 50 is also unclear. Was it the mob who descended on Jesus who then fled, or was it Jesus' disciples? Probably the latter.

THE FLIGHT OF THE NAKED YOUNG MAN

> 14:51 And a certain young man was following him, having a linen cloth thrown on his naked body. And they seized him,

> 52 But he left the linen cloth behind and ran away naked.

These two verses are particularly puzzling. Who was this otherwise nameless young man? Was he following Jesus after his arrest and after the disciples had already fled in fear? The story appears to serve no particular purpose, which may suggest the reliability of this rather minor detail following Jesus' arrest.

The young man is obviously unknown to the evangelist's audience. He appears to have arrived on the scene late and was dressed only in a linen cloth over his otherwise naked body. The mob that arrested Jesus seizes the young man, but he is able to run away naked, thereby escaping arrest. It is not clear why the mob wanted to seize him, inasmuch as Jesus' chief accomplices, his disciples, had apparently already fled.

These two verses are generally considered a legend or a construction of the evangelist. However, it is not clear whether they were drawn from an old tradition or were a creation of the evangelist. Whatever the source of this story, its significance and purpose remain a mystery.

JESUS' TRIAL BEFORE THE HIGH PRIEST AND THE COUNCIL

> 14:53 And they led Jesus away to the high priest; and all the chief priests and the elders and the scribes assembled.

CHAPTER 14

— — —

14:54 And Peter followed him from a distance, right into the high priest's courtyard. And he was sitting with the attendants and was warming himself at the fire.

— — —

14:55 But the chief priests and the entire council were looking for testimony against Jesus in order to put him to death; and they found none.

56 For many gave false testimony against him, and their testimonies were not consistent.

57 And some stood up and gave false testimony against him, saying,

58 "We heard him say, 'I will destroy this temple that is made with hands, and in three days I will build another which is not made with hands.'"

59 And not even then was their testimony consistent.

60 And the high priest stood up in the center and asked Jesus, saying, "Have you nothing to say with regard to what they are testifying against you?"

61 But he remained silent and did not answer anything. Again the high priest asked and said to him, "Are you the Messiah, the Son of the Blessed One?"

62 And Jesus said, "I am. And you will see the Son of Man sitting at the right hand of the Power and coming with the clouds of heaven."

63 But the high priest tore his clothes and said, "What further need do we have of witnesses?

> 64 You heard the blasphemy! How does it appear to you?" But they all condemned him to be deserving of death.
>
> 65 And some began to spit on him and to blindfold him and to strike him and to say to him, "Prophesy!" And the attendants struck him with the palms of their hands.

It was clearly the intention of the evangelist's written source was to show that the execution of Jesus was a miscarriage of justice by both Jews and Romans. This pericope is particularly interesting, because it reports the first of several trials that place blame for Jesus' death on either Jewish or Roman authorities. Jewish authorities of the time probably did not have the authority to execute (by stoning) someone who violated Jewish law. Crucifixion was a Roman form of execution for a capital offense, generally for someone who conspired against Roman rule by sedition or revolt. Such a punishment could be carried out only by an appropriate Roman imperial authority. In the case of Jesus, that would be Pontius Pilate, the procurator of the Roman province of Judea from 26–36 CE. If Pontius Pilate was ultimately responsible for Jesus' execution as an enemy of Rome, then it is incumbent upon us to try to understand the specific charges that led to his crucifixion. Are there clues in this gospel to enable us to understand why Jesus was crucified?

This pericope may provide some indication regarding the formal charges against Jesus. There is nothing that we have confronted thus far in this gospel to suggest that Jesus was a political revolutionary who questioned the authority of Roman rule in Palestine. In fact, we are reminded of Jesus' pronouncement "Render to Caesar what belongs to Caesar and to God what belongs to God" (12:17). If Jesus was not a political threat to Roman rule, then it is unclear whether the charges against him were legitimate or falsified. Alternatively, did the evangelist completely falsify the portrait of Jesus throughout the gospel in order to eliminate the anti-Roman political revolutionary that Jesus, in fact, was? As unlikely as that is, we should at least keep that possibility in mind as we examine the texts that allegedly deal with Jesus' multiple trials.

The high priest to whose house Jesus was presumably taken was Caiaphas, who served as high priest 18–36 CE, although Caiaphas is not mentioned by name in the story. The text suggests all of the chief priests, elders, and scribes assembled on short notice. Or perhaps they had already assembled at Caiaphas's home in anticipation of a prearranged plan that Jesus would be taken to them by the mob that likely included members of the temple police.

The arrival of Peter into the high priest's courtyard (v. 54) seems improbable and is likely inserted between verses 53 and 55 in order to prepare for Peter's denial of Jesus (vv. 66–72), the story immediately following the account of Jesus' trial. Verse 54 actually introduces the story of Peter's denial of Jesus, which begins in verse 66, suggesting that the evangelist deliberately inserted the account of Jesus' trial (vv. 55–65) within the literary unit of verses 54 and 66–72. This technique of inserting one story within another (interspersion or intercalation) appears elsewhere in this gospel: in 5:21–42, the miracle stories of the Woman Healed of the Flow of Blood and of the Girl Restored to Life; and in 11:12–25, the Cursing of the Fig Tree and the Cleansing of the Temple. The insertion of the story of Jesus' trial within the story of Peter's denial may be a literary device to imply that the two events occurred simultaneously and to enable the audience to contrast the behavior of the two stories' principal characters: Jesus and Peter.

Verse 53 follows naturally upon Jesus' arrest in verse 46, confirming the likelihood that verses 47, 48–50, and 51–52 were added by the evangelist and that the story of Jesus' trial (14:53, 55–65) immediately followed the story of the betrayal and arrest (14:43–46) in the evangelist's written source.

Verse 55 marks the actual beginning of Jesus' trial. The assembled group represents a meeting of the Jewish court, the Sanhedrin, headed by the high priest and composed of heads of priestly families (the chief priests), scribes, and lay elders for a total of seventy-one members. Jewish law prohibited meetings of the Sanhedrin at night in criminal cases, so the details of the story are questionable. The purpose of the meeting is stated clearly at the beginning of the trial in verse 55: namely, to collect evidence that would result in putting Jesus to death. It is interesting that the intended verdict is stated at the outset. The Sanhedrin was clearly looking for evidence to put Jesus to death, but the witnesses' evidence was contradictory, and two witnesses were required to convict (Deut 19:15). The testimony that was eventually provided was that Jesus will destroy the temple and rebuild it in three days (v. 58).

Verses 57–59 may be little more than the evangelist's commentary on verse 56. Verse 58 is curious, especially in the mouths of Jesus' accusers: Jesus intended to destroy the temple and rebuild it in three days. The allusion to Jesus' death and resurrection is eminently clear, so it is unlikely that Jesus said anything like this. Or, if the words in verse 58 are taken literally (Jesus could destroy and rebuild the temple), this was clearly a grave offense to the Jewish leaders. Jesus does not reply to the accusations (vv. 60–61a). His silence may reflect the influence of Isa 53:7 and hence point to the hand of the church in composing this story:

> He was oppressed, and he was afflicted,
> > he did not open his mouth;
> like a lamb that is lead to the slaughter,
> > and like a sheep that before its shearers is silent,
> so he did not open his mouth.

Yet even then (v. 59), the testimony of those who heard Jesus did not agree, and Jesus remained silent (vv. 60–61a). The material in this part of the story is reminiscent of passages from Psalms, which the evangelist's source may have had in mind in composing this pericope:

> Ps 27:12: Do not give me up to the will of my adversaries,
> > for false witnesses have risen against me,
> > and they are breathing out violence.
> Ps 35:11: Malicious witnesses rise up;
> > they ask me about things I do not know.
> Ps 38:14: Truly, I am like one who does not hear,
> > and in whose mouth is no retort.

The events of Jesus' trial before the Jewish authorities are laid out in the gospel as being in fulfillment of the Jewish Scriptures.

In verse 61b, the high priest asks Jesus directly, "Are you the Messiah, the Son of the Blessed One?" Jesus now speaks without delay, "I am" (Greek *ego eimi*), an expression of divine self-revelation in the Jewish Scriptures (see Ex 3:13–14 and Isa 43:10). Is Jesus simply replying in the affirmative to Caiaphas's question, or is he saying something more about himself? I suspect that the hand of the church is evident in Jesus' statement, inasmuch as he is now disclosing to the high priest and the council what had heretofore been a secret—his messiahship, his divine nature in the most exalted language imaginable: Jesus is the (adopted) Son of God, a claim reminiscent of the baptism story (1:11: "You are my Son, the beloved; in you I take delight"). The evangelist is likely reading deep meaning into Jesus' claim. Some manuscripts of our gospel read in verse 62a: "You said that I am," thereby putting the words into the mouth of the high priest, not Jesus—possibly the original reading of this passage.

Jesus continues his answer to the high priest: "You will see the Son of Man seated at the right hand of Power and coming with the clouds of heaven," a conflation of Ps 110:1 and Dan 7:13. The high priest tears his clothes and asks the council what further need they have of witnesses. The words of Daniel announcing the arrival of the eschatological Son of Man conform to teaching of the historical Jesus, but clearly not in the context of this story.

The response of the high priest and the others is to seek the death sentence for Jesus, even though the actual charges against him are not clear. That is not surprising. Even if there had been a trial before the council, who would have provided a record of the events to the church? None of Jesus' disciples was present at the trial. The story in its current form is a legend, a likely construct of the early church, an account based on imaginative early tradition, perhaps already in written form in a Passion Narrative available to the evangelist.

The reference in verse 63 that "the high priest tore his clothes" was a ritual response to Jesus' blasphemy. Although a claim to messiahship was not considered blasphemy, speaking the divine name was. Was Jesus' uttering of "I am" in Aramaic or Hebrew understood by the evangelist and his audience as a reference to the divine name? That too is not entirely clear. In any event, in the story the high priest asks the others if they agree that Jesus deserves the death sentence to which they assent although they had no authority to carry out such a sentence. Neither could the council under Jewish law recommend a punishment for a criminal offense at a meeting held at night. The evangelist may be unfamiliar with such important details. In any event, it is clear that Jesus did something or said something that provoked the leaders of the Jewish establishment to turn him over to the Roman authorities on a drummed-up allegation of rebellion against Rome.

The spitting, blindfolding, and beating in verse 65 seem an improbable response by members of the council and may be an addition inspired by a passage like Isa 53:3–5:

> 3 He was despised and rejected by others;
>> a man of suffering and acquainted with infirmity;
> and as one from whom others hide their faces
>> he was despised, and we held him of no account.
> 4 Surely he has borne our infirmities
>> and carried our diseases;
> yet we accounted him stricken,
>> struck down by God and afflicted.
> 5 But he was wounded for our transgressions,
>> crushed for our iniquities,
> upon him was the punishment that made us whole,
>> and by his bruises we are healed.

Although the evangelist's account of Jesus' Trial Before the High Priest and the Council is probably not historically credible, it likely reflects the authority of the high priest to assign to Jesus the charge of blasphemy, an insult to God, and, therefore, to request Jesus' death. The words that the evangelist assigns to Jesus in verse 62 indicate that Jesus claimed to be Messiah, and perhaps even more than Messiah. They also indicate that Jesus would be exalted to God's right hand, a position of the highest honor. Moreover, Jesus' prediction of his second coming as the eschatological Son of Man will subsequently serve for members of the council as proof of Jesus' messiahship, his power, and his glory. Total blasphemy! The evangelist apparently believed that the penalty for blasphemy was death, and that the Sanhedrin had this power, if only through misrepresentation of the charge to the Romans.

It should be remembered that the evangelist's audience already knew that Jesus had been crucified and believed that Jesus had been raised from the dead and exalted to God's right hand, and that he would return sometime soon as the eschatological Son of Man. In this story, Jesus is prophesying about himself *ex eventu* (*out of* or *after* the event), with the advantage of the church's and the evangelist's hindsight about what had already transpired. The evangelist represents Jesus as knowing in advance at his trial what members of the church already knew and believed.

Acknowledging these details means that the evangelist is not reporting accurately what unfolded at Jesus' trial. The evangelist and probably his written source represent Jesus as knowing in advance the details of what is about to unfold in Jesus' death and beyond.

PETER'S DENIAL OF JESUS

14:66 And when Peter was below in the courtyard, one of the high priest's female servants came.

67 And when she saw Peter warming himself, she looked at him attentively and said, "You too were with the Nazarene, this Jesus."

68 But he denied it, saying, "I neither know nor understand what you are saying." And he went out into the entrance hall, and a rooster crowed.

69 And the same female servant saw him and began again to say to those who stood by, "This man is one of them."

70 But he denied it again. And a little later those who stood by again said to Peter, "You certainly are one of them, for you are a Galilean."

71 But he began to invoke a curse on himself and to swear, "I do not know this man about whom you are talking!"

72 And immediately a rooster crowed a second time. And Peter remembered the statement Jesus said to him, "Before a rooster crows twice, you will deny me three times." And when he thought about it, he wept.

We have already seen that verse 54 was probably an original part of this story, which in this form is a legend. The Greek word *paidiske* (vv. 66 and 69) probably means a female slave. The tone of her words to Peter is almost scornful: "You too were there with the Nazarene, this Jesus" (v. 67). Peter's reply is his first denial: "I neither know nor understand what you are saying" (v. 68). And a cock crowed in fulfillment of Jesus' prediction in 14:30. The female servant confronts Peter again: "This man is one of them" (v. 69), and Peter denies it again (v. 70). A bystander identifies Peter as a Galilean (v. 70), and this time Peter swears, as if God is his witness, that he does not know Jesus (v. 71). A cock crows a second time, and Peter remembers what Jesus told him (v. 72). Peter wept, the last we hear about Peter and the disciples in the gospel until the notice given to the women at Jesus' empty tomb in 16:7.

It is difficult to imagine that this story is pure fantasy, as it casts a dark shadow on the most important of Jesus' disciples, who is guilty of denying he even knew Jesus. Perhaps even more important, however, is the importance of this story for members of the evangelist's church, who were sometimes tempted to abandon their newfound faith in the risen Lord. Even Peter doubted or denied Jesus and was restored, so members of the community should be forgiving of those who may also have lapsed. In short, the story forewarns the Christian community of the challenges and dangers of backsliding, disloyalty, or desertion.

CONCLUSIONS AFTER CHAPTER 14

The anonymous evangelist likely had access to a written Passion Narrative for material in the final chapters of the earliest gospel. This source was probably built not primarily on historical memory, but rather on some memory but primarily on proof texts from Jewish Scriptures. The literary form of the original Passion Narrative to which the evangelist had access may have been inspired by an interest in the deaths of famous people of the period in Greek, Latin, and Jewish literature and also by the story of the death of the prophet Zechariah in 2 Chronicles.

Chapter 14 begins with the Plot of the Priests and the Scribes to Kill Jesus (14:1–2), something they are represented as having been contemplating for some time. These verses may be the invention of the evangelist, or more likely of his written source, an early version of the Passion Narrative.

There follows the Anointing at Bethany (14:3–9), perhaps originally a pronouncement story. The evangelist likely inserted this story within the Passion Narrative because of the allusion to Jesus' death and burial. In its present form this story has characteristics of the missionary message of the Gentile-Christian church and likely has no historical value.

Judas Agrees to Betray Jesus (14:10–11) may have followed directly on the story of the plot in verses 1–2. That Judas betrayed Jesus seems likely, but no motive is given for the betrayal. The offer of money did not precede but followed Judas's offer of betrayal to the chief priests. My best guess is that Judas (and probably other disciples and even Jesus himself) did not expect this drastic downturn in Jesus' ministry in Jerusalem and that Judas's disillusionment with Jesus then turned into betrayal.

The story of the Preparations for the Passover Meal (14:12–16) follows. It contains some inconsistencies and is probably a composition of the evangelist, inserted here in the narrative to provide a proper setting for the celebration of the Lord's Supper.

But first there is the Prophecy of Judas's Betrayal (14:17–21), which is set in the context of the final meal. Once again this story is likely a *vaticinium ex eventu*, a prophecy *out of* or *after* the event, a composition of the evangelist, who could not imagine that Jesus did not know in advance what was about to happen to him almost immediately following the meal.

The Institution of the Last Supper (14:22–25), the verses that are perhaps most written about in the two-thousand-year history of Christianity, is also probably not a reliable record of an historical event. It is more likely drawn from an early Christian liturgy of Palestinian origin. The story in its present form served the evangelist as a way of interpreting the meaning of Jesus' death within the context of his final days before the dreadful events unfolded. It is, however, not clear whether the story of the Institution of the Lord's Supper was already in the evangelist's written source or whether it was added to the Passion Narrative by the evangelist. The fact that Paul already attributed the Institution of the Last Supper to Jesus on the night that he was betrayed suggests this story was probably already in the version of the Passion Narrative available to the evangelist. I still maintain, however, that it is probably not an historical account of an actual event presided over by Jesus.

Peter's Denial Foretold (14:26–31) is still one more example of *vaticinium ex eventu*, a prophecy *out of* or *after* the event. In fact, Jesus predicts in this story that all of his disciples will "fall away," not simply Peter.

The story Jesus Prays in Gethsemane (14:32–42) may have as its single historical component the fact that it was in Gethsemane that Jesus was arrested. The details of the story are quite elaborate, yet all of the possible witnesses to the events are represented in the story as being asleep most of the time. The principal purpose of the story appears to be to serve as the setting (v. 36) for Jesus to submit totally to the events that are about to unfold inasmuch as they are the will of God. Although Jesus may have begun to understand by now what was unfolding, this story is probably a poetic recreation of Jesus' emotion in accepting what was already happening. The story of Gethsemane represents Jesus' total submission to God's will in the form of his forthcoming sacrificial death—far more than Jesus could have understood at this time. The story presupposes the church's belief in Jesus' salvific death and resurrection.

The Betrayal and Arrest of Jesus (14:43–50) is likely grounded in an actual event. It appears Judas probably did lead a mob of people, commissioned by the Jewish authorities, to Jesus in Gethsemane, because he knew where Jesus and the disciples would be that evening. The details of the story are likely not historical, especially the cutting off the ear of the high priest's slave (v. 47). It is reported in this story that the arrest was the occasion for the desertion of Jesus' disciples, perhaps a reliable detail.

The Flight of the Naked Young Man (14:51–52) is a total enigma. Whether it reflects an actual event or is a composition of the evangelist is unclear. The story seems to serve no historical or theological purpose.

Jesus' Trial Before the High Priest and the Council (14:53, 55–65) is a creative account of the first of Jesus' trials, this one before the Jewish authorities, the Sanhedrin. Although there likely was such a trial after Jesus' arrest in Gethsemane, the details of this story are probably a construction of the church. Although the high priest likely had the authority to charge Jesus with blasphemy, it is certainly not clear what the basis of such a charge might have been. This story was probably available to the evangelist in written form in the Passion Narrative to which he had access.

Peter's Denial of Jesus (14:54, 66–72) may also have some basis in fact, if we set aside the predictive element of the crowing of the rooster. Jesus' disciples had apparently already fled at the time of Jesus' arrest in Gethsemane. Perhaps Peter, the disciple who was closest to Jesus, went to the house of the high priest to see what would unfold.

I find it likely that there was a relatively early written Passion Narrative, probably created for liturgical purposes within the early church, perhaps in Palestine. The evangelist had access to that narrative, but he likely reworked it and added to it to suit his purpose in retelling the story of the events that led to Jesus' death.

Chapter 15

JESUS' TRIAL BEFORE PONTIUS PILATE

15:1 And immediately, early in the morning, the chief priests held a consultation with the elders and scribes and the entire council, bound Jesus, led him away, and delivered him over to Pilate.

2 And Pilate questioned him, "Are you the King of the Jews?" He answered and said to him, "You say so."

3 And the chief priests accused him of many things.

4 But Pilate again questioned him, saying, "Have you no answer? See how many accusations they bring against you."

5 But Jesus still answered nothing, so that Pilate marveled.

6 But at each festival he was accustomed to release to them a prisoner, whomever they requested.

7 But there was one named Barabbas, who was chained with the rebels, who had committed murder in the rebellion.

8 And the crowd went up and began to ask him to do just as he had always done for them.

9 But Pilate answered them, saying, "Do you want me to release to you the king of the Jews?"

10 For he knew that the chief priests had handed him over because of envy.

> 11 But the chief priests incited the crowd, so that he would instead release Barabbas to them.
>
> 12 But Pilate again answered and said to them, "What then do you want me to do with the king of the Jews?"
>
> 13 But they again cried out, "Crucify him!"
>
> 14 But Pilate said to them, "Why, what evil has he done?" But they cried out all the more, "Crucify him!"
>
> 15 But Pilate, wanting to pacify the crowd, released Barabbas to them; and he delivered Jesus, after he had whipped him, so that he might be crucified.

JESUS' TRIAL BEFORE PONTIUS Pilate shares an interesting feature with Jesus' Trial Before the High Priest and the Council (14:53, 55–65) and Peter's Denial of Jesus (14:54, 66–72): all three passages contain three questions (or charges). We likely witness in these three passages the evangelist's use of the written version of the Passion Narrative he used as a source as well as his own literary style, as he shaped the narrative to serve his own purposes.

It is difficult, if not impossible to know whether the story of Jesus' trial before Pontius Pilate reflects something that actually happened or whether it is fantasy. More specifically, we know of no external source that acknowledges the practice of forgiving a Jewish prisoner on the occasion of the Passover festival. Neither do we know anything about Barabbas (whose Aramaic name means "son of the father"). What is clear is there must have been some sort of trial before Pilate, because only he could order a crucifixion, not the Jewish authorities and certainly not the crowd. As the story of Jesus' passion circulated, probably first orally and then in written form, individual stories likely circulated and eventually attached themselves to the narrative, making our work of separating fact from fiction and the evangelist's written source from the final gospel narrative particularly difficult.

It appears in verse 1 that this passage marks the end of the meeting of the Sanhedrin the night before. Or perhaps there was a second meeting of the council to confirm in the daytime the capital decision reached the night before: namely, that Jesus should be executed. The high priest apparently ordered that Jesus be delivered to Pilate, the Roman procurator of Judea from 26–36 CE. We do not know what charges the high priest passed on to Pilate, but they must have been something like insurrection, a drummed-up charge for what was more likely Jesus' challenge of the Jewish authorities in the confrontational incident in the temple precinct following his arrival in Jerusalem.

The evangelist portrays Pilate as being prepared to release Jesus, likely because the evangelist wanted the principal blame for Jesus' crucifixion to be placed, for political reasons, not on the Romans, but squarely on the Jewish authorities in Jerusalem. The implication of the text is that Pilate did not regard the charges of the council to be legitimate, but that he succumbed to pressure from the Jewish authorities and from the mob that was obviously sympathetic to the Jewish authorities.

Pilate's question to Jesus "Are you the king of the Jews?" implies that Jesus had claimed the role of the political Messiah before the Sanhedrin, a claim that might sound to the Romans like a subversive crime of political rebellion or subversion. The exchange of words between Jesus and Pilate in the text is obviously a construct, as no one was there to record this exchange.

The incident regarding Barabbas (vv. 6–15) may be part of the original legend, or it may be an insertion by the evangelist, to contrast the true insurrectionist Barabbas with Jesus, who was not a political criminal despite the claims of the high priest and the Sanhedrin.

It is likely that the evangelist's written source already interpreted the Suffering Servant of Deutero-Isaiah in messianic terms because it was believed relatively early in the history of the church that these scriptural passages provided a meaningful explanation of the final days in Jesus' life.

THE MOCKERY BY THE SOLDIERS

> 15:16 But the soldiers led him away into the courtyard, that is, the praetorium (the provincial governor Pilate's official headquarters), and they called together the whole cohort.
>
> 17 And they clothed him in a purple robe and placed a twisted crown of thorns on him.
>
> 18 And they began to salute him, "Hail, king of the Jews!"
>
> 19 And they struck his head with a reed and spat on him and fell to their knees in homage to him.

> 20 And when they had mocked him, they took the purple robe off of him and put his clothes on him. And they led him out to crucify him.

Although it is possible that soldiers mocked Jesus based on the apparently false charge by the Jewish authorities that he had claimed to be king of the Jews, the story of the Mockery by the Soldiers has little purpose except to serve as a link between the Trial Before Pontius Pilate (15:1–15) and the Crucifixion of Jesus (15:21–32). It may be a legend or an addition to the Passion Narrative by the evangelist. The story expresses the thoughtless cruelty of the Roman soldiers, a cohort of which would number between 500 and 600 soldiers, obviously an exaggeration.

The crown of thorns (v. 17) mockingly suggests Jesus' royal dignity, as does the soldiers' saluting Jesus as king of the Jews (v. 18) and kneeling before him in homage (v. 19). The striking of Jesus on the head and spitting on him (v. 19) are reminiscent of Isa 50:6:

> I gave my back to those who struck me,
> > and my cheek to those who pulled out the beard;
> I did not hide my face from insult and spitting.

This unit ends with the soldiers' removing the purple robe and dressing Jesus once again in his own clothes (v. 20), so that they might now crucify him. There is, of course, irony in this story, inasmuch as the evangelist's audience obviously already understood what the Roman soldiers did not understand: namely, that Jesus actually was the messianic king of the Jews.

THE CRUCIFIXION OF JESUS

> 15:21 And they compelled a certain man, Simon, a Cyrenian, the father of Alexander and Rufus, as he was coming out of the country and passing by, to carry his cross.
>
> 22 And they brought him to the place Golgotha, which is, translated, "Place of a Skull."
>
> 23 And they tried to give him wine, mixed with myrrh, but he did not take it.

24 And they crucified him and divided his garments, casting lots for them to determine what each man should take.

25 But it was the third hour (9 a.m.) and they crucified him.

26 And the inscription of the offense was written above: "THE KING OF THE JEWS."

27 And with him they crucified two robbers, one on his right and the other on his left.

[28 And the Scripture was fulfilled which says, "And he was counted with the transgressors."]

29 And those who passed by mocked him, shaking their heads and saying, "Aha! You who would destroy the temple and rebuild it in three days,

30 save yourself, and come down from the cross!"

31 Similarly, the chief priests also mocked him among themselves along with the scribes and said, "He saved others; himself he cannot save.

32 Let the Messiah, the King of Israel, come down now from the cross, so that we may see and believe." Even those who were crucified with him insulted him.

To some extent, everything that precedes in this gospel anticipates the passion and crucifixion of Jesus. The crucifixion is always on the mind of the evangelist, and there are several instances when events in the Passion Narrative are actually predicted by Jesus in some detail (e.g., 8:31; 9:31; 10:33). More than any other part of the earliest gospel, the Passion Narrative, and most specifically the Crucifixion of Jesus and the Death of Jesus (perhaps a single unit), are built on and created out of passages from the Jewish Scriptures.

    The conformance of the Crucifixion of Jesus and the Jewish Scriptures is so intricate that there is little question that a version of the crucifixion and death of Jesus was composed relatively early in the history of the church on the basis of proof texts from the Jewish Scriptures. A written narrative, probably close to the original form, was apparently available to the evangelist.

15:21–32	Jewish Scriptures
15:21 And they compelled a certain man, Simon, a Cyrenian, the father of Alexander and Rufus, as he was coming out of the country and passing by, to carry his cross.	
22 And they brought him to the place Golgotha, which is, translated, "Place of a Skull."	
23 And they tried to give him wine, mixed with myrrh, but he did not take it.	Prov 31:6 Give strong drink to one who is perishing, and wine to those in bitter distress.
24 And they crucified him and divided his garments, casting lots for them to determine what each man should take.	Ps 22:18 They divide my clothes among themselves, and for my clothing they cast lots.
25 But it was the third hour (9 a.m.) and they crucified him.	
26 And the inscription of offense was written above: "THE KING OF THE JEWS."	
27 And with him they crucified two robbers, one on his right and the other on his left.	Isa 53:12b . . . he poured out himself to death, and was numbered with the transgressors.
[28 And the Scripture was fulfilled which says, "And he was counted with the transgressors."]	[see Isa 53:12 and Ps Sol 16:5]
29 And those who passed by mocked him, shaking their heads and saying, Aha! You who would destroy the temple and rebuild it in three days,	Ps 22:7 All who see me mock at me; they make mouths at me, they shake their heads. Ps 109:25 I am the object of scorn to my accusers; when they see me, they shake their heads. Lam 2:15 All who pass along the way clap their hands at you; they hiss and wag their heads at daughter Jerusalem.
30 save yourself, and come down from the cross!" 31 Similarly, the chief priests also mocked him among themselves along with the scribes and said, "He saved others; himself he cannot save.	Wis Sol 2:17–18 Let us see if his words are true, and let us test what will happen at the end of his life; for if the righteous man is God's child, he will help him and will deliver him from the hand of his adversaries.

15:21–32	Jewish Scriptures
32 Let the Messiah, the King of Israel, come down now from the cross, so that we may see and believe." Even those who were crucified with him insulted him.	Ps 22:8 "Commit your cause to the LORD; let him deliver—let him rescue the one in whom he delights.

That the Romans crucified Jesus is indisputable fact. Why the Romans crucified Jesus is less clear, and the details of the story of Jesus' crucifixion in fulfillment of Jewish Scriptures are probably grounded in early Christian theological motives. Unable to explain Jesus' unexpected death, his followers turned to the Jewish Scriptures to demonstrate that Jesus' crucifixion and death were in fulfillment of God's purpose. The search for an explanation of Jesus' inconceivable and unthinkable death was probably early Christian apologetic addressed to a Jewish audience, perhaps originally in the Jerusalem church and in Aramaic.

The only portions of the story of the crucifixion that were not generated from the Jewish Scriptures are: (1) that Simon, the Cyrenian, the father of Alexander and Rufus carried Jesus' cross (15:21); (2) that the site of the crucifixion was Golgotha, Aramaic for "Place of a Skull" (15:22); (3) that the crucifixion took place at the third hour, i.e. at 9 a.m. (15:25); and (4) that there was an inscription on the cross that read "THE KING OF THE JEWS" (15:26). The timing of the crucifixion at the third hour (#3) is likely part of the evangelist's narrative scheme (see also vv. 33 and 34 below), so we are reduced to three possible historical details: Simon of Cyrene carried Jesus' cross; the site of the crucifixion was Golgotha; and an inscription on the cross read "THE KING OF THE JEWS." Pretty basic details, but enough to confirm that the Romans crucified Jesus, presumably for claiming that he was the Jewish Messiah, a spurious charge likely fabricated by the Jewish leadership, who considered Jesus a threat to their authority.

The reference to Simon from Cyrene in northeast Libya is probably historical. There is a reference in Acts 6:9 to a synagogue of the Freedmen (i.e., former slaves) in Jerusalem for Jews from Africa (Cyrene and Alexandria) and Asia Minor (Cilicia and Asia). Simon (Hebrew Simeon) and his sons may have migrated from Cyrene to Jerusalem and joined this synagogue. The story of Simon carrying Jesus' cross was possibly carried forward by his sons Alexander and Rufus, who may have been known to the evangelist and to some of his audience. The evangelist's written source probably included the elements inspired by Jewish Scriptures. The Crucifixion of Jesus is a carefully crafted story designed to show that Jesus' crucifixion and death were evidently the will of God and had been prophesied in the past.

Psalms seems to have been a major source for the construction of this section of the Passion Narrative. The fact that it was believed in Jesus' time that King David was the author of most of the Psalms may be significant. It is David, the exemplar of kingship in Israel, who was already bearing witness a millennium earlier to Jesus' messiahship. The link between the Scriptures and the unfolding events is intentionally striking. Clearly a major objective of the evangelist and of the Passion Narrative he used was to disclaim the previous understanding of messiahship as political and to create a new understanding of messiahship in light of Jesus' suffering and death by means of references to the Jewish Scriptures.

The Passion Narrative made it clear Jesus could have saved himself (vv. 30–32) but chose not to do so. Consider, for example, the miracles he performed early in his ministry (chapters 1–8). Jesus was simply being obedient to God's will by suffering and dying in fulfillment of God's word through David and the prophets in the Jewish Scriptures. The culmination of this fact is confirmed below in verse 39, when the Roman centurion ironically says, "Truly this man was a Son of God" or "This man was God's Son."

Verse 28 was probably not in the original text of this gospel, hence the brackets. Some less important manuscripts added it later, reflecting their acknowledgment of the allusion to Isa 53:12 (and to Ps Sol 16:5).

In summary, it is virtually impossible to dissect the story of the crucifixion of Jesus into its various strata. Certainly, the story goes back to the period of oral tradition, perhaps in the Aramaic-speaking Jerusalem church, and was subsequently incorporated into a written Aramaic and then later Greek narrative, which the evangelist adapted to his own purposes in writing the earliest gospel.

THE DEATH OF JESUS

15:33 And when the sixth hour (12 noon) had come, there was darkness over the whole land until the ninth hour (3 p.m.).

34 And at the ninth hour (3 p.m.) Jesus cried out with a loud voice, "*Eloi, Eloi, lema sabachtani,*" which is, translated, "My God, my God, why have you forsaken me?"

35 And some of those who stood by, when they heard that, said, "Look, he is calling Elijah!"

CHAPTER 15   233

36 But someone ran, filled a sponge with sour wine, placed it on a reed, and held it up for him to drink, saying, "Let us see whether Elijah is coming to take him down."

37 But Jesus uttered a loud cry and expired.

38 And the curtain of the temple was torn in two from top to bottom.

To some extent, everything that precedes in this gospel points to the passion, crucifixion, and death of Jesus. The ending was always in the mind of the evangelist. More than any other section in the earliest gospel, the story of the passion, crucifixion, and death is built on passages from the Jewish Scriptures.

15:33–38	Jewish Scriptures
33 And when the sixth hour (12 noon) had come, there was darkness over the whole land until the ninth hour (3 p.m.).	Amos 8:9 On that day, says the Lord GOD I will make the sun go down at noon, and darken the earth in broad daylight.
34 And at the ninth hour (3 p.m.) Jesus cried out with a loud voice, "*Eloi, Eloi, lema sabachtani*," which is, translated, "My God, my God, why have you forsaken me?	Ps 22:1 My God, my God, why have you forsaken me?
35 And some of those who stood by, when they heard that, said, "Look, he is calling Elijah!"	
36 But someone ran, filled a sponge with sour wine, placed it on a reed, and tried to give it to him to drink, saying, "Let us see whether Elijah is coming to take him down."	Ps 69:21 They gave me poison for food, and for my thirst they gave me vinegar (sour wine) to drink.
37 But Jesus gave a loud cry and expired.	Ps 18:6 In my distress I called upon the LORD; to my God I cried for help. From his temple he heard my voice, and my cry to him reached his ears.
38 And the curtain of the temple was torn in two from top to bottom.	

Once again, the incidence of the relationship of the text of the gospel and the Jewish Scriptures is so intricate that there can be no question that the story of the Death of Jesus was composed relatively early and was available in something close to its final form in a written source available to the evangelist.

The darkness that hung over the entire land during the three hours that Jesus hung alive on the cross is not only in fulfillment of the prophecy of Amos. It is a sign of cosmic mourning as God's will is carried out in the death of Jesus in the period between noon and 3 p.m.

Jesus' cry from the cross at 3 p.m. is a rendering of Ps 22:1, clearly an element found in the written Passion Narrative reflecting the influence of the early Christian community, perhaps already in Jerusalem, but with no historical value. The cry in both Aramaic and Greek may imply that some in the evangelist's community could understand Aramaic and some not, perhaps one more bit of evidence in support of Antioch of Syria as the place of composition of this gospel. Yet, in the text one of the bystanders, presumably a Jew, suggests Jesus is calling for Elijah, the prophet who was a miracle worker and whose arrival would proclaim the arrival of God's rule. Here it seems Elijah would take Jesus down from the cross, a rather strange suggestion.

Jesus made a loud cry and died, and the curtain of the temple—the veil between the nave of the temple and the Holy of Holies in which God dwelt—was torn in two, probably symbolizing the opening of the way to God or the departure of Israel's God from the Holy of Holies. Whatever the meaning, and that is not entirely clear, the evangelist is suggesting that Jesus' death obviously had eschatological significance. This is the end of the old order. In fact, verse 38 may be the end of the Passion Narrative available in written form to the evangelist. This section certainly marks the end of the building of the narrative based on passages from the Jewish Scriptures.

THE ROMAN CENTURION AND THE WOMEN

15:39 But when the centurion, who was standing by opposite him, saw that he had expired in this way, he said, "Certainly this man was a Son of God!"

40 But there were also women looking on from a distance, among whom were both Mary of Magdala, Mary the mother of James the younger and of Joses, and Salome,

41 who followed him when he was in Galilee and served him, and many other women who had come up with him to Jerusalem.

The confession of the centurion in verse 39 that Jesus was truly "a Son of God" (not *the* Son of God) is probably a construction of the evangelist to provide further evidence of Jesus' innocence and of his messianic sonship. This additional acknowledgement of Jesus as a Son of God provides justification for an early claim in this gospel: that, at the time of Jesus' baptism, God adopted Jesus as his Beloved Son (1:11). The words "Son of God" in verse 39 may also be the reason the words "Son of God" were added to the superscription in 1:1 in some later manuscripts: "Beginning of the good news of Jesus Christ, [Son of God]."

Verses 40–41 seem anticlimactic and are probably a construction of the evangelist in anticipation of the accounts of the Burial of Jesus (15:42–47) and the Discovery of the Empty Tomb (16:1–8). There were at the crucifixion three women, all followers of Jesus, and many other women as well (v. 41): (1) Mary from Magdala on the northwest side of the Sea of Galilee; (2) Mary the mother of the younger or the smaller (Greek *mikros*) James and of Joses; and (3) Salome. Mary of Magdala appears in this gospel again only in 15:47 and in 16:1 (and also in 16:9, which is not an original part of the gospel but a later addition known only since the end of the second century). Mary the mother of Joses (but no mention of the younger or smaller James) appears again in 15:47 and 16:1. Both Marys serve in this gospel as witnesses of where Jesus was buried (15:47). Mary's sons James and Joses are otherwise unknown in this gospel, although they may perhaps have been known to members of the evangelist's community. Salome is also otherwise unknown in this gospel, although she reappears, together with the two Marys, at the empty tomb (16:1–8). The three women fled in terror and amazement after their encounter with the young man in the empty tomb *and said nothing to anyone* (16:8). Surprisingly, only women who knew Jesus were present at the crucifixion. There is no mention of men who knew him. We know that the disciples are said to have abandoned Jesus at the time of his arrest in Gethsemane, but were there no other men among Jesus' followers in Jerusalem?

THE BURIAL OF JESUS

15:42 And when evening had already come, because it was a Day of Preparation, that is the day before the Sabbath,

43 Joseph of Arimathea, a prominent member of the council, who was also himself awaiting the kingdom of God, took courage and went in to Pilate and asked for the corpse of Jesus.

44 But Pilate was surprised that he was already dead; and summoning the centurion, he asked him whether he had been dead for some time.

45 And when he found out from the centurion, he gave the corpse to Joseph.

46 And he bought a piece of fine linen, took him down, and wrapped him in the linen cloth and laid him in a tomb that had been hewn out of rock, and rolled a stone across the entrance of the tomb.

47 But Mary of Magdala and Mary the mother of Joses observed where he was laid.

The Day of Preparation (v. 42) refers to the daylight hours before the arrival of the Sabbath at sunset on Friday, which the evangelist explains, presumably for Gentiles in his audience. The evangelist wants to make it clear that Jesus was taken down from the cross and buried before the onset of the Sabbath. The appearance of Joseph of Arimathea comes as a surprise. Who was he? Is there any likelihood that a member of the Sanhedrin would ask for Jesus' corpse to give it a proper burial?

The stories of the women at the crucifixion and burial of Jesus and of the role of Joseph of Arimathea may be little more than an effort on the part of the evangelist to afford Jesus a decent burial. The story of the women is complicated by the fact that they are described three times (15:40; 15:47; and 16:1), and each time somewhat differently. Was the evangelist weaving together three different legendary traditions involving women, since the men, Jesus' disciples, had all run away? It was essential to have people present at the events involving Jesus' burial and the discovery of the empty tomb.

Moreover, there is no mention of the ritual washing of the body or the anointing of the body with oil or spices. As mentioned previously, this may have been the reason for the story of the anointing with expensive oil by the woman at Bethany in 14:3–9 above. Verse 47 (from which Salome is missing) may be little more than an addition by the evangelist to prepare for the story of the empty tomb in chapter 16. The statement in verse 47 that the women were at the burial was essential in order to explain how the women would have known where to go later to find the empty tomb.

CONCLUSIONS AFTER CHAPTER 15

It is likely that the evangelist's source for the material in chapter 15, a written Passion Narrative, already interpreted Jesus' life and ministry in messianic terms in order to account for the horrific events in the final days of Jesus' life. Psalms (especially Ps 22) was a major source, perhaps the earliest source, of an originally oral and later-written Passion Narrative.

It is challenging, and perhaps impossible, to put all of the pieces of the Passion Narrative into a coherent historical reconstruction of what actually unfolded in the final days of Jesus' life, and then how the oral and subsequent written tradition originated and developed. Although the Passion Narrative in the earliest gospel is not a reliable record of details in Jesus' final days, some things are relatively clear. At some point Jesus accepted his inevitable death, but when was that? Shortly after the cleansing of the temple? At a final Passover meal with his disciples? In Gethsemane at the time of his arrest? At a trial before the high priest and the Sanhedrin? There is no way to know with any certainty which, if any, of these stories reflects actual events in Jesus' final days and which are merely legendary constructions of the church or the evangelist.

After Jesus' death and the subsequent belief of some of his followers that Jesus had been raised from the dead and exalted to God's right hand, someone skillfully created a narrative to explain the inexplicable: why Jesus had suffered, been crucified, and died a humiliating death. There is nothing in contemporary Jewish literature to suggest that anyone at that time expected a suffering Messiah. That meant that it fell to Jesus' followers to explain the significance of what had happened during those final days after Jesus and his disciples arrived in Jerusalem for the Passover festival, with absolutely no expectation of what was about to unfold. The principal resource for that exercise was apparently a detailed search through Jewish Scriptures by followers of Jesus in order to find meaning in the ignominious events of Jesus' suffering, crucifixion, and death.

The Passion Narrative constitutes a significant portion of the earliest gospel and may in some form have been the oldest written document incorporated by the evangelist into his gospel after substantial editing and rewriting. The Passion Narrative is surely the cornerstone of Christianity. Some have suggested that the earliest gospel is nothing more than a Passion Narrative with a long preface. To some extent that is likely true.

The Trial before Pontius Pilate (15:1–15) was necessary for Jesus to be crucified, but the written account is probably legendary or fictitious in its detail. There were no witnesses who might have delivered the details of such a meeting to Jesus' followers. Also the crowd shouting to free Barabbas may have as its motive merely to contrast Jesus with a real political insurrectionist, in order to place the blame for Jesus' execution not on the Romans but on the Jewish leadership and their supporting crowd.

The Mockery by the Soldiers (15:16–20) appears to be a story in fulfillment of Isa 50:6 and introduces an element of literary irony into the narrative. The Roman soldiers mockingly salute Jesus as king of the Jews, while those listening to a reading of the gospel, the evangelist's audience, already know that Jesus is, in fact, the messianic king of Israel.

The Crucifixion of Jesus (15:21–32) is the culmination of everything that precedes in the gospel. It is obvious that this portion of the Passion Narrative was composed initially on the basis of proof texts from Jewish Scriptures, most especially from Psalms, especially Ps 22, and, perhaps subsequently from material from the Songs of the Suffering Servant in Deutero-Isaiah. A proto-Passion Narrative may have been composed in the first or second decade after Jesus' death, perhaps in Jerusalem and perhaps originally in Aramaic.

We know that the Essenes, the people of the Dead Sea Scrolls, already sought understanding of events surrounding their own founding and history in the Jewish Scriptures and recorded such fulfillment of Scriptures in their writings, most especially in a commentary on Habakkuk (1QpHab). Early Christians were doing something very similar by trying to find scriptural passages that afforded an explanation of Jesus' suffering and death. They believed that biblical prophecies were now being fulfilled in the life and ministry of Jesus and in the events of the early Christian community. It is likely that the original author of such a story was a Palestinian Jewish Christian writing in Aramaic to a Jewish Christian community, perhaps the church in Jerusalem. Such a written interpretation of Jesus' suffering and death served to vindicate Jesus and his followers in their struggle against strong Jewish and Roman opposition.

A component of this Passion Narrative in our gospel, specifically the times of day referred to in 15:25, 33, and 34, may reflect not historic memory of events in Jesus' final hours but may rather reflect a crucifixion liturgy within the church. Converts to Christianity were about to die to their old selves in anticipation of being born again into Christ during the days and hours leading up to their baptisms at Easter, the date when the church celebrated Jesus' resurrection and the baptism of new converts to Christianity.

The Death of Jesus (15:33–38) is the culmination of all that preceded. Although I have commented on material in the Passion Narrative in bits and pieces, primarily for the sake of reflecting more clearly on smaller units one at a time, my divisions of the Passion Narrative are probably somewhat artificial.

The final sections in chapter 15, the Roman Centurion and the Women (15:39–41) and the Burial of Jesus (15:42–47) are probably constructions of the evangelist, afterthoughts needed to provide witnesses—female witnesses since the disciples had already fled for their lives—to the death and burial of Jesus in order to explain their presence at the Empty Tomb just two days later (16:1–8).

Chapter 16

THE DISCOVERY OF THE EMPTY TOMB

16:1 And when the Sabbath was over, Mary of Magdala, and Mary the mother of James, and Salome bought aromatic oils, so that they might go and anoint him.

2 And very early in the morning on the first day of the week, they went to the tomb just after the sun had risen.

3 And they were saying to one another, "Who will roll away the stone from the entrance of the tomb for us?"

4 And when they looked up, they saw that the stone had been rolled away, for it was extremely large.

5 And as they entered the tomb, they saw a young man sitting on the right side wearing a white robe; and they were astonished.

6 But he said to them, "Do not be astonished. You are looking for Jesus the Nazarene, who was crucified. He has been raised! He is not here. Look, the place where they put him!

7 But go and say to his disciples and to Peter, 'He is going ahead of you into Galilee; there you will see him, just as he said to you.'"

8 And they went out and fled from the tomb, for terror and amazement had seized them. And they said nothing to anyone, for they were afraid.

CHAPTER 16

THERE IS CONSIDERABLE DISAGREEMENT among scholars regarding the material in chapter 16 of the gospel. According to the evangelist, the three women who were present at Jesus' crucifixion (15:40) and burial (15:47)—Mary of Magdala, Mary the mother of James, and Salome—came to the tomb where Jesus lay in order to anoint his body with oil. In 15:30, Mary the mother of James is described as "Mary the mother of James the younger (or the smaller) and of Joses," and in 15:47 as "Mary the mother of Joses." Do these differences reflect the evangelist's use of different sources for these three stories? Perhaps, but the evidence is inconclusive.

The three women arrived at the tomb to anoint Jesus' body two nights and a day after Jesus' death, knowing that there was a huge rock covering the entrance to the tomb, and wondered who would roll the rock back for them to enter the tomb. These details in the story already raise questions about its historical value. Why would the women go to the tomb after the passing of two sunsets, knowing that the anointing should take place before sunset on the day of Jesus' death and that they could not roll back the stone from the entrance of the tomb? Moreover, in 14:8, Jesus declared that his body had already been anointed for burial by the woman in Bethany (see 14:3–9 above).

When the three women entered the tomb, they did not see Jesus' body. They saw, instead, a young man dressed in a white robe, who told them not to be afraid, because Jesus had been raised from the dead (the verb is in the passive voice). The young man is probably an angelic or heavenly figure, as he is dressed in white clothing. The women were instructed by the young man to tell the disciples, and Peter, that they would see Jesus in Galilee, just as he had already told them. Although Jesus told his disciples in 8:31; 9:31; and 10:33 that he would rise again (the verb is in the active voice in these three passages), there is no mention in these three verses that Jesus would appear to the disciples. The reference in verse 7 is apparently to 14:28: "But after I am raised up, I will go before you to Galilee." This verse appears in the context of the Denial of Peter and likely implies that the earliest appearances of the risen Lord may have occurred in Galilee. This detail may be the only reliable fact in this otherwise legendary account and serves to explain the prediction of appearances in Galilee in 14:28, an example of *vaticinium ex eventu*, prophecy *out of* or *after* the event.

And why, if Jesus announced to his apostles three times that he would rise again after his death, was no one at his tomb to test or to verify Jesus' prediction? After all, Jesus' three predictions of his suffering and death were all accurate in some detail. It is, of course, clear that the hand of the church and/or of the evangelist created these predictive stories after the fact (*vaticinia ex eventu*, prophecies *out of* or *after* the event).

Ironically, the story ends (16:8) by saying that the women said nothing to anyone in spite of the young man's order to tell the disciples and Peter. What then was the source of this information, if not the three women? The earliest gospel ends on the note that the women were terrified. There are no resurrection appearances to anyone in this gospel, merely the hint that there will be appearances in Galilee (more specifically, Jesus is going ahead of his disciples into Galilee).

Chapter 16 is simply an account of the three women, the empty tomb, and the mysterious young man. The three later gospels of Matthew, Luke, and John all have detailed accounts of resurrection appearances, although the accounts in the three later gospels are very different from one another (compare Matt 28:9-10, 16-20; Luke 24:13-53; and John 20:11—21:19). The earliest gospel is totally devoid of detailed legendary resurrection appearances.

The material in this chapter was likely composed by the evangelist, apparently based on early Christian belief in the preaching (*kerygma*) of the church that Jesus had been crucified and buried and that he had been raised or exalted on the third day in accordance with the Scriptures (1 Cor 15:4; see also Acts 2:24; 2:32-33; Rom 1:4). These passages in Paul and Acts, together with the words of the evangelist in chapter 16, probably reflect the earliest preaching of the church: that God had raised Jesus from the dead in fulfillment of the words of King David in Ps 16:8-11 and, perhaps, most especially in Ps 110:1:

> The LORD said to my lord,
>   "Sit at my right hand
> until I make your enemies your footstool."

God could not abandon Jesus to the land of the dead, so he exalted him to his right hand, a position of honor and power, and made him Lord and Messiah. This claim appears to be the most primitive form of the church's belief in the exaltation or the resurrection of Jesus. The message was clear: evil could not triumph over good. God had the final word in exonerating Jesus by elevating him to a position of honor and power and glory in fulfillment of the Jewish Scriptures.

We are, of course, no longer speaking about events in history. We are witnessing a confession of faith. There is no attempt by the evangelist to describe the actual resurrection or to describe appearances of the risen Christ, features evident in the three other canonical gospels and in the apocryphal *Gospel of Peter*. The earliest gospel is more restrained, probably because it relies on a more primitive, less-developed tradition. Nevertheless, the earliest evangelist apparently translated primitive theology into imaginative history or legend by adding to the primitive theology the detail of the empty tomb.

The ending of the gospel in verse 8 has puzzled scholars: Greek *ephobounto gar* ("for they were afraid"). The conjunction translated as "for" is the final word of the gospel, an ending that seems peculiar to many scholars. There are many examples in Greek literature from Homer to Plato to Justin Martyr of ending a sentence with the conjunction *gar* (for), but no example of ending a book with this conjunction. Some have speculated that a page of the original ending of the gospel was broken off and lost or that the evangelist died before he finished writing the gospel. Clearly, the later evangelists, especially the authors of the gospels of Matthew and Luke who used the earliest gospel as a source for their own writing, found the ending "for they were afraid" unacceptable and added endings of their own, although very different endings to be sure. The earliest gospel likely ended in 16:8, because the evangelist had nothing more to say. The tomb was empty; Jesus had been raised from the dead; Jesus would appear to the apostles in Galilee. The evangelist was probably unaware of stories of specific resurrection appearances. Such stories were apparently created after the earliest gospel was already in circulation.

It is important to look briefly at the meaning of the word "resurrection" in the Judaism of Jesus' time. Suffice it to say that not all Jews in this period believed in the resurrection of the dead, most specifically the Sadducees. And those who did believe did not always agree on the nature of the resurrection. Some apparently believed it was the earthly person who would arise, including the earthly body (Greek *soma*). Others believed that it was rather the inner person, the spirit (Greek *pneuma*) or the soul (Greek *psyche*), that would arise. It was also not clear where the dead would live after the resurrection. The belief that some might perish in hell while others were rewarded in heaven was only beginning to spread in this period.

Earliest Christianity probably believed that Jesus' exaltation into heaven was spiritual, but the earliest gospel reflects the more material resurrection of the body, a view that is more fully developed in the gospels of Matthew, Luke, and John, which report detailed appearances of Jesus in bodily form. Mainstream contemporary Christianity seems to maintain two very different views: (1) that immediately after death the soul (Greek *psyche*) or the spirit (Greek *pneuma*) goes to a place of reward or punishment, heaven or hell, and (2) that at some time in the uncertain future, when Christ returns, there will be a resurrection of the physical body (Greek *soma*).

There is no discussion here of the longer or shorter endings of this gospel following 16:8, because the longer and shorter endings are almost universally considered later additions to the gospel.

CONCLUSIONS AFTER CHAPTER 16

The earliest evangelist was apparently the first person to write an extended narrative of the "good news" (*euangellion*) of Jesus Christ. As such, he was the first to try to represent the church's belief in Jesus' life and ministry, and his suffering, death, and exaltation or resurrection (they are the same) to the right hand of God. Accordingly, the anonymous evangelist may have been the first to report that the tomb in which Jesus had been buried following his crucifixion was empty when the women went to anoint his body. The explanation for the empty tomb came to the women in the words of the mysterious young man: the crucified Jesus has been raised from the dead; look, he is no longer in the tomb. The women were afraid. The end of the gospel!

CONCLUSION

THE LITERARY FORMS OF THE GOSPEL

The material in our earliest gospel is diverse and rich, making it important to identify the various literary forms that were incorporated into the gospel. Identifying these literary forms provides us with valuable information about the oral and/or the written source or sources to which the evangelist presumably had access. Only then can we understand better the building blocks of the earliest gospel. In identifying these forms, it is important for the reader to know that this is sometimes an easy task, and it is sometimes not so easy. Not every story, not every pericope, falls clearly into one of the categories discussed below, although most do.

PRONOUNCEMENT STORIES

In the Introduction to this volume, I identified five literary forms. The first of these is the pronouncement story, which generally involves a discussion or dialogue between Jesus and an adversary in which Jesus resolves the issue with a final saying or pronouncement. Inasmuch as the critical element in the pronouncement story is the final saying or pronouncement of Jesus, it is important to ask whether the introductory dialogue recalls the actual setting for the saying; or, alternatively, if the pronouncement story is merely a creation of the church during the period of the oral and/or written transmission of some individual sayings of Jesus. Perhaps pronouncement stories were created for use in preaching or teaching in the church, in which case the dialogue was probably created by the church to provide a suitable context for some sayings of Jesus. The following are examples:

    2:5–10a   Jesus has Authority to Forgive Sins

    2:15–17   Jesus Eats with Sinners and Tax Collectors

2:18-20	The Question about Fasting
2:23-27	Jesus' Pronouncement about the Sabbath
3:1-6	The Man with the Paralyzed Hand
3:20-26	Jesus and Beelzebul
3:31-35	Jesus' True Family
7:1-8	The Tradition of the Elders
7:9-13	More on the Tradition of the Elders
9:33-35	Which Disciple is the Greatest?
9:38-39	Another Exorcist
10:1-9	Jesus' Teaching about Divorce
10:13-16	Jesus Blesses the Children
10:17-31	The Rich Man, True Riches, and the Kingdom of God
11:27-33	The Question of Jesus' Authority
12:13-17	On Paying Taxes to Caesar
12:18-27	The Question of the Resurrection
12:28-34	The Greatest Commandment
12:41-44	The Poor Widow's Contribution
13:1-2	Jesus Predicts the Destruction of the Temple
14:3-9	The Anointing of Jesus at Bethany

The pronouncement stories are not randomly spread throughout the gospel. They are grouped into clusters, some of which may be arranged somewhat topically: 2:5—3:35 (seven stories); 7:1-13 (two stories); 9:33—13:2 (eleven stories). The grouping into clusters suggests the evangelist probably had access to one or more written sources that contained only pronouncement stories, which he spread throughout the gospel, but in clusters. The order of stories may actually reflect the arrangement in which the pronouncement stories appeared in the evangelist's source(s), but we cannot know that with any degree of certainty. Stated simply, the evangelist apparently had access to one or more written sources that contained only pronouncement stories that may originally have served the catechetical interests of the church. The evangelist spread these stories throughout his gospel in clusters or groupings.

MIRACLE STORIES

The second literary form identified in the Introduction is miracle stories, accounts of wondrous events attributed to Jesus by the church. Some of these stories are based primarily on the fulfillment of alleged proof texts in the Jewish Scriptures. In fact, many are modeled after miracle stories in the Old Testament about Moses, Elijah, and Elisha. In the Introduction, I reminded the reader that it is essential to distinguish between miracles and miracle stories. A miracle story is not positive evidence of an actual miracle. It is exactly what the name implies: it is a story. The following are examples:

1:21–28	Jesus Heals the Man with the Unclean Spirit
1:29–31	The Healing of Peter's Mother-in-law
1:40–45	The Cleansing of the Man with the Scaly Skin
2:1–4, 10b–12	The Healing of the Paralyzed Man
4:35–41	The Stilling of the Storm
5:1–20	The Healing of the Gerasene Demoniac
5:21–23, 35–43	The Girl Restored to Life
5:25–34	The Woman Healed of the Flow of Blood
6:30–44	The Feeding of the Five Thousand Men
6:45–52	Jesus Walks on the Water
6:53–56	The Healing of the Sick in Gennesaret
7:24–30	The Syro-Phoenician Woman's Request for her Daughter
7:31–37	Jesus Cures a Deaf Man
8:1–9	The Feeding of the Four Thousand
8:22–26	Jesus Cures a Blind Man at Bethsaida
9:14–29	The Exorcism of the Epileptic Boy
10:46–52	Jesus Heals the Blind Man Bartimaeus in Jericho

As in the case of the pronouncement stories, so too the miracle stories seem to be grouped into clusters: 1:21—2:12 (four stories); 4:35—6:44 (five stories); 6:45—8:9 (five stories); 8:22—10:52 (three stories). The grouping of the miracle stories into clusters also suggests the author had access to one or more written sources that contained only miracle stories that he spread through the gospel, but in clusters. The miracle stories confirmed for the church Jesus' status as Messiah and Son of God and fulfilled such Scriptures as Isaiah 35:6a:

> Then the eyes of the blind shall be opened,
> > and the ears of the deaf unstopped;
> Then shall the lame leap like a deer,
> > and the tongue of the speechless sing for joy.

PARABLES

The third literary form identified in the Introduction is parables, common in both Jewish and Greco-Roman circles. A parable is a short story told to illustrate a simple truth, in this gospel often a truth about the coming kingdom of God or the period of God's rule. Parables in this gospel often draw their stories from nature or agriculture. The following are examples:

4:1–9	The Parable of the Sower
4:10–12	The Purpose of Parables
4:13–20	The Interpretation of the Parable of the Sower
4:26–29	The Parable of the Growing Seed
4:30–32	The Parable of the Mustard Seed
11:12–14, 20–21	The Cursing of the Fig Tree
11:15–19	The Cleansing of the Temple
12:1–12	The Parable of the Evil Winegrowers
13:28–29	The Lesson of the Parable of the Fig Tree
13:34–36	The Parable of the Absent Householder

As in the case of pronouncement stories and miracle stories, so too the parables are grouped: 4:1–4:32 (three parables, plus a statement about the purpose of parables and the interpretation of a parable) and 11:12—13:36

(three parables, plus the explanation of a parable, and one enacted parable [the Cleansing of the Temple], which might also be classified as a legend). These groupings of parables also suggest that the evangelist had access to one or more written sources that contained only parables that he chose to incorporate into his gospel in clusters.

SAYINGS

The fourth literary form identified in the Introduction is sayings. As the name implies, sayings refers to individual sayings or to clusters of sayings, usually attributed to Jesus. They generally reflect specific teaching of Jesus, not mere conversation. However, the fact that a saying is attributed to Jesus does not necessarily mean that it reflects something that Jesus actually said. Prophets in the early church continued to speak in the name of Jesus guided by the Spirit or the Holy Spirit. The following are examples:

1:14–15	The Beginning of Jesus' Teaching in Galilee
2:21–22	New and Old
2:28	Humankind is Master of the Sabbath
3:27	On the Strong Man
3:28–29	On Blasphemy
3:30	An Unclean Spirit
4:21	The Lamp
4:22	Nothing Hidden
4:23	Ears to Hear
4:24	With what Measure You Give
4:25	He Who has
7:14–23	Multiple Sayings on Defilement and Ritual Cleanness
8:34	On Cross-bearing
8:35	Whosoever Wants to Save his Life
8:36	What will it Profit a Man?
8:37	What can a Man Give in Exchange?
8:38	Whoever is Ashamed

9:1	There are some Standing Here
9:36–37	Whoever Receives a Child
9:40	Whoever is Not Against Us
9:41	A Cup of Water
9:42	On Causing Little Ones to Sin
9:43	Hand
9:45	Foot
9:47–48	Eye
9:49	Salted with Fire
9:50a	Salt is Good
9:50b	Salt in Yourselves
10:11–12	On Divorce and Adultery
10:31	Many Who are First
10:42–44	Whoever Wants to be First
10:45	The Son of Man Came to Serve
11:22	Have Trust in God
11:23	It will Happen if You Believe
11:24–25	On Prayer
12:35–37	The Question about David's Son
12:38–39	Criticism of the Scribes
12:40	Taking Advantage of Widows
13:7–8	Signs of the Beginning of the End
13:9–13	On Persecution
13:14–20	The Abominable Desecration
13:21–23	Warnings against False Messiahs and False Prophets
13:24–27	A Prophey of the Coming of the Son of Man
13:30–31	The Certainty of Imminent Consummation
13:32	On the Unknown Hour and Day

13:33	An Exhortation to be Alert
13:37	The Application is to Everyone

It is evident that the evangelist had access to one or more collections of sayings of Jesus. In some instances one or more sayings are appended to a pronouncement story (9:40–50) or to other narratives (11:22–25). Sometimes collections of sayings are connected by catchwords (4:21–25; 9:37–50; etc.), or multiple sayings on the same subject are connected (7:14–23; 8:34—9:1; 9:43–50; etc.). Many of the sayings in chapter 13 may already have been available to the evangelist in a separate collection of apocalyptic material that served as a source of this gospel. It is probable that the evangelist had access to more than one collection of sayings compiled for teaching purposes in the church or for the instruction of catechumens, new members of the church. Some such collections of sayings may have been arranged on the basis of subject matter.

LEGENDS

The fifth literary form identified in the Introduction is legends, or stories about Jesus (or in a few cases stories about someone else, such as John the Baptist or one of Jesus' disciples). These stories report alleged events in the life of Jesus or someone close to Jesus and are often but not always surrounded by supernatural events. In some instances a story may refer to an actual event (e.g., Jesus' Baptism by John, or the Betrayal and Arrest of Jesus in Gethsemane, or Jesus' Trial Before Pilate), but the account of the event in the gospel may have little or no historical value with regard to its detail. In those instances, the account in the gospel is rather a creation of the church or perhaps a construction of the evangelist. It is particularly difficult to distinguish between legends and constructions of the evangelist (our next category). The legends or stories in the gospel have no distinctive literary form. The following are examples of probable legends:

1:2–11	The Preaching of John and the Baptism of Jesus
1:12–13	The Temptation of Jesus in the Wilderness
1:16–20	The Call of Jesus' First Disciples
2:13–14	Jesus Calls Levi to be his Disciple
6:1–6a	The Rejection of Jesus at Nazareth
6:14–29	The Death of John the Baptist

8:10–13	The Demand for a Sign
8:27–30	Peter's Declaration about Jesus
8:31–33	Jesus Foretells His Death and Resurrection
9:2–8	The Transfiguration of Jesus
9:33–36	Which Disciple is the Greatest?
9:38–39	Another Exorcist
10:35–41	James and John Ask Jesus for Precedence
11:1–11	Jesus' Triumphal Entry into Jerusalem
11:15–19	The Cleansing of the Temple
14:3–9	The Anointing of Jesus at Bethany
14:12–16	The Preparations for the Passover Meal
14:22–25	The Institution of the Lord's Supper
14:32–42	Jesus and the Disciples in Gethsemane
14:43–50	The Betrayal and Arrest of Jesus
14:51–52	The Flight of the Naked Young Man
14:53–65	Jesus' Trial before the High Priest and the Council
14:66–72	Peter's Denial of Jesus
15:1–15	Jesus' Trial Before Pontius Pilate
15:16–20	The Mockery by the Soldiers
15:21–32	The Crucifixion of Jesus
15:33–38	The Death of Jesus
15:39–41	The Roman Centurion and the Women
15:42–47	The Burial of Jesus
16:1–8	The Discovery of the Empty Tomb

Several legends appear in chapters 1 and 2, specifically regarding the ministry of John the Baptist (1:2–8), the baptism of Jesus (1:9–11), the temptation of Jesus in the wilderness (1:12–13), and the beginning of Jesus' ministry in Galilee (1:14–15), including the call of Jesus' First Disciples (1:16–20; and perhaps 2:13–14). Although the broad outline of these events (apart from the mythical Temptation in the Wilderness in 1:12–13) may be somewhat factual, the details almost certainly are not.

The purpose of a legend is often transparent. Peter's declaration about Jesus as Messiah (8:27–30) is almost certainly a story designed to say that Peter, who was the first to see the risen Lord after Jesus' crucifixion and death, actually recognized Jesus as Messiah during his lifetime. And the story of the transfiguration of Jesus (9:2–8) confirms Peter's confession of Jesus as Messiah for the inner circle of disciples: Peter, James, and John.

Beginning already in chapter 11 with Jesus' triumphal entry into Jerusalem (11:1–11), we are introduced to events in Jesus' final days in Jerusalem, a prelude to the more detailed Passion Narrative (14:3—16:8). Half of the material identified above as legends was probably drawn from a single written source, known as the Passion Narrative (chapters 14–16), perhaps the earliest written material in the church. The division of the material in the Passion Narrative in chapters 14–16 into smaller units is topical and is done for the convenience of discussion. It is the Passion Narrative specifically, and much of the legendary material more generally, that are designed to introduce the reader to the theme of the Suffering Messiah, the Christian answer to Jesus' ignominious death.

According to the earliest gospel, Jesus' suffering and death were part of God's plan for Jesus and humanity. This plan was already foretold in the Jewish Scriptures. It is not a coincidence that The Crucifixion of Jesus (15:21–32) and The Death of Jesus (15:33–38) are the most detailed stories in the entire gospel, built almost entirely on passages from the Jewish Scriptures.

From the beginning of the gospel, the reader (or listener) knows who Jesus is, but his identity is kept as a secret from others, thereby explaining why it was not fully known and understood until after his death by virtue of his resurrection. It may be the evangelist himself who created the device of the Messianic Secret in the gospel in order to explain why Jesus' true identity was clear, even to his disciples, only after his death.

Storytelling in this gospel is in large measure a creation of the church or, in many instances, a creation of the evangelist. Distinguishing between legends and constructions of the evangelist (our next category) is particularly difficult, and in some instances virtually impossible. A few pericopes are actually listed in more than one category when there is apparent overlap or uncertainty. These lists are guideposts. They are not carved in stone.

CONSTRUCTIONS OF THE EVANGELIST

In addition to these five literary forms, there are several others narratives that do not conform to these literary forms and that appear to be constructions of the evangelist. Some of them are little more than transition stories, narratives of a verse or two designed to move Jesus from one geographic place to another. Some are brief introductions to pericopes in order to provide a time or a setting for the story. Not all of these transitional phrases have been broken off from the pericope to which they belong, so they are not all listed here. They are, however, generally so identified in the discussion of each relevant pericope. The following are examples of generally more detailed constructions of the evangelist:

1:1	The Superscription or Title
1:21–22	Jesus Teaches in the Synagogue
1:32–34	The Healing and Exorcism of Many
1:35–39	Jesus Departs on a Preaching Tour of Galilee
2:13–14	Jesus Calls Levi to be His Disciple
3:7–12	The Multitude at the Seaside
3:13–19	Jesus Appoints the Twelve
4:33–34	Concluding Statement about Jesus' Parables
5:24	Expresses Jesus' Movement
5:43	Feature of the Messianic Secret
6:6b–13	Jesus Sends the Twelve Out on a Missionary Journey
6:30–34	Relocation of Jesus to a Deserted Place
6:53–56	Relocation and the Healing of the Sick in Gennesaret
8:14–21	The Yeast of the Pharisees and of Herod
9:9–13	The Coming of Elijah
9:30–32	For a Second Time Jesus Foretells his Death and Resurrection
10:10	Relocation into the House
10:32–34	For a Third Time Jesus Foretells His Death and Resurrection
11:20–21	Relocation to the Fig Tree

13:3–4   Four Disciples Question Jesus Privately

13:5–6   Jesus' Warning about Imposters

14:1–2   The Plot of the Priests and Scribes to Kill Jesus

14:10–11   Judas Agrees to Betray Jesus

14:17–21   The Prophecy of the Betrayal

14:26–31   Peter's Denial Foretold

16:1–8   The Discovery of the Empty Tomb

There are also the multiple elements of the motif of the Messianic Secret likely added by the evangelist to pericopes in his sources (1:34, 43–44; 3:11–12; 5:43; 7:36; 8:30; 9:9, 30–32. See also 8:26; 8:31; 10:32–34).

Inasmuch as the evangelist presumably drew from many written sources that contained clusters of pronouncement stories, miracle stories, parables, sayings of Jesus, and legends, he often had to provide a temporal transition from one story to the next in order to create a coherent narrative. Also, since the evangelist wanted to indicate that Jesus moved from one place to another, he also had to provide the material for geographical movement. In other words, the evangelist created the glue that tied together the material from his multiple sources into a coherent narrative.

It is particularly difficult to draw a distinction between the legends (or the stories about Jesus) that may have been in one or more of the evangelist's sources and constructions of the evangelist, because both contain brief stories about Jesus or someone else. Nevertheless, I am convinced there is considerable evidence to conclude that the building blocks of the earliest gospel consisted of several written sources, including (1) one or more sources that contained about twenty-one pronouncement stories; (2) one or more sources that contained about seventeen miracle stories; (3) one or more sources that contained about seven parables, some with explanations or follow-up; (4) multiple sources that contained many dozens of sayings, some grouped into clusters because they contain similar subject matter; and (5) one or more sources that contained about thirty legends or stories about Jesus and others. Among the so-called legends, much if not most of the material in chapters 14–16 was probably already available to the evangelist in a distinct written Passion Narrative that may have served as a liturgical setting for the week before the church's celebration of Easter. If these conclusions are correct, and I believe they are, the evangelist drew from multiple written sources, perhaps as many as ten or even more.

THE TEXT OF THE GOSPEL

Unfortunately, we do not have the original Greek text of the gospel, the evangelist's so-called autograph. We have copies of copies of copies etc., handwritten by scribes who over a period of centuries made both inadvertent and deliberate changes to the manuscripts they were copying. The changes during the first century of transmission were understandable, because the scribes before 200 CE had no idea that they were preserving books that would, centuries later, be regarded as sacred Scripture. But even after 200 CE, when the church began to think of the gospel as Scripture, scribes intentionally continued to modify the text. Notwithstanding, from the thousands of ancient Greek manuscripts and early translations of the gospel into Syriac, Latin, Coptic, Georgian, Ethiopic, Nubian, Sogdia (a Middle Iranian language), Gothic, Old Church Slavonic, etc., textual critics have attempted to reconstruct something close to what they believe is the evangelist's original Greek text. However, many scholars, including myself, believe it is more likely that textual critics have been able to construct, at best, a text that was current in about 200 CE, but not necessarily any earlier, at least in the case of the Synoptic Gospels. This construct by textual critics is the Greek text with which I worked and which I translated, as best as I could, into English—trying, when possible, to preserve the sense and sometimes the awkward style and grammar of the original Greek.

Working with an English translation of the gospel rather than with the Greek text is especially problematic, as words in the original Greek sometimes have a wide range of meanings, the subtlety or ambiguity of which cannot be preserved in translation into any language. We must also remember that Jesus and his disciples probably did not speak Greek or Latin, but rather Aramaic, an ancient Semitic language spoken by people in Roman Palestine. Therefore, even if we have access to something close to the autograph of the Greek text, it is sometimes difficult to understand the original meaning of the text, especially with respect to alleged sayings of Jesus that presumably passed from Aramaic into Greek and now into English. The commentary addresses some of these issues in the context of specific passages.

THE LITERARY FORM OF GOSPEL OR BIOGRAPHY

The word "gospel" comes from the Old English *godspel*, which means "good news," exactly the same meaning as the original Greek word *euaggelion* in the superscription or title of the book in 1:1. At the time that the evangelist wrote, gospel was not a literary form. The designation of "gospel" as a literary form developed toward the end of the second century, about a hundred thirty years after the evangelist wrote this earliest proclamation of "the good news of Jesus Messiah." The Greek of the superscription is ambiguous. The original Greek can refer to Jesus' proclamation of the good news, or to the church's proclamation of the good news about Jesus. The evangelist probably leans toward the second meaning.

The earliest gospel is similar in literary form to Greco-Roman biographies. Such biographies were not intended to provide an accurate historical record of a person's life and work. Rather they presented a positive account of the person's character in order to provide readers with examples of how to lead meritorious lives. Greco-Roman biographies provided a portrait of an individual's greatness. Exaggeration, falsification, overstatement, hyperbole, aggrandizement, and outright falsehood were commonplace in Greco-Roman biographies. This gospel is no exception in style and context. The author's purpose was to promote the good news, not to provide a historically accurate life of Jesus.

THE AUTHOR OF THE GOSPEL

The gospel is anonymous. There is no claim to authorship, and the author was likely no one known to us from the New Testament or from early Christian literature. In fact, he was not actually an author but rather a collector of existing written sources, from which he created a coherent narrative that mimics Greco-Roman biography.

The author was probably a person of standing in his church and was obviously able to read and write Greek. His Greek is, however, sometimes awkward, suggesting that Greek may not have been his mother language, or that he was bilingual in Aramaic and Greek. The evangelist was obviously not an eyewitness to the events recorded in the gospel; neither did he have personal access to an eyewitness. The earliest gospel is largely a collection of already-existing written sources. The evangelist was a collector, an organizer, and an editor of multiple written documents to which he likely had access in his church.

THE PLACE OF COMPOSITION

It is not entirely clear where the author lived and wrote the gospel. He frequently explains Jewish customs to his readers or listeners and translates

Aramaic words into Greek, suggesting at least some of his audience were not Jewish Christians but rather Gentile Christians. The gospel also uses some Latin words or Latinisms, suggesting, as the place of composition, either Rome or a Roman province, perhaps in Italy or Syria. Rome has often been considered the place of composition of the gospel, and many scholars still make the case for Rome. Alexandria has also been suggested by some scholars.

Syria is, in my opinion, also a likely candidate for the gospel's place of composition, especially if there is any significance to the mention in 12:42 of the coins "*lepta*" and "*quadran*," which probably point to one of the eastern Roman provinces. Moreover the story of the Syro-Phoenician woman (see 12:42 and commentary) may also point to Syria. Frequent Old Testament imagery in the gospel suggests a church made up of both Jewish Christians and Gentile Christians, a church in which both Aramaic and Greek were spoken. All of this points to Syria in my opinion.

The evidence is thin and the clues minimal, but I am inclined to believe the earliest gospel was written by a member of the church in Antioch of Syria for a mixed community of Jewish and Gentile Christians. The evidence is not compelling, but cosmopolitan Antioch, with a population of more than 500,000 when Christianity arrived, was the third-largest city in the Greco-Roman world behind Rome and Alexandria. An important Christian community in Antioch of Syria dates probably from the first decade in the history of the church and served as the sponsor of early Gentile Christian missionary activity.

THE DATE OF COMPOSITION

The date of composition is also not self-evident. Scholars have usually pointed to the text of chapter 13 for clues about events unfolding at the time of the gospel's composition. The situation in 13:5–23 probably points to a time after Nero's persecution of Christians in Rome in 64 CE. Moreover, there is probably a hint of the events of the Jewish war against Rome that began in 66 CE and ended in 74 CE. The author is probably writing before the fall of the Jerusalem temple in 70 CE, as that major event is not mentioned. Hence, a date after 66 CE and before 70 CE seems likely. A date of composition of 67–69 CE is reasonable, but by no means certain.

CHAPTER 16

THE CHRISTOLOGY OF THE GOSPEL

In order to understand the author's Christology, his understanding of who Jesus was, it is helpful to look at the some of the titles of Jesus in this gospel. The less theological titles that are applied to Jesus in this gospel are:

Teacher

(4:38; 9:17, 38; 10:17, 20, 35; 12:14, 19, 32; 13:1; 14:14)

Jesus is portrayed eleven times in the gospel as a teacher, an innocuous title implying that he was regarded by some as an instructor, a dispenser of valuable teaching.

Rabbi

(9:5; 11:21; 14:45)

Jesus is portrayed three times in the gospel as rabbi, a synonym for teacher, often used by a person's disciples or followers, as a term of respect, to imply a teacher's greatness.

Shepherd

(14:27)

The term shepherd appears only once in the gospel with respect to Jesus and then only metaphorically in a quotation from Zech 13:7. See also the reference in 6:34 of the gospel.

Jesus of Nazareth or Jesus the Nazarene

(1:9, 24; 10:47; 14:67; 16:6)

Jesus is represented five times in the gospel as Jesus the Nazarene or as Jesus of Nazareth, his presumed place of birth and upbringing and likely his most recent home.

Son of Mary

(6:3)

Jesus is referred to only once in the gospel as Son of Mary. It is more usual to refer to someone as the son of his father than as the son of his mother (see immediately below).

Son of the Carpenter (i.e., Joseph)

(6:3 in the original text)

Some of the oldest and best manuscripts of the gospel read in 6:3: "Is this not the son of the carpenter and of Mary," implying that Joseph and Mary were Jesus' parents. It is eminently clear that the evangelist assumed Mary and Joseph were Jesus' parents. There is no birth narrative, and there is no knowledge of the virgin birth in this gospel. These claims appear only later in the gospels of Matthew and Luke.

By way of summary, it is likely that "teacher" and "rabbi" were titles that were used of Jesus by his disciples and other followers during his lifetime. Jesus was apparently also known as the son of Mary and Joseph and was known to have been born and probably still lived in Nazareth. At that time, Nazareth was a small, unimportant agricultural village of 400 to 500 people in the Roman district of Galilee, about 20 miles from the Mediterranean Sea to the west and the Sea of Galilee to the east.

The more theological titles that are applied to Jesus in the gospel are:

Christ or Messiah

(1:1; 8:29; 9:41; 12:35; 13:21; 14:61; 15:32)

Christ (Greek *Xristos*) is the word in the gospel that translates the Hebrew word *Messiah*, meaning "the anointed one." It is used seven times in the gospel with reference to Jesus. In the first century, the word usually referred to a political figure, a descendant of King David, who was anointed by God and who would liberate Israel from foreign rule. Although the term appears already in the title or superscription of the gospel and is used of Jesus several times, it is unlikely this title was used of Jesus during his lifetime. In fact, Acts 2:36 makes it clear that God *made* Jesus Lord and Messiah *after* his death.

I am

(14:62)

It is not entirely clear what the evangelist intended by having Jesus answer "I am," when the high priest asked if he was the Messiah, the Son of the Blessed One. Was Jesus simply answering in the affirmative, or was he invoking the divine name I AM from Exod 3:14, when Yahweh answered Moses' question by saying "I AM has sent me to you?" In any event, it is unimaginable that the historical Jesus would have invoked such a divine claim for himself, whatever the intention of the evangelist.

The Coming One

(8:38; 11:9–10)

The title the Coming One or its equivalent appears twice in the gospel. In 8:38, Jesus is obviously referring to someone other than himself, specifically to the eschatological Son of Man, who will soon come and usher in the kingdom of God, the period of God's rule. Verses 11:9–10 recall Ps 118:25–26, when referring to Jesus upon his triumphal entry into Jerusalem. The evangelist clearly wants the reader or listener to understand Jesus is fulfilling the prophecy in Ps 118. The hand of the church is evident in this reference. The Coming One was obviously not a title applied to Jesus during his lifetime.

Son of David

(10:47–48; 12:35)

Son of David appears twice. It was a title used by some Jews of the period to refer to a royal, presumably political Messiah. In 10:47–48 it is the blind man Bartimaeus who calls Jesus "Son of David." The evangelist would like the reader or listener to believe that Jesus was already recognized as Messiah during his lifetime. The hand of the church is evident in this reference. It is highly unlikely that the term was used of Jesus during his lifetime. The reference in 12:35 is not specifically to Jesus, but to the Messiah in general.

Son of Man

(2:10, 28; 8:31, 38; 9:9, 12, 31; 10:33, 45; 13:26; 14:21, 41, 62)

The phrase or title Son of Man appears thirteen times in the gospel, but not always with reference to Jesus. As mentioned in the text, the phrase "Son of man" can mean in Aramaic simply "man" or "humankind," and it appears with that meaning twice in the gospel. Two of the thirteen passages, both sayings of Jesus, refer to the rights or authority of humankind: (1) to forgive sins (2:10); and (2) to be lord of the Sabbath (2:28). Three of the sayings refer to the eschatological Son of Man who will usher in the kingdom of God (8:38; 13:26; and 14:62), references that likely reflect the genuine teaching of the historical Jesus. The remaining eight references (8:31; 9:9, 12, 31; 10:33, 45; 14:21, 41) refer to Jesus in his role as the suffering Son of Man. These eight references clearly reflect the teaching of the church after Jesus' death or, in some instances, perhaps the hand of the evangelist. These references reflect the effort of the church to explain how Jesus' suffering was a sign of his messiahship. The evangelist drew from proof texts that the church found especially in Psalms and in the songs of the suffering servant in Deutero-Isaiah, some of which may have been collected somewhat earlier into *testimonia*. The church apparently also believed that when the eschatological Son of Man finally appeared, he would be none other than Jesus himself, who *during his lifetime* was the suffering Son of Man.

King of the Jews

(15:2, 9, 18, 26)

The title King of the Jews appears in the gospel four times, basically all in the same context: Jesus' trial before Pontius Pilate and the crucifixion. The title implies that Jesus was crucified for claiming to be a political Messiah, an insurrectionist, a threat to Roman rule. It is unlikely that Jesus ever made such a claim about himself and that the claim was delivered to the Romans by Jewish authorities in Jerusalem, who considered Jesus a threat to them.

King of Israel

(15:32)

The title King of Israel appears only once in this gospel and is a synonym for King of the Jews.

Son of God

(15:39)

The title appears only once in this gospel, when a Roman centurion says at the crucifixion, "Truly this man was a Son of God." Such a statement seems highly unlikely and clearly reflects the hand of the church or of the evangelist. Paul states in Rom 1:4 that "Jesus was declared to be Son of God with power according to the spirit of holiness by resurrection from the dead." The title is post-resurrection and obviously a claim of the church. The title also appears in some manuscripts of the gospel in the title or superscription (1:1), but it is not original in that context and was added subsequently by a scribe.

Son of the Blessed One

(14:61)

This title appears only once in the gospel and like Son of God was a title bestowed by the church.

My Son, the Beloved

(1:11; 9:7; 12:6)

This title appears three times in the gospel:

1. In the context of Jesus' baptism, which combines elements of Ps 2:7 and Isa 42:1 and implies that God *adopted* Jesus as his Son at his baptism (adoptionist theology);

2. On the occasion of Jesus' Transfiguration (9:2–8), when Jesus' divine sonship was revealed on a high mountain to Peter, James, and John; and

3. In the metaphoric language of the Parable on the Evil Winegrowers (12:1–9). This title is also a post-resurrection claim of the church.

Prophet

(6:4, 15; 11:32)

The title appears in the gospel only three times, twice with reference to Jesus. It is first used by Jesus in 6:4 when, in the context of his rejection in Nazareth, he says, "A prophet is not without honor except in his own country and among his own relatives, and in his own house." (See also 3:21, 31–32). That Jesus was rejected in Nazareth appears probable. Why would the church otherwise create such a story? Although Jesus fits many of the qualities of a prophet, it is not clear that he ever claimed the title himself. The passage in 6:15 suggests some people considered Jesus a prophet during his lifetime, a reasonable possibility. In 11:32 the title prophet applies to John the Baptist.

By way of summary, it appears that, when applied to Jesus, the titles Christ or Messiah, the Coming One, Son of David, Son of Man, Son of God, Son of the Blessed, and the Son the Beloved reflect the belief of the post-resurrection church and not of the historical Jesus. I AM in a divine sense is certainly not something Jesus could have ever said of himself. It smacks of outright blasphemy. That Jesus was referred to mockingly as King of the Jews or King of Israel at his crucifixion is quite possible, perhaps even likely.

As we have seen, the title Son of Man is especially problematic. I am convinced Jesus used the title not of himself but of the eschatological Son of Man, whose imminent arrival Jesus apparently proclaimed. The title Son of Man was subsequently applied to Jesus by the church during the post-resurrection period, when Christians were trying to explain Jesus' suffering and used the title Son of Man as the equivalent of a suffering Messiah. The church also apparently believed Jesus would return again, sometime soon, as the eschatological Son of Man in a Second Coming.

THE PURPOSE OF THE EVANGELIST IN WRITING THIS GOSPEL

The purpose of the evangelist seems clear. Likely a convert from Judaism and, therefore, already skilled in the Jewish Scriptures and likely an important member of his church, the evangelist had access to written materials that contained sayings of Jesus and stories about Jesus. But the individual stories and/or the collections of stories had no context. Their value was probably in their recitation as part of the liturgy of the church (perhaps in connection with sermons as they are used even today) or in *Vade Mecums*. *Vade Mecum* is Latin for "go with me" and has been used at least since 1629 of a portable handbook or guide, perhaps a catechism for converts preparing for baptism at Easter.

Using the model of Greco-Roman biography, the evangelist set out to write a life of Jesus by creating a framework for the collections of pronouncement stories, miracle stories, parables, sayings, and legends to which he had access in written sources, probably in his own church. Like a Greco-Roman biography, the gospel is not a reliable historical record of events in the life and ministry of Jesus. In fact, it was not intended to provide an accurate historical record of Jesus' life and work. Rather this "Life of Jesus" presented a positive account of Jesus' person and character in order to provide readers or listeners in the evangelist's church and elsewhere with an example of how to lead a good life. The gospel provides a picture of Jesus' greatness. And as in Greco-Roman biographies, exaggeration, falsification, overstatement, hyperbole, aggrandizement, and outright falsehood are commonplace in the gospel.

THE HISTORICAL JESUS

This volume would not be complete without at least trying to draw from the earliest gospel a picture of the historical Jesus, the man who lies behind this gospel that proclaims the good news about this amazing man. Scholars have developed criteria that enable them to reach behind the gospels to discover what they can about the historical Jesus.

The five principal criteria that scholars have formulated are:

1. *The criterion of dissimilarity or embarrassment* maintains that a saying of Jesus or a tradition about Jesus that does not reflect the claims of the church about Jesus has a greater likelihood of being accurate than a saying or tradition that mirrors the church's *kerygma* or preached message, or that reflects the theological bias of the church. A dissimilar or embarrassing saying of Jesus or tradition about Jesus is unlikely to have been fabricated by the church. Although this criterion has its limits, it is probably the single most important criterion in trying to uncover the historical Jesus.

2. *The criterion of multiple attestation* maintains that to be credible, a saying of Jesus or a tradition about Jesus should be attested by two or more independent witnesses. Inasmuch as we have been looking in this volume at only the earliest gospel, this criterion is not helpful. Moreover, the authors of the Gospels of Matthew and Luke clearly used the earliest gospel as one of their sources, so repetition of a saying of Jesus or a tradition about Jesus in the earliest gospel that appears again in Matthew and/or Luke does not qualify as multiple attestation.

3. *The criterion of contextual credibility* maintains that documents must be understood within the historical, political, social, and religious

contexts to which they belong. Therefore, any reconstruction of the life and ministry of Jesus must be consistent with and conform to the historical, political, social, and religious situation in first-century Roman Palestine. Jesus was first and foremost a Galilean Jew, and he must be understood as such.

4. *The criterion of Semitism or Aramaism* maintains that a saying or tradition that reflects, exhibits, or displays Aramaic or Semitic qualities or tendencies has a greater claim to authenticity than material that makes sense only in a Greek setting.

5. *The criterion of coherency or conformity* refers to sayings of Jesus or traditions about Jesus that are similar to material whose credibility or reliability has already been established by one of the other four criteria.

In using these criteria, it is important to understand that we can establish only what Jesus probably said and probably did, as we make an effort to understand what may have happened during the course of his life and ministry. This task is not an exact science, and our conclusions are, therefore, drawn solely within the limits of historical reason. What is reasonable? What is probable? That is, of course, a major question.

The evidence suggests Jesus was probably born shortly before the beginning of the common era in Nazareth of Galilee to Joseph and Mary. His father may have been a carpenter, which implies that Jesus would probably have learned the trade growing up. Jesus apparently had four brothers—James, Joses, Judas, and Simon—and at least two nameless sisters (6:3). Jesus apparently heard in Nazareth about the teaching of John the Baptist, and sometime around 29 CE he went to be baptized in the Jordan River by John into his baptism for the forgiveness of sins. John was a prophetic-type figure and may have understood himself as the forerunner of the eschatological Son of Man, whose imminent arrival he may have proclaimed.

Upon John's arrest, Jesus seems to have taken up John's message and to have begun to proclaim it throughout Galilee, attracting a following and apparently even some disciples. The imminence of the eschatological Son of Man and of the kingdom of God or God's rule led Jesus to proclaim a radical but simple social ethic that challenged aspects of the Jewish law. In anticipation of the end of history, as we understand it, Jesus taught his followers to love God and to love their neighbors as they would love themselves. Jesus' teaching on a multitude of subjects (on the Sabbath, blasphemy, defilement, adultery, prayer, and on just about every subject) often challenged traditional Jewish teaching reflected in the Law, the Jewish Torah, as interpreted by established Jewish authorities. Jesus apparently believed that the purpose of the Law was to serve humankind; it was not the purpose of humankind to serve the Law.

Jesus apparently decided to take his radical message to Jerusalem at the time of the Passover pilgrimage (perhaps in 30 CE). Jesus' challenge to the Jewish authorities in the temple precincts apparently led to their decision to arrest him, to bring him to trial, and to seek his execution. The Jewish authorities apparently took an official charge of insurrectionism to the Roman prefect Pontius Pilate, who ordered Jesus' crucifixion, probably on April 5, 30 CE of the Gregorian calendar.

THE AFTERMATH

The earliest gospel ends with the women's discovery of the empty tomb, but we cannot understand the gospel unless we address what transpired in the immediate aftermath of Jesus' death and burial. There are three things that happened that are critical to an understanding of the beginnings of Christianity, of the shaping of the tradition that underlies the gospel, and of the actual writing of the earliest gospel.

First and perhaps foremost, someone or perhaps several of Jesus' followers—not necessarily one or more of the twelve disciples—came to believe, following Jesus' death, that God would not allow evil to triumph over good. It was outwardly evident that the Jewish authorities and the Roman government had succeeded in killing Jesus. It was clear that evil was victorious. But that verdict could not stand. That was not the end of the story. God would not allow Jesus to die this ignominious death, and so God had the final word. God raised Jesus from the dead and declared him to be *Son of God* with power by resurrection from the dead (Rom 1:4). God exalted Jesus at his right hand, a position of power, and *made him Lord and Messiah* (Acts 2:32–36). In other words and in nonmythical language, good ultimately triumphed over evil. However, in the mythical language of first-century apocalyptic Judaism, God raised Jesus from the dead, undoing the apparent victory of evil over good, thereby reversing the events of Jesus' crucifixion and death.

Second, to understand better what had transpired and how and why Jesus had suffered and died, someone or several people realized that God's will could best be understood in light of the Jewish Scriptures. And so there began a search through the Scriptures to understand how and why Jesus, a faithful servant of God, had died such an undeserved and ignominious death. Passages in the Jewish Scriptures, perhaps first in Psalms, provided clues. The songs of the suffering servant in Deutero-Isaiah afforded additional insights, and so there began a process that probably extended over several years, maybe over several decades, to discover what the Jewish Scriptures predicted about what *would* happen and, therefore, what *must have happened*. The Scriptures informed and shaped the growth of the church's tradition about Jesus.

Thirdly—although not necessarily third in sequence—first Peter and then others believed that they had seen the resurrected Lord. The earliest belief of the church regarding the resurrection of Jesus was probably not belief in a resuscitated corpse. That apparently came much later, perhaps even after the writing of the earliest gospel. In Gal 1:11–12 Paul writes: "For I want you to know, brothers and sisters, that the gospel that was proclaimed by me is not of human origin; for I did not receive it from a human source, nor was I taught it, but I received it through a revelation of Jesus Christ." Once again in Gal 1:15–16a, Paul says, "But when God, who had set me apart before I was born and called me through his grace, was pleased to reveal his Son *to me*, so that I might proclaim him to the Gentiles . . . ." A footnote in the text of the NRSV indicates that the phrase "to me" (italicized above) actually says in Greek "in me," or perhaps even better "within me." In other words, Paul describes in his own words the inner experience or the subjective nature of his revelation of the risen Lord. The risen Christ "appeared" *in* or *within* Paul, language not unlike what one hears today in some Evangelical Christian circles in the United States and elsewhere. The risen Lord was present with and within Paul, even as the risen Christ had probably appeared first *to* and *in* and *within* Peter and then others, perhaps first in Galilee. In fact, some may have seen the risen Lord in dreams, a not uncommon vehicle for religious visions in ancient times. Whatever the details, there can be no doubt that Jesus' followers, one by one, came to believe that the risen Lord had appeared *to* or *in* or *within* them. We may not fully understand the nature of their experience, but early Christians clearly underwent a religious experience or conversion that they described in mythical language that made sense to them. Psychologists of religion can and have contributed more on this subject than I can deal with in this volume.

Finally, the development of tradition about Jesus occurred in an atmosphere in which those who created, transmitted, and put the tradition into writing already believed what occurred in the aftermath of Jesus' crucifixion and death. This belief that Jesus was Son of God, Lord, and Messiah colored the way in which the tradition developed and evolved, making it almost impossible to get beyond the risen Lord to recover the historical Jesus. The sources available to our evangelist were already colored and influenced by the church's belief in and about Jesus, as was the evangelist himself. The importance of these details explains better how and why the gospel is what it is: not a history book as we understand history, but a proclamation of the *good news* about Jesus Messiah. From our perspective, it is, unfortunately, a work of limited historical value.

ISSUES FOR FURTHER CONSIDERATION OR DISCUSSION

I think of myself primarily as an historian, someone who tries to reconstruct the past as accurately as possible, based on as much evidence as is available, and within the limits of historical reason. In a significant way, I have in what precedes been involved in what may seem to many readers to be a deconstruction (or even a destruction) of the earliest gospel and its message. The results of my work may seem negative to some, perhaps even to most.

I like to believe that something positive can emerge from this exercise, even for people who consider themselves observant Christians. I do not believe for a moment that Christianity is committed to belief in a resuscitated corpse or to the belief that one man's death can bring salvation to others. Such beliefs remind me of the religious value in antiquity of animal sacrifices and even of human sacrifices. Surely an outdated worldview!

I think I can, however, say that Jesus died and apparently rose again into the church's *kerygma* or preaching. The ancient message of the gospel is very clear: evil does not triumph over good, even when it appears to do so. There is a certain timelessness in this message and in Jesus' message that the law is here to serve humankind; humankind is not here to serve the law, especially those portions of the law that are little more than human devices of one group to maintain control over another group. Jesus' teaching to love God and to love one's neighbor is not two distinct laws. They are a single law, a single commandment. It is not possible to say one loves God unless one loves one's neighbor. In fact, one might say that loving and serving one's neighbor is what Jesus' teaching was ultimately about. His life serves as a rare and invaluable model for the good life. If religion has any value, it must speak to what is timeless or eternal, and not be governed by an obsolete worldview, an ancient mythology and cosmology that we should have left behind several centuries ago. Let us try to discover and then focus on what is timeless in this gospel. That would be the good news.

BIBLIOGRAPHY

Aland, Kurt, ed. *Synopsis of the Four Gospels*, Greek-English Edition of the Synopsis Quattuor Evangeliorum, 10th ed. London: United Bible Societies, 1993.
The Analytical Greek Lexicon Revised, edited by Harold K. Moulton. Grand Rapids: Zondervan, 1978.
Bellinzoni, Arthur J. *The New Testament: An Introduction to Biblical Scholarship*. Eugene, OR: Wipf & Stock, 2016.
Bultmann, Rudolf. *The History of the Synoptic Tradition*, translated by John Marsh. Oxford: Basil Blackwell, 1962.
Charles, R. H., ed. *The Apocrypha and Pseudepigrapha of the Old Testament in English*, 2 vols. Oxford: Clarendon, 1963.
Charlesworth, James H., ed. *The Old Testament Pseudepigrapha*, 2 vols. Garden City, NY: Doubleday, 1985.
Collins, Adela Yorbo. *Mark: A Commentary*. Hermeneia. Minneapolis: Fortress, 2007.
Dibelius, Martin. *From Traditon to Gospel*, translated by B. L. Wolff. London: Ivor Nicholson & Watson, 1934.
Ehrman, Bart. *The New Testament: A Historical Introduction to the Early Christian Writings*. New York: Oxford University Press, 1997.
Gaster, Theodor. *The Dead Sea Scrolls in English Translation*. Garden City, NY: Doubleday Anchor, 1957.
A Greek-English Lexicon of the New Testament and Other Early Christian Literature, translated by William F. Arndt and F. Wilbur Gingrich. Chicago: The University of Chicago Press, 1957.
Josephus, Flavius. *Antiquities of the Jews.* Cambridge, Massachusetts: Harvard University Press, 1961.
Kittel, Gerhard, and Gerhard Friedrich, eds. *Theological Dictionary of the New Testament*, translated by Geoffrey W. Bromiley. Grand Rapids: Eerdmans, 1985.
Liddell, Henry George, and Robert Scott. *A Greek-English Lexicon*. Oxford: Clarendon, 1948.
Mann, C. S. *Mark, A New Translation with Introduction and Commentary*. The Anchor Bible. Garden City, NY: Doubleday, 1986.
Marcus, Joel. *Mark 1-8: A New Translation with Introduction and Commentary*. The Anchor Bible. New York: Doubleday, 2000.
Marxsen, Willi. *Mark the Evangelist: Studies on the Redaction History of the Gospel*, translated by James Boyce, et al. New York: Abingdon, 1969.

Novum Testamentum Graece, Nestle-Aland, 27th ed. Stuttgart: Deutsche Bibelgesellschaft, 2006.

Page, T. E., et al. *The Apostolic Fathers*, 2 vols. The Loeb Classical Library. Cambridge, MA: Harvard University Press, 1948, 1952.

Perrin, Norman. *Rediscovering the Teaching of Jesus*. New York: Harper & Row, 1967.

Robinson, James M. *The Problem of History in Mark and Other Markan Studies*. Philadelphia: Fortress, 1982.

The RSV Interlinear Greek-English New Testament. The Nestle Greek Text with a Literal English Translation by Alfred Marshall. Grand Rapids: Zondervan, 1978.

Schweitzer, Albert. *The Quest of the Historical Jesus*, translated by W. Montgomery with a new introduction by James M. Robinson. New York: Macmillan, 1968.

Strauss, David Friedrich. *Das Leben Jesus (The Life of Jesus)*. Quoted in Albert Schweitzer, *The Quest for the Historical Jesus*, translated by W. Montgomery. New York: Macmillan, 1968.

Streeter, Burnett Hillman. "The Priority of Mark," *The Four Gospels: A Study of Origins*, London: Macmillan and Co., 1924.

Taylor, Vincent. *The Formation of the Gospel Tradition*. London: Macmillan, 1933.

———*The Gospel According to St. Mark, The Greek Text with Introduction and Notes*. London: Macmillan, 1955.

Wrede, Wilhelm. *The Messianic Secret*, translated by J. C. G. Grieg. Cambridge: James Clark & Company, 1971.

SCRIPTURE INDEX

Biblical References are listed according to their order in the Bible

OLD TESTAMENT

Genesis
2:2–3 — 31

Exodus
3:13–14 — 218
3:13–15 — 83
3:14 — 261
14:21–29 — 82
16 — 103
16:4–8 — 79
20:12 — 90
21:17 — 90
23:20 — 10
24:15 — 81
24:15–18 — 123
24:18 — 81
31:14–15 — 34
33:18–19 — 81

Leviticus
13–14 — 20
18:16 — 75
19:18b — 175
20:9a — 90
20:10 — 138

Numbers
15:32–36 — 34

Deuteronomy
5:16 — 90
6:4 — 175
6:5 — 175
13:1–3 — 189
19:15 — 217
22:22 — 138
23:25 — 31
24:1–4 — 138
25:5–6 — 173
29:2–4 — 107

Joshua
3:7–17 — 82

Judges
11:12 — 16

1 Samuel
21:1 — 31
21:2 — 31

1 Kings
17:8–16 — 79
17:17–24 — 65
17:18 — 16
19:11–13a — 81

2 Kings
2:8 — 82
2:11 — 76

2 Kings (continued)

2:13–14	82
3:13	16
4:1–7	79
4:18–37	65
4:42–44	79

2 Chronicles

24:20–22	197
35:21	16

Job

19:25–27	173

Psalms

2:7	11, 263
16:8–11	242
18:6	233
22	237, 238
22:1	233, 234
22:7	230
22:8	231
22:18	230
27:12	218
35:11	218
38:14	218
42:6	211
42:11a	211
43:5	211
69:21	233
73:24–25	173
89:20–37	177
109:25	230
110:1	113, 177, 181, 218, 242
117:23	169
117:26a	156
118:22–23	169
118:25	156
118:25–26	261

Proverbs

31:6	230

Isaiah

5:1–7	167–68
6:9	106
6:10	47–48
9:7	177
11:1–9	177
13:13	185
14:30	185
19:2	185
25:6	207
26:19	173
29:13	89
29:18	109
35:3–6a	99
35:5–6a	109
35:6a	248
40:3	10
42:1	263
43:10	218
47:8	82
47:10	82
50:6	228
52:13—53:12	114, 128, 145
53:3–5	219
53:6	201
53:11b-12	149
53:12	213, 230, 232
56:7c	159
66:24	133

Jeremiah

5:21	106
8:13	158
31:31–34	206
31:33	102
33:6–7	177
33:14–18	177

Lamentations

2:15	230

Ezekiel

5:12	185
12:2	106
34:23–24	177
37:1–14	173
37:24	177

Daniel

7—13	194
7:13	218
7:13–14	113, 157

7:21	204
8:13–14	188
9:27	188
11:31	188
12:2	173
12:11	188
13:7	190

Hosea
6:2	113
6:6	176
9:16–17	158

Joel
3:1	102

Amos
8:9	233

Micah
6:8	95

Haggai
2:6	185

Zechariah
8:23	102
13:7	208, 259
14:4	156, 185

Malachi
2:10a	138
3:1	10, 76
4:4	122
4:5	110
4:15	76

OLD TESTAMENT APOCRYPHA

1 Maccabees
1:54	188

Wisdom of Solomon
2:17–18	230

OLD TESTAMENT PSEUDEPIGRAPHA

Sibylline Oracles
3.635–36	185

4 Ezra
13:31	185

2 Esdras
13	113

1 Enoch
37–71	113
62:14	207
99:4	185

2 Baruch
27.6–7	185
29:5–8	207
70.3	185
70.8	185

Psalms of Solomon
16:5	230, 232
17:4–45	177

NEW TESTAMENT

Matthew
1:1–17	177
6:9	162
6:14	162
6:15	162
10:1–4	36
20:16	144
20:28	149
28:9–10	242
28:16–20	242

Mark
1:1	3, 8–9, 22, 49, 85, 254, 256, 260, 263
1:2–3	31
1:2–8	252

Mark (*continued*)		2:4	43, 45		
1:2–11	9–11, 251	2:5	43		
1:7–8	12, 13	2:5–10a	245		
1:9	102, 259	2:5—3:35	246		
1:9–11	252	2:10	31, 113, 262		
1:10	42	2:10b-12	247		
1:11	110, 122, 168, 218, 235, 263	2:12	69, 73		
		2:13	45		
1:12	39	2:13–14	26–27, 32, 36, 251, 252, 254		
1:12–13	11–12, 251, 252				
1:14–15	12–13, 75, 249, 252	2:14	14, 43, 143		
1:15	45, 75	2:15–17	27–28, 32, 245		
1:16	26, 42, 45	2:16	204		
1:16–20	13–14, 37, 183, 251, 252	2:16–17	29		
		2:17	43		
1:18	42, 143	2:18–20	32, 246		
1:19	42	2:18–22	28–30		
1:20	143	2:21–22	161, 249		
1:21	33, 45, 70, 129	2:23	45, 70		
1:21–22	22, 70, 254	2:23–27	246		
1:21–28	15–18, 21, 24, 61, 247	2:23–28	30–31		
1:21—2:12	248	2:24	70		
1:22	45, 73	2:27	21, 25, 70		
1:23	61	2:27–28	25		
1:24	61, 110, 259	2:28	113, 161, 249, 262		
1:25	20, 60, 61	3	26, 42		
1:27	73	3:1	45		
1:27–28	69	3:1–6	33–34, 36, 42, 246		
1:29	42, 73	3:2	70, 73		
1:29–31	17, 21, 247	3:4	70		
1:30	143	3:5	43, 139		
1:31	42, 98	3:6	42, 43, 47, 88		
1:32	73	3:7–12	35, 42, 254		
1:32–34	17–18, 22, 254	3:9	45		
1:34	20, 110	3:12	60		
1:35	42	3:13–14	32		
1:35–39	18–19, 22, 254	3:13–15	72		
1:39	20	3:13–19	14, 36–38, 42, 201, 254		
1:40–45	19–21, 26, 108–09, 247	3:14–15	38		
1:41	42, 98	3:15–17	32		
1:44	60	3:16–17	122		
1:45	45, 69, 73	3:16–19	26, 32		
2:1	33, 42, 45	3:18	26		
2:1–4	24, 247	3:20	45		
2:1–12	23–26, 32	3:20–26	42, 246		
2:1—3:6	24	3:20–30	38–40, 41		
2:2	49	3:21	43, 264		
2:3	73	3:23	43		

SCRIPTURE INDEX

3:27	42, 249	5:1–20	58–62, 77, 86, 102, 247
3:27–30	161		
3:28	180	5:2b-20	67
3:28–29	42, 249	5:14	73
3:30	42, 73, 249	5:15	73
3:31–32	264	5:17	45, 73
3:31–35	40–41, 42, 246	5:19	67
3:32	45, 73	5:20	45, 69, 73
3:33	43	5:21	45, 67
3:34	43	5:21–23	78, 86, 102, 247
4:1	56, 73	5:21–42	217
4:1–2	45, 54	5:21–43	62–65
4:1–9	44–46, 248	5:22–23	67
4:1–32	88, 248	5:23	98
4:3–8	54	5:24	45, 67, 254
4:9	54, 91	5:24–34	86, 102
4:10	54	5:25–34	67, 77, 84, 247
4:10–12	45, 48, 51, 248	5:27	45
4:11	46, 54	5:30	45
4:11–12	53, 54	5:31	45
4:12	91	5:34	67
4:13	54, 107	5:35–42	67, 78
3:13–19	201	5:35–43	86, 102, 247
4:13–20	45, 48–50, 248	5:37	122, 210
4:18	91	5:41	98, 99
4:20	91	5:43	55, 60, 67, 254
4:21	54, 57, 249	6:1–6a	69–71, 84, 86, 251
4:21–25	50–51, 54, 251	6:1–29	86
4:22	57, 249	6:2	45, 73, 98
4:23	54, 57, 91, 249	6:3	110, 260, 266
4:24	54, 57, 67, 91, 249	6:4	263
4:25	57, 249	6:5	98
4:26	54	6:6	45
4:26–29	46, 54, 57, 248	6:6b-13	71–73, 85, 86, 254
4:30	54	6:7	45, 73
4:30–32	46, 52–53, 54, 57, 248	6:7–13	14, 72
4:33	91	6:14	73, 86
4:33–34	51, 53–54, 254	6:14–16	110
4:34	55	6:14–29	73–76, 85, 86, 124, 251
4:34b	54		
4:35–41	54–56, 66, 77, 83, 86, 102, 247	6:15	71, 263
		6:17	13
4:35—6:44	248	6:17–18	13
4:36	45	6:17–28	106
4:38	259	6:30	45
4:41	69, 110	6:30–34	254
5:1	56	6:30–44	66, 76–80, 83, 85, 86, 102, 119, 205, 247
5:1–2a	67		

Mark (continued)		7:32–35	108
6:34	45, 73	7:36	60
6:35–36	103	8:1–9	66, 102–04, 119, 205, 247
6:35–44	102		
6:38	104	8:1–10	79
6:41	103, 104, 205	8:6	205
6:45	78, 109	8:10	106, 119
6:45–52	66, 80–83, 85, 86, 102, 109, 119, 247	8:10–13	104–05, 119, 252
		8:11	73, 106
6:45—8:9	78	8:12	139, 180
6:45—8:26	66	8:14–21	105–07, 119, 254
6:46	78	8:17	128
6:47	78	8:18	91, 108
6:52	106, 119, 128	8:22	106
6:53	81, 86	8:22–26	81, 108, 119, 247
6:53–56	66, 83–84, 102, 254	8:22—10:52	248
6:54	86	8:23	98
6:55	45, 73, 86	8:25	98
6:56	86	8:27–30	109–12, 119, 252, 253
7:1	90, 94	8:27—10:45	145
7:1–8	87–89, 246	8:28	71
7:1–13	104, 246	8:29	151, 260
7:1–23	88, 99	8:31	73, 112, 113, 114, 124, 127, 145, 152, 163, 208, 229, 241, 262
7:2	88, 91		
7:2b-4	90		
7:5	91, 94	8:31–33	107, 112–14, 252
7:5–8	90	8:31–34	119
7:9–13	90, 246	8:32	73
7:14	45, 90	8:34	249
7:14–15	94	8:34—9:1	114–18, 119, 190, 251
7:14–16	91–92	8:35	249
7:14–23	94, 249, 251	8:36	249
7:15	90, 91, 94, 99	8:37	249
7:17	92	8:38	113, 190, 195, 249, 261, 262
7:17–20	92–93		
7:17–23	94	9:1	121, 180, 190, 195, 250
7:18	21, 99, 108, 128		
7:18b-20	90	9:2	121, 210
7:19	95, 99	9:2–8	121–23, 134, 252, 253, 263
7:20	99		
7:21–23	90, 93–95	9:5	259
7:23	99	9:7	263
7:24	90	9:9	208, 262
7:24–30	66, 95–97, 99, 102, 247	9:9–13	123–25, 134, 254
		9:12	262
7:31	45	9:14–29	125–27, 134, 247
7:31–37	66, 97–99, 100, 102, 108, 247	9:17	259
		9:23	161

9:27	98	10:27	163
9:30–32	127–28, 135, 254	10:28	73
9:31	112–13, 114, 145, 152, 229, 241, 262	10:28–30	141, 143–44
		10:28–31	41, 151
9:33	137	10:29	143, 180
9:33–35	246	10:31	141, 144, 250
9:33–36	252	10:32	73
9:33–37	128–29	10:32–34	144–46, 152, 254
9:33–50	128, 135	10:33	128, 229, 241, 262
9:33—13:2	246	10:33–34	112–13, 114, 147
9:36–37	250	10:34	208
9:37	132, 133	10:35	259
9:37–50	132	10:35–41	152, 253
9:38	132, 259	10:35–45	146–49
9:38–39	246, 252	10:38–39a	209
9:38–41	129–30, 133	10:41	73
9:39	132	10:42–44	152, 250
9:40	250	10:45	152, 250, 262
9:40–50	251	10:46–47	156
9:41	132, 133, 180, 250, 260	10:46–52	150–51, 156, 247
		10:47	73, 259
9:42	132, 133, 250	10:47–48	261
9:42–50	130–34, 148	11	164, 180
9:43	132, 250	11–13	153
9:43–50	251	11:1	153, 199
9:45	132, 250	11:1–6	202
9:47	132	11:1–11	153, 154–57, 164, 252, 253
9:47–48	250		
9:48	132	11:1–25	153
9:49	132, 250	11:2	156
9:50	132	11:9–10	261
9:50a	250	11:10	156
9:50b	250	11:11	157
10:1–9	246	11:12	153
10:1–12	136–39	11:12–14	153, 157–58, 161, 164, 248
10:1–31	151		
10:2–12	151	11:12–19	153
10:3	163	11:12–25	217
10:10	254	11:12—13:36	248
10:11–12	161, 250	11:15	73, 160
10:13–16	139–40, 151, 246	11:15a	160
10:15	180	11:15–19	153, 154, 158–60, 164, 213, 248, 252
10:17	259		
10:17–22	141, 151, 181	11:16	159
10:17–30	141	11:17	160
10:17–31	140–44, 148, 246	11:17–21	203–04
10:20	259	11:18	160, 163, 199
10:23–27	142–43, 151	11:19	160

Mark (continued)

Reference	Pages
11:19–20	153
11:20	158
11:20–21	153, 158, 160, 161, 164, 248, 254
11:20–25	160–62
11:20—13:37	153
11:21	259
11:22	160, 161, 250
11:22–23	161
11:22–25	153, 164, 250
11:22—13:44	153
11:23	180, 250
11:23–24	160–61
11:24	161
11:24–25	161, 250
11:25	161, 162
11:26	162
11:27	163, 170, 177
11:27–28	168
11:27–33	153, 162–64, 164, 246
11:28	169
11:31	163
11:32	263
12	164, 180, 181
12:1	73
12:1–9	167, 169, 180, 263
12:1–12	153, 166–69, 248
12:6	169, 263
12:9	169
12:10–11	169, 180
12:10–12	169, 180
12:11	169
12:12–14	191
12:13	170
12:13–17	153, 169–71. 180, 246
12:14	259
12:17	216
12:17–22	181
12:18–27	153, 172–74, 181, 246
12:19	259
12:20–24	191
12:23	172, 191
12:24	174
12:25	173
12:26–27	173
12:27	174
12:28–34	174–76, 177, 246
12:29–34	181
12:30	175
12:31	175
12:32	259
12:33	175
12:35	176, 261, 261
12:35–37	153, 176–78, 181, 250
12:37b	179
12:38–39	178, 179, 250
12:38–40	153, 177, 178, 181
12:40	250
12:41–44	154, 179–80, 181, 246
12:42	5, 258
12:43	179
13	164, 182, 194
13:1	259
13:1a	183
13:1–2	154, 183, 246
13:1–37	154
13:3	210
13:3–4	54, 183, 255
13:4	184
13:5	73, 184
13:5b-27	191, 193
13:5–6	154, 184, 189, 255
13:5–8	189
13:5–23	5, 258
13:5–27	191
13:6–37	183
13:7–8	154, 184–86, 250
13:8	186
13:9–13	154, 186–87, 250
13:14–20	154, 187–89, 250
13:17	102
13:19	102
13:20	189
13:21	260
13:21–23	154, 189, 250
13:24	102
13:24–27	154, 189–91, 250
13:26	113, 262
13:26–27	192, 194
13:28–29	154, 191, 248
13:30	180
13:30–31	154, 192, 194, 250
13:32	154, 192, 194, 250
13:32–37	191
13:33	251

13:33–36	154, 195	14:55–65	223, 226
13:34–36	248	14:61	260, 263
13:37	154, 194, 251	14:62	113, 192, 261
14	157	14:64b	145
14—16	253	14:65	73, 145
14:1	153	14:66–72	198, 220–21, 224, 226, 252
14:1-2	198–99, 201, 222, 255		
14:1-52	198	14:67	259
14:3-9	199–201, 222, 223, 236, 241, 246, 252	14:69	73
		14:71	73
14:3—16:8	253	15:1	145
14:8	241	15:1–15	225–27, 238, 252
14:9	180	15:2	262
14:10–11	201, 222, 255	15:8	73
14:12–16	202–03, 222, 252	15:9	262
14:13–16	202	15:15	145
14:14	259	15:16–20	227–28, 238, 252
14:17	79, 202, 203	15:18	73, 262
14:17–21	203, 222, 255	15:20	145
14:17–23	103	15:21–32	228–32, 238, 252, 253
14:17–25	85	15:24	145
14:18	180	15:25	238
14:19	73	15:26	262
14:21	262	15:30	241
14:22	78, 79	15:32	260, 262
14:22–25	78, 104, 202, 204–07, 222, 252	15:33	231, 238
		15:33–38	232–34, 239, 252, 253
14:23	79	15:34	231, 238
14:25	180	15:37	145
14:26–31	207–09, 223, 255	15:39	232, 263
14:27	259	15:39–41	234–35, 239, 252
14:28	208, 241	15:40	236, 241
14:30	180, 221	15:42–47	235–37, 239, 252
14:32–42	209–11, 223, 252	15:47	235, 236, 241
14:33	73, 122	16:1	200, 235, 236
14:33–34	139	16:1–8	145, 235, 239, 240–43, 252, 255
14:34a	211		
14:36	223	16:6	259
14:37	37	16:6–7	208
14:41	262	16:7	208, 221
14:43	201	16:8	208, 235
14:43–50	212–14, 223, 252	16:9	235
14:45	259	16:18	98
14:47	223		
14:51–52	214, 223, 252	Luke	
14:53	145, 223, 226	3:23–38	177
14:53–65	198, 214–20, 252	6:12–16	36
14:54	224, 226	13:30	144

Luke (continued)

22:37	213
24:13–53	242

John

6:1–15	83, 119
6:16–21	83, 119
6:22–59	119
6:67	36
6:70	36
6:71	36
7:42	177
20:11—21:19	242
20:24	36
20:30–31	85
20:31	7

Acts

1:12–14	36
2:24	242
2:32–33	242
2:32–36	113, 267
2:33	111
2:36	11, 111, 195, 260
3:16	130
4:10	130
6:9	231
9:2	170
9:13–17	130
11:26b	30
16:18	130
18:25	170
19:1–7	12
19:9	170
19:23	170
22:4	170
24:14	170
24:22	170

Romans

1:3	177
1:3–4	169
1:4	11, 111, 113, 195, 242, 263, 267
1:13	41
13:1	171
13:6–7	171
16:1	41

1 Corinthians

5:8	106
5:12–13	47
7:10–11	139
11:23	205
11:24	205
11:23–24	78
11:23–26	204–05
11:25	205
11:26	205
12:27–31	130
15	213
15:3–4	10, 213
15:3–5	111
15:4	242
16:20	40

2 Corinthians

1:8	41
13:11	41

Galatians

1:11–12	268
1:15–16a	268
5:7–10	106

Ephesians

6:21	41

Colossians

1:2	41
4:5	47

1 Thessalonians

1:10	114
2:19	114
3:13	114
4:12	47
4:15	114
5:1–2	114
5:26	41

2 Timothy

2:8	177

Hebrews

8:6–12	206

James
5:14–15a   130

Revelation
6:8   185
11:13 185
16:18 185

OTHER ANCIENT WRITINGS

Flavius Josephus, *Antiquities of the Jews*
    12.5.4   188
    18.5.1–2   75n1

Papyrus Egerton 2   171

www.ingramcontent.com/pod-product-compliance
Lightning Source LLC
Chambersburg PA
CBHW070235230426
43664CB00014B/2310